COACHES CLINICS

INSTANT REVIEW

BASKETBALL NOTEBOOK

VOLUME 9

Edited by

Bob Murrey

ISBN: 1-57167-363-6
Library of Congress Catalog Card Number: 97-81339

Book Layout : Christy Uden
Diagrams: James Hunt and Mark Hileman
Cover Design: Dody Bullerman
Cover Photos: Photos courtesy of University of Tennessee and University of Kentucy
Editor: Bob Murrey

Coaches Choice Books is a division of: Sagamore Publishing, Inc.
                                          P.O. Box 647
                                          Champaign, IL 61824-0647
                                          Web Site: http://www.sagamorepub.com

NCAA

MEN'S

WOMEN'S

DIVISION I
UNIVERSITY OF KENTUCKY
TUBBY SMITH

UNIVERSITY OF TENNESSEE
PAT SUMMITT

DIVISION II
UNIV. OF CALIFORNIA - DAVIS
JOHN WILLIAMS

UNIV. OF NORTH DAKOTA
GENE ROEBUCK

DIVISION III
UNIV. OF WISCONSIN - PLATTEVILLE
BO RYAN

WASHINGTON UNIVERSITY (MO)
NANCY FAHEY

NAIA

DIVISION I
GEORGETOWN (KY)
HAPPY OSBORNE

UNION (TN)
DAVE BLACKSTOCK

DIVISION II
BETHEL (IN)
MIKE LIGHTFOOT

WALSH (OH)
KARL SMESKO

NJCAA

DIVISION I
INDIAN HILLS CC
TERRY CARROLL

CENTRAL ARIZONA COLLEGE
LIN LAURSEN

DIVISION II
KIRKWOOD CC
CHRIS JONES

ILLINOIS CENTRAL COLLEGE
LORENE RAMSEY

DIVISION III
FERGUS FALLS CC
DAVE RETZLAFF

ANOKA-RAMSEY CC
PAUL FESSLER

CONTENTS

CONTENTS

PREFACE

The excitement at college basketball's national championship Final Four continues to be at an all-time high. It is thought that more people watch the Final Four double-header than any other single sports event.

At the end of a long day, Kentucky and North Carolina emerged as winners for the men's division with Tennessee and Louisiana Tech being the winners in the women's division.

The national championship honors went to Kentucky and Coach Tubby Smith, as the Wildcats defeated North Carolina 78-69 for their seventh title. Tennessee and Coach Pat Summitt won the women's title, defeating Louisiana Tech 93-75 for their third straight title. This was the sixth national title for Coach Summitt.

In this 35th annual edition of the *Instant Review Basketball Notebook*, you will find greater in-depth articles on most phases of basketball. All coaches are looking for drills, and there are many in this book, as well as discussions on organization, player relationships, offenses, defenses, pressure defense, zone defense, zone offense, late-game situations and game strategy.

The fact that you are reading the *Instant Review Basketball Notebook* at this moment is a testimony to your interest in the game of basketball. Many people made the production of this book possible, beginning with the coaches who spoke at our clinics, sharing their knowledge and expertise. Burt Droste and Tom Desotell spent many hours recording the notes at the clinics, then presented them to Mary Jane Grellner, who transcribed all the notes and assisted in editing them.

Enjoy the book. When you think about books, videotapes and clinics, we hope you will call us at 1-800-COACH-13. We are here to serve you.

Sincerely,

Bob Murrey

Bob Murrey
President and Editor

1998-1999

STEVE ALFORD - Southwest Missouri State

At SMS since the spring of 1995 (age of 30 years old, second youngest in Division I), bringing with him a very direct, hands-on approach to winning. With a full recruiting year to take into his second season with the Bears, he pushed SMS into the 20-win circle and postseason tournament play for the first time since 1993 with a 24-9 record.

BILL BAYNO - UNLV

Three years as head coach at UNLV. Bayno was the first man hired by John Calipari at UMass in 1988 when John took over. His recruiting ability has been credited for their outstanding success. He also played for UMass. In 1987, Bayno worked with Larry Brown at Kansas.

DAVE BLISS - New Mexico

Coach Bliss is the reason basketball is so hot at New Mexico. In his ninth year at the helm, they are enjoying success and good fortune like no other time in their 94-year history. His record at NM is 197-91 (.684) and overall 416-254 (.621).

JOHN BRADY- Louisiana State University

Came to LSU in March, 1997 after six successful years as head coach at Samford. With his 89-77 record while there, he was the winningest coach in Samford history. His teams won TAAC West Division in 1996 and 1997. His coaching philosophy is all about player relationships.

HUBIE BROWN - NBA - TNT- Analyst

One of the NBA's most respected and well-known coaching figures. Served as head coach for the Hawks and the Knicks. This is his ninth season as analyst on TNT's NBA telecasts, and previously he was with CBS for eight years. A master teacher and motivator. Does clinics in foreign countries in addition to the numerous ones in this country.

NEIL DOUGHERTY - Kansas

Joined the Kansas staff in 1994. With Eddie Fogler at Vanderbilt four years and South Carolina two years. Also an assistant at Drake one year and at his alma mater, Cameron University four years. His first two years were spent at West Point where he played for Mike Krzyzewski.

NORM ELLENBERGER - Indiana

Spent seven years at IU with Bob Knight as an assistant coach and administrative assistant. At UTEP with Don Haskins for four years and helped lead them to a 16-8 WAC mark and NCAA bid. Head coach at New Mexico seven years (134 wins, 2 WAC titles, 2 NCAA and 2 NIT bids).

BRUISER FLINT - UMass

After seven years as an assistant at UMass, he just finished his second year as head coach after succeeding John Calipari. The team overcame a 6-9 start to finish at 19-14. He followed up last season with a 21-11 record. Two NCAA bids. Named District I Co-Coach of the Year with Jim Calhoon.

BILL FOSTER - BIG 12 Conference

First coach Division I to take four teams to 20-win seasons. Coach of the Year in 1978 (Duke-Final Four). Past president of the NABC. Member and Board Chairman of the Naismith Basketball Hall of Fame. Director of Basketball Operations for The Big Twelve Conference.

PETE GAUDET - Vanderbilt

First year as an assistant at Vanderbilt after 15 years at Duke. He was there when Duke had its great run with two consecutive NCAA titles in 1991 and 1992. Was responsible for scouting and player development, worked primarily with the big men. Former head coach at West Point.

MARK GOTTFRIED - Alabama

New coach at Alabama. While at Murray State they won back-to-back OVC crowns, guiding them back to the NCAA Tournament for the 5th time in the 1990s and the 8th time in program history. Assistant at UCLA seven years, which included a National Championship in 1994-95.

RAY HARPER - Kentucky Wesleyan

KWU was the Division II Runner-up in 1998 (30-3). In Harper's two years as head coach, their record is 51-11-.82%. National Champions in '90 when he was Associate Head Coach (seven years). His teams play an uptempo offense and a full-court defense.

JIM HARRICK - Rhode Island

At Rhode Island since May 1997. In 17 years as a head coach (358-260 (.691) record) with 12 NCAA Tournament and 2 NIT berths. His 1994-95 UCLA squad won the NCAA National Championship. Previously head coach at Pepperdine from 1979-'88, posting a 167-97 (.633) mark.

BILL HERRION - Drexel

Seventh year at Drexel. Averaging 22 wins per year. Three straight NCAA appearances. Three times Conference Coach of the Year. Former assistant at George Washington and Boston University. Highly competitive young coach, intense and focused. Never had a losing season.

JOE HOLLADAY - Kansas

He just finished his sixth year on the staff and is involved in all phases of the program. He was a highly successful and respected high school coach, teacher and administrator for 23 years. While at Jenks, OK, 40 state champions in eight years and a record 10 state titles in 1990-91.

GENE KEADY - Purdue

At Purdue 18 years. One of the top collegiate coaches in the nation. With six Big Ten championships and five National Coach of the Year District awards. He is the third winningest coach, percentage-wise, in Big Ten history (.663) and the fifth all-time in Big Ten victories (203).

RUDY KEELING - Northeastern

At Northeastern since 1996, after spending eight successful years at Maine, creating one of America East's strongest basketball programs. By '91 they advanced all the way to the NAC Tournament title game, and in '94, they went 20-9, making another NAC championship appearance.

BOB KNIGHT - Indiana

America's premier coach. His defensive and offensive strategies have been used by coaches at all levels throughout the world. Three NCAA Championships, NIT, '84 Olympic Gold, '79 Pan American Games Gold and over 700 victories are some of his achievements. Excellent teacher.

DON MEYER - Lipscomb

Twenty-two years at Lipscomb (614-162). The Bisons have averaged 28 wins a season (79.2). In 1997, they captured the TranSouth Conference regular-season title, their 11th conference title, and in '96, he guided them to the Final Four of the NAIA National Championship.

KEVIN O'NEILL - Northwestern

An intense competitor, a program builder and a natural-born recruiter, O'Neill accepted the challenge of resurrecting the Northwestern program in 1997 after spending three successful years at Tennessee and three at Marquette, leading them to one NIT and two NCAA tournaments.

QUICK CLIP BIOS

DAVE PORTER - Lafayette H.S. (St. Louis)

He just finished one of his best seasons ever as they reached the state championship finals. Porter's all-senior team was bolstered by 6'10" Robert Archibald, a native of Scotland. His teams have won over 425 games while coach at Lafayette, Sedalia Smith-Cotton and Poplar Bluff.

EARNEST RIGGINS - Former AAU/College Coach

He has coached girls teams in age groups, high school (203-14 with an Illinois State championship and #1 national rating) and the women's team at San Diego State ('83-'89). He coached the famed Jackie Joyner-Kersey.

KEVIN STALLINGS - Illinois State

In five years, he has led his teams to 107 wins, two NCAA Tournaments and two National Invitation Tournaments, regular and postseason championships at ISU. Spent five years at Kansas (four NCAA's) and six years at his alma mater, Purdue (six NCAA's and three Big Ten Titles).

TIM WELSH - Providence

Starting his first year after a highly successful three years at Iona (70-22-.761), where he led the team to three straight first-place finishes in the conference. Two NIT bids, and one NCAA bid. Served as an assistant at Iona, Syracuse and Florida State.

DENNIS WOLFF - Boston

Four years at Boston, during which time he has brought the program full cycle, accumulating a 77-43 record (.641), including an impressive 49-21 (.700) mark in league play. The past two seasons, his teams have placed first in the conference. NCAA bid in '97. His trademark has been a tenacious defense.

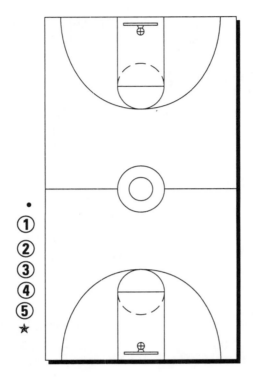

○ = **Offense**

X = **Defense**

◐ = **Player with the Ball**

– – → = **Direct Pass**

———| = **Screen**

∼∼∼→ = **Dribble**

———→ = **Cut of Player without the Ball**

++++++→ = **Shot**

Defensive Drills And Concepts

We got beat on a half-court shot in our league tournament that kept us from going to the NCAA tournament. The kid who shot the ball got a loose ball and never saw the basket when he shot it. It was the first three-pointer in his career. But it went in. Because we didn't get to that loose ball, we didn't advance. If we had gotten to that loose ball, we would have won. We use that as a teaching tool for our kids. It wasn't just a lucky shot. Think about how he got to that ball to get off the shot. Loose balls are a big part of defense.

We make sure that our players know what our philosophy is. This sign is on the back of our locker room door. "WORK HARD—WORK SMART—HAVE FUN." It sounds very simple. It's saying that what kids struggle with today is simplicity without explanation. If I just put this up without explaining, most of our kids will concentrate on the "have fun" first, and that can't happen first. They are in this order for good reason. You can't truly have fun with this game until you understand what a work ethic is, and you really need to understand the game to play it. Most kids don't. Most don't understand work ethics. You can push them right up to a line, but you can't get them across. You will tell them that practice is from 3:00 to 5:00, and they will be there from 3:00 to 5:00. Few come at 2:00 or stay after practice.

When I played with Michael Jordan on the Olympic Team, there was a huge gap between his ability and the ability of the other great players on that team. But what impressed me was that he was always the first one on the floor and the last one to leave. He would grab Chris Mullins and me, the two designated slow spot-up shooters, and challenge us to "horse." We could beat him early in the season because at that time he really couldn't shoot that well. But by the end of the summer it was different. He wanted to improve his shooting. And that's the kind of improvement he showed over several months time by just playing competitive games of horse. I think that our motto applies to him. When you truly understand what work is about, and you truly understand the game you are playing, then you truly understand what fun is all about.

We have another slogan: "EXPECT TO WIN BECAUSE YOU HAVE PREPARED TO WIN." You can have the first three words as a slogan, but you need to explain why. You don't just show up and expect to win. You expect to win because of the way that you have worked. We have a board of TEAM GOALS.

TEAM GOALS
(Opponent)

Offense	Defense	Combined
51% FG ( )	42% FG ( )	+ 10 FT ( )
80% FT ( )	Hold under 65 pts ( )	58% RB ( )
10 or fewer Turnovers ( )		Force 20 or more Turnovers ( )
Scored first each half ( )	Nobody gets 20 points ( )	

We have this on a dry erase board. We fill in the parentheses for each game. Where it says "opponent," we put in the name of the team we are playing. If they beat us, the numbers are red; if we win, the numbers are black. All good things go in black. You can adjust this to your level of coaching. I took this from Indiana and changed it a little. I go over this before our film sessions. Do this on a game by game basis.

We try to stress the little things. "Little things lead to big things."

We have this board in our locker room.

GOES TO WORK

GAME OPPONENT TOTAL		SEASON CUMULATIVE
( )	Charges Taken	( )
( )	Loose Balls	( )
( )	+5 Free Throws Made	( )
( )	Rebounds	( )
( )	Put-Backs	( )
( )	Assists	( )

These six things are important and they must become important to your players. It will only become important if it is written down. The number of the top player for that game can go into the parentheses. This is one way to get on your leading scorer if he doesn't show in any of these categories, and it also shows the other players how important their roles are even if they aren't the leading scorer.

DEFENSIVE CONCEPTS

Perimeter
- Active and aggressive. We want active and aggressive hands and an aggressive attitude.

- Weight more back than front.

- Normal pick up is the time line. This varies with each team and the scouting reports.

- Force to the sideline. Deny the top or reversal pass (keep the ball on one side).

- Stay in stance. Force the backcut or catch the ball high on floor.

- *Always* jump to the ball. Many young players don't understand this concept. We spend a lot of time on this.

- Communicate on all screens and cuts.

- Our wings force to the baseline, not the basket, baseline.

(Diagram 1)   We don't want the ball in this area.

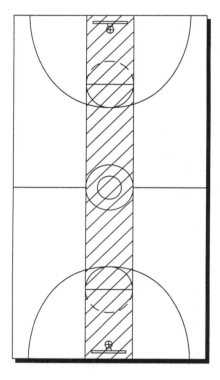

Diagram 1

- Be aware of rules, guard drop.

- Block out, find your man, the outlet is eliminated if you guard the rebounders.

- Fake traps—use everywhere—ballhandler—shooter—post feeds.

- Challenge all shots. Be aware of rules, guard drop.

- Block out, find your man, the outlet is eliminated if you guard the rebounders.

- Fake traps—use everywhere—ballhandler—shooter—post feeds.

- Challenge all shots.

Post
- We like to 3/4 front—then adjust to opponent.

- Beat your man to spot—(Diagram 2) If he likes to post at six feet, make him go nine feet. Don't let him in the area within one big step off the block.

- Scout his best move—turn right or left shoulder.

- Don't give up the angles.

- Teach the stance after your man catches.

- On flash cuts play chest to chest.

- Make the cutter go behind.

- Challenge all shots.

- Secure all rebounds.

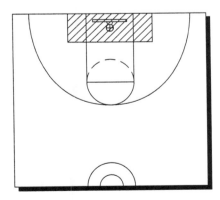

Diagram 2

HELP SIDE RULES

(Diagram 3)   If the ball is above the free-throw line extended, we are one step man side.

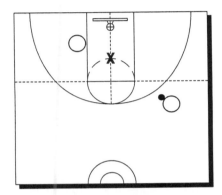

Diagram 3

(Diagram 4)   If the ball is below the free-throw line extended, we are one step ball side.

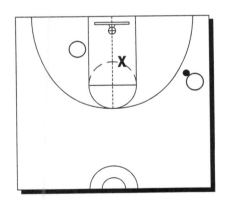

Diagram 4

- Communication

- All loose balls are ours. We chart these for practice.

- Don't stand and watch—talking (helping)—pressure—blocking out

- Give up a maximum of one shot.

ATTITUDE

- Be tough mentally.

- Be hard to play against.

- Get stops.

(Diagram 5)   Defensive slide drill. Players in opposite corners. Slide to the backboard and tap the backboard three times. Then backpedal to mid-court. We teach how to backpedal. We do not backpedal straight up. We are bent in the stance. Players now slide to the sideline at the hash mark, then sliding to the baseline, not to the basket. Change lines. We will then do the same drill by adding the dribble. We will dribble the baseline, make three backboard taps, dribble to the sideline and the baseline. We will do it more like a zigzag drill, one-on-one. Force the dribbler sideline and then baseline.

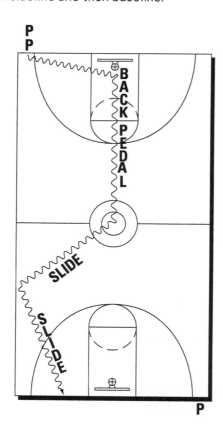

Diagram 5

(Diagram 6)   "Roll the ball side." Slide along the baseline, then the sideline. Face the baseline and sideline as if he were guarding a man. When he gets to the hash mark, plant the inside foot. A second player rolls him the ball. He must bend, pick it up, and attack the basket. Use both sides of the floor at the same time. First, take a layup. Then include a shot fake and make a layup. Next shoot the three-point shot.

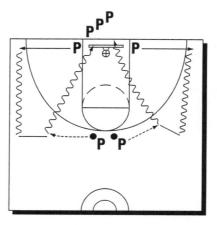

Diagram 6

(Diagram 7)   "Roll the ball under." P1 rolls the ball to the free-throw line extended. While he is doing that, P2 is sliding block-to-block. P1 follows the ball, bends down for ball and then pivots. P2 plays defense and they go one-on-one. This can be done many ways. P1 can get the ball, pivot, and shoot with P2 contesting the shot and blocking out. Then emphasize not getting beat middle. If the defensive man has his hand down as he is closing out, it is an automatic shot. It is difficult to get the defense to close-out with hands up. You must take away the shot first. Then go live one-on-one. If he makes it, he takes it again.

(Diagram 8)   One-on-one starting at mid-court. Offense at mid-court, defense on the three-point line. We want the offensive man to explode right at the defense. The defense must break the offense down off the dribble and keep him out of the middle.

The more we did this, the harder our players went. Make it competitive.

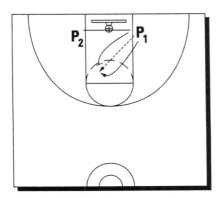

Diagram 7

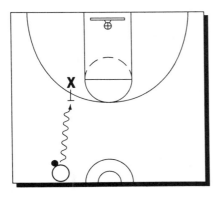

Diagram 8

(Diagram 9)   Close-out drill. The defense starts with the ball under the basket. The offense starts on the three-point line. The defense makes an underhand, hard, chest pass and closes out. If he doesn't get there, he goes again. The defense keeps the ball out of the middle. Force the dribbler to the baseline. Sometimes we limit the offense to one dribble, two dribbles or else go one-on-one.

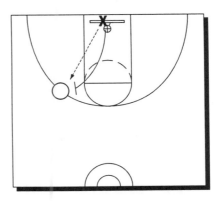

Diagram 9

(Diagram 10)   Twelve-Stops Defensive Drill. (1) Drill starts with a defensive man playing the dribbler, ball pressure. (2) As the ball is passed to the wing, the defensive man jumps to the ball. (3) The offensive man cuts to the post and the defensive man plays post defense. (4) After a count of two, the offensive players cross the lane, and the defense is in help position. (5) The player on the wing starts to dribble toward the baseline, and now the defense takes the charge. (6) The ball is dribbled back out, and the defensive man jumps to his feet and again assumes the help position. (7) The ball is passed crosscourt to the opposite wing, and the defensive man closes out. (8) The wing passes back to the coach and the defensive man jumps to the ball. (9) The coach starts to dribble to the elbow, and the defensive man helps and recovers. (10) Coach passes the ball back to the wing, and the defensive man closes out. (11) Wing goes one-on-one with defensive man. (12) Wing takes a shot and the defense blocks out.

(Diagram 11)   If you run this drill for the big men, at (10) you go into the post and get the feed and play one-on-one from the post.

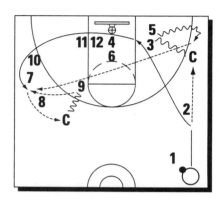

Diagram 10

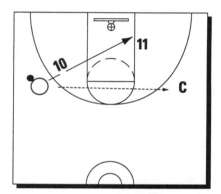

Diagram 11

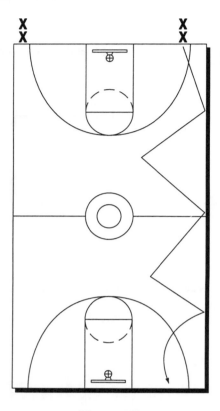

Diagram 12

(Diagram 12)   Zigzag. We go with partners, but no ball. Down and back with hands behind the back. Then down and back with active hands. The third time down, the defense takes the charge at mid-court. Get up and resume the drill and take another charge near the end line. Then, we add a ball. Again, no hands, then active hands, then charges. Now we do two trips of live, full-court, one-on-one. This is where we let them be creative as players.

(Diagram 13)   Sideline, baseline. This is conducive to our basic rules. We teach sideline, baseline. We spread the players, with partners. Slide hash to baseline, not basket, baseline. Then slide hash to mid-court. Do this for 30 seconds, hands behind the back, and you must be talking. If they don't talk, we add 10 seconds to the drill. Every player goes to every position. That in itself is a very good drill. Now repeat with active hands. Some days we have one man dribble during this drill.

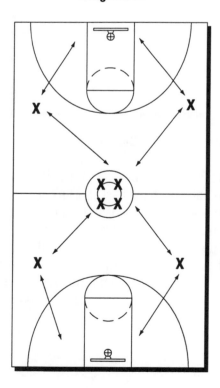

Diagram 13

(Diagram 14)   Lane slides. A lot of people do lane slides, but we give the players a ball. The ball must be beneath the knees. Anytime the ball comes up to knee level, we start over. This will keep them in a good stance. They must put a foot on the line before they change direction.

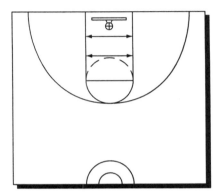

Diagram 14

(Diagram 15)   Post defense. Two coaches, with an offensive player on each block. The defense must chop the feet the entire time. The defensive man is playing 3/4 front, but constantly chopping his feet. If the coach holds the ball and says "over," then he must go over the post. If the coach says "under" then the defensive man must go under the post. If the pass is thrown from coach to coach, he must sprint to the other side and play defense with chopping feet. If the coach dribbles baseline, the defense must get to the low side.

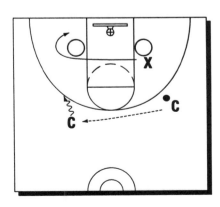

Diagram 15

(Diagram 16)   3/3 defensive cut-throat. You can do this 3/3 or 4/4. Three squads: blue, maroon, and white. Maroon is on defense. Blue is on offense. Play to 5. If maroon gets a stop, they drop the ball and sprint down to the other end and white comes on. All white players must get inside the paint, get the ball and attack maroon. Blue is off. You get points by getting stops. If you get a stop you stay. If white scores on maroon, then maroon goes off while white sprints back on defense and blue comes on offensively.

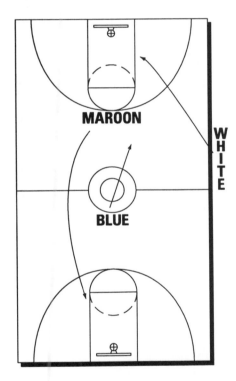

Diagram 16

We also play 5/5 D Stop Buildup, white vs. maroon. White must get one stop. When white gets one stop they get the ball. Now maroon must get one stop. When white is on defense again, they must get two stops in a row before they are on offense. Then maroon must get two stops. Now white must get three stops in a row, etc. When we scrimmage, we go about 6 minutes at a time. Because at the college level there is a TV timeout every four minutes in a game. We will also put limits on the offense; no dribbles, 2 dribbles, or have the defense with the hands behind the back. Then the offense must catch and drive.

(Diagram 17)   Transition drill, Name game. 3/3. Three offensive men on the baseline, three defensive men at the free-throw line extended. Coach has the ball. As he passes the ball to one of the offensive men, he calls the name of one of the defensive players. That player must sprint to the endline, touch, and get back on defense. The others play 3/2 until he gets there, playing the ball and the basket. At times, the coach can call two names.

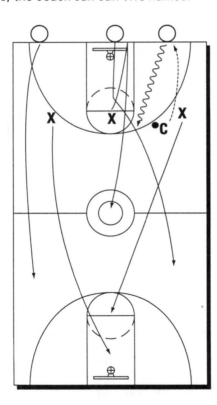

Diagram 17

(Diagram 19)   5 defense, 2 offense on the baseline. Coach has the ball. This is 5/3, 5/4 and 5/5 transition. Coach shoots, one man rebounds. The two men on the baseline are big and little. The big man protects the basket, the little man the ball. The rebounder sprints to get into the action as the other five men run the break. This is a 5-on-3 drill. Then 5-

on-4 with two men rebounding. With 5-on-5, three men rebound.

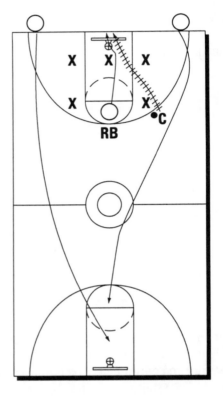

Diagram 18

(Diagram 19)   Box drill. 4/4 on the corners of the lane. Work down-screen, back-screen, and cross-screen. Make the guard-to-guard pass and screen down. The defense jumps to the ball and then lets your teammate through.

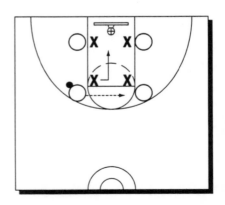

Diagram 19

(Diagram 20)   Then run the back-screen on the guard-to-guard pass.

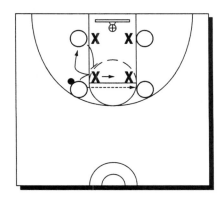

Diagram 20

(Diagram 21)   If the player whom we are defending is a shooter, we will chase over the back-screen.

Diagram 21

(Diagram 22) Cross-screen in the post area. What really upsets the cross-screen is when you get off of your man. Our defensive rule says that when the ball is below the free-throw line, we are one step ball side on the help side. This distorts the screening angle.

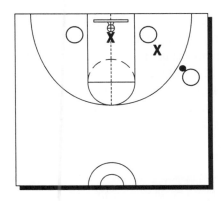

Diagram 22

INDIVIDUAL WORKOUT

- Shoot without dribble (12-15 shots)—plus 10 free throws.

- Shoot with dribble (10-12 shots)—plus 10 free throws.

- Bank shots (10-15 shots)— plus 10 free throws.

- Ballhandling—two balls and lines (2-4 minutes)—plus 10 free throws.

- Point moves/post moves (12-15 shots)—plus 10 free throws.

- Three-point shots (10-12 shots)—plus 10 free throws.

- Movement without the ball (8-12 shots)—plus 10 free throws.

- Ballhandling, attack dribble and control (2-4 minutes)—plus 10 FTs.

- Rope, jump lines, slides, backboard tips (4-5 minutes)—plus 10 FTs.

- Repeat worst drill of workout—plus 10 free throws.

I don't think it matters what they do as much as them doing it, and doing it daily. The skill development occurs in the off-season. This is a seven days a week workout. If you do this, you will get better. This was my workout. I would do it over and over again. For my team, we have three different workouts, a Monday/Wednesday/Friday workout, a Tuesday/Thursday workout, and a Sunday workout. It is basically the same workout, but we change it around. This is what we want them to do and they must chart these things so that they mean something.

(Diagram 23)   This explains #7, movement without the ball. Put chairs on the floor. Start with a ball. Drop the ball and cut away. While you are cutting away, the ball is bouncing lower and lower. When the player gets back, he must bend over to get the ball. This puts him in his stance. He squares up and shoots. He rebounds, comes back, continuous movement. The diagram shows three possible positions. Then include a shot fake with one dribble. If the strength factor isn't there, move it back to the three-point line and do it again.

Diagram 23

Half-Court Offense

It's easier to get kids to play hard on defense than it is on offense. We stress early offense and transition. It makes life easier if you get some easy baskets. The better athletes you have, the more you can play up tempo and run. There is a fine line between controlling tempo and getting your kids to take good shots as opposed to just giving them the freedom to run. Easy baskets are crucial. We run a lot of set plays called "quicks." We may run 20 different plays throughout the course of the year, but we run them all out of the same set. All of our offensive moves go back to what we call our individual work; half-court, transition, motion, posting, etc. We teach our kids to attack the basket.

We have four rules for our individual work:

• We must simulate game situations. Our first look is to take the ball to the rim. If you can't get there, then we teach the short jumper.

• You must change speeds both in the post and on the perimeter.

• You must go body to body, and you must initiate contact. It is human nature to avoid contact. We want the shoulder in the chest of the defensive man.

• Be ready to shoot the ball before you catch it. Have your hands ready.

We must make each player better individually, or we won't be that good as a team. You must teach each player individually. Just going out and playing 5-on-5 isn't enough. Half-court offense is screening and reading screens. Teach your kids to set illegal screens. Teach them to move with the defense. Anticipate the movement of the defense. Teach the body position that you want, but you move until you make contact, then stop. Teach your kids to play without the ball. The next thing we emphasize is moving the ball and being unselfish. You must post the ball, no matter what the size. We are trying to get the best shot we can get.

Before the season starts our staff sits down and I ask these questions. What do we want to accomplish offensively with the personnel we have? Do we want to run or just play half-court? This year we scrapped our motion offense and went from transition to set plays.

What are our strengths and weaknesses? What are your attributes? Are your kids smart? Do we have a post presence? The fewer limitations you have, the more you can run. We do individual work every day.

(Diagram 1) "Perfection." This is transition related. Every drill is timed, so that they play under the pressure of the clock. We keep track of the mistakes. Three balls. The first segment is a speed dribble and a layup, as fast as you can go. Even at the high school level you should get there in four or five dribbles. The next man goes when the first man gets to half-court. Everything we do is with two hands. After making the layup, take it out of the basket with two hands. If a player misses, he goes again. You do it until everyone makes a speed dribble right-handed layup. 4 is waiting for 1's shot. Then do the same drill on the left. They must dribble with the left hand. If they dribble with the right hand, they go again. If they can't make a left-handed layup, have them make a jump stop and go up with both hands.

(Diagram 2) 2-on-0 full-court. If the ball hits the floor, start over. Make the shot.

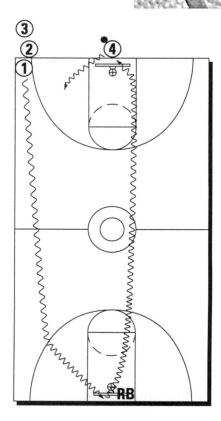

Diagram 1

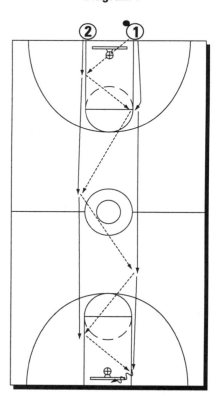

Diagram 2

(Diagram 3)   3-on-0. "Michigan." 1 and 2 pass the ball back and forth while 3 sprints down the side. 1 makes a jump shot and makes the pass ahead to 3, or perhaps 2 makes the pass to 3. 2 and 3 touch the baseline as 1 rebounds. The shooter goes to the outlet, the passer must follow and get the ball before it hits the floor. The outlet pass is made and then one pass going in the opposite direction for the layup. If they miss, they go again.

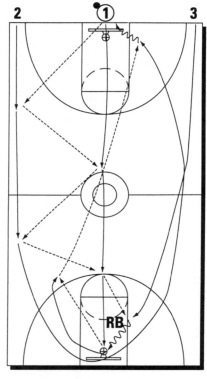

Diagram 3

(Diagram 4)   3-on-0 with a weave. They go full-court in three passes for the layup. If they miss, go again. Then, we do the same drill except we now shoot a jumpshot. The weakside man rebounds and makes the outlet pass.

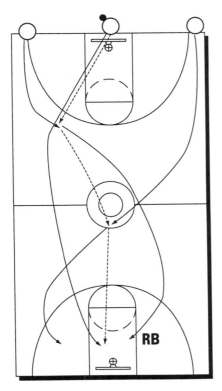

Diagram 4

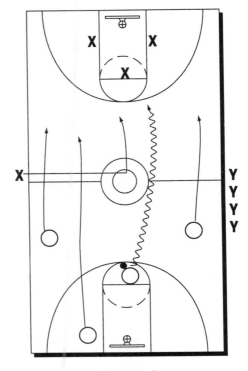

Diagram 5

(Diagram 5)   "Knick Drill." This is a transition drill with three teams of four players each. Start with three X's on defense and four O's on offense. Four Y's are on the side. As the four O's cross mid-court, the 4th X runs in and touches the center circle and gets into the game. Thus, a 4-on-3 becomes 4-on-4 if the shot isn't taken quickly.

(Diagram 6)   When X's have the ball, they go the other way against the Y's, 4-on-3 until they cross mid-court when the 4th Y comes in, touches the center circle and gets into the act. Keep a three way score.

(Diagram 7)   "Cut and Fill." 2-on-0. We split the court into four quadrants to help them understand spacing. Two coaches and a manager. 1 passes to a coach. Teach them to change speeds. They must work hard on offense. 1 makes a fake screen and cuts to the basket for the return pass from the coach. 2 has made a V-cut and comes to the elbow for a pass from the other coach for a jumpshot. A manager fouls the player taking the layup.

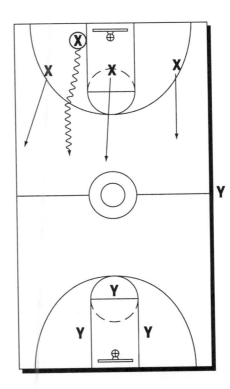

Diagram 6

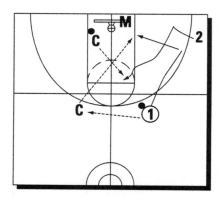

Diagram 7

(Diagram 8)   The next drill is similar except 1 does screen for 2. 2 comes off the screen and 1 rolls to the basket, each getting a pass from a coach.

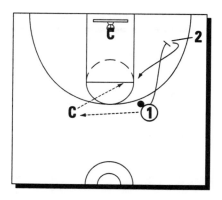

Diagram 8

(Diagram 9)   The next move is a curl. 2 curls and gets fouled by the manager as he gets the short shot. 1 sets the screen and then comes to the elbow for the ball.

(Diagram 10)   Fade. 1 sets the screen. 2 fakes coming off the screen and goes to the deep corner, not the short corner. 1 comes back to the ball.

(Diagram 11)   Back-screen. 1 passes to the coach, 2 sets a back-screen for 1 who goes to the corner for the skip-pass from the coach.

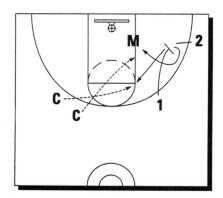

Diagram 9

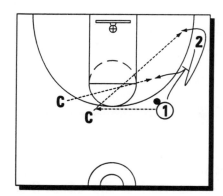

Diagram 10

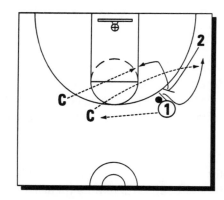

Diagram 11

(Diagram 12)   "High and Wide." 3-on-0 is done on occasion. No set pattern. Teach the spacing, stay high and wide. They must make six passes, and they have one dribble to improve their angle. Hit, screen, curl. Do something different; you control it.

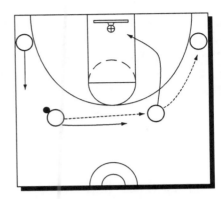

Diagram 14

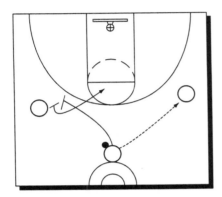

Diagram 12

(Diagram 13)   We usually do 4-on-0, "Wing Cutter." Every time the wing made a pass into the corner, he cut. The others replaced.

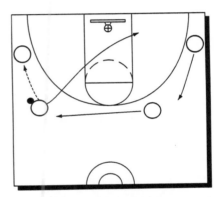

Diagram 15

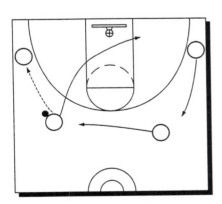

Diagram 13

(Diagram 16)   Can also cut down the middle on the guard-to-guard pass.

(Diagram 14)   When the ball is reversed, the same thing.

(Diagram 15)   Cut and replace. Make them take five or six passes before a shot.

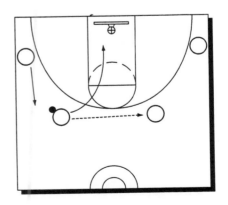

Diagram 16

(Diagram 17)   Quick hitters. "Chop." This is out of our transition. On transition, 2 and 3 run the wings, 5 goes to the ball-side block, 4 takes the ball out and inlets to 1. We go directly from transition to quick hitters. 1 passes to 3. If 3 can't hit 5, he reverses back to 1 to 4 to 2. 5 back-screens for 3 who comes off for the pass from 2. 4 screens down for 5 after making the pass to 2.

Diagram 17

(Diagram 18)   Option is for 4 to set a ballscreen for 1 and run a screen and roll. 1 can come off for a shot or a pass to 2. 5 screens for 3 and then gets a down-screen from 4. 5 breaks high. Anytime 4 and 5 are on the same side of the court, there is a back-screen or a down-screen.

Diagram 18

(Diagram 19)   "Up." This is run on the right side. Same play except that 2 runs the cut off of 5 into the lane, then comes back out on the same side. After 4 sets a ballscreen for 1, he screens down for 2 who comes off the screen for the pass from 1. This is a good three-point shot for 2.

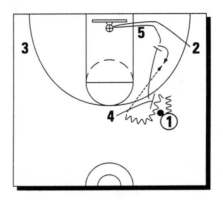

Diagram 19

(Diagram 20)   If 2 doesn't get the shot, he dribbles corner, 4 posts up with 5 crossing the lane.

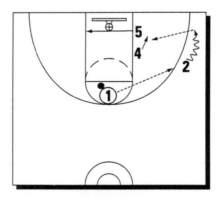

Diagram 20

(Diagram 21)   "Chase" a decoy off of the "Up." Starts the same way with 1 dribbling off of 4's screen. 2 goes into the lane, and then comes back out the same side just as before. 4 screens down for

2. X5 will try to help guard 2 coming off the screen. 5 then crosses the lane, and steps through and comes to the ball. 1 uses the "back-off dribble" (see next diagram). If 2 doesn't have the shot, he is looking to 4 or 5.

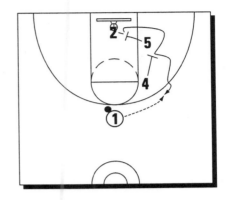

Diagram 23

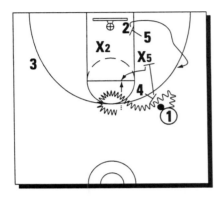

Diagram 21

(Diagram 24)　This puts X5 on 4, and X4 on 2. And X2 on 5. So we pass from 2 to 5.

(Diagram 22)　In individual work, we teach what we call the "back-off dribble." The guards sprint with the ball, stutter-step, put your back or hip into the defense, drive them hard and back off to create space, and then make the pass into the post.

Diagram 24

(Diagram 25)　"Kansas." This is a screen the screener out of transition. 3 screens for 5. 4 screens down for 3 who comes high. 1 passes to 5 or 1 to 3 to 2. 3 could have a foul line jump shot.

Diagram 22

(Diagram 23)　You can't switch this because 5 will end up being guarded by a little man. 2 comes off the staggered-screens of 5 and 4.

Diagram 25

Diagram 27

(Diagram 26)   "Hand off." 1 dribbles to the wing, 2 fades to the corner and then comes back off of the staggered-screen of 5 and 4. 3 spots up at the post. 2 curls.

Diagram 28

Diagram 26

(Diagram 27)   If you want the three-point shot, 2 comes off the staggered-screen and fades.

(Diagram 28)   If they switch, 4 breaks to the basket for the pass from 1.

(Diagram 29)   Also, 4 can spot up at the foul line and get the pass from 1 and go one-on-one.

Diagram 29

(Diagram 30)   An option to this is for 2 to come off the staggered-screen and get the pass from 1. 1 and 5 set a double-screen for 3 who curls. 1 fades to the corner, 5 ducks in. 4 dives to the basket. The ball can go from 1 - 2 - 4 or 1 - 2 - 3 or 1 - 2 - 5.

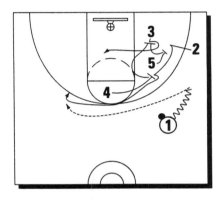

Diagram 30

(Diagram 31)   You can run this for 3 on the other side. 5 comes high as 1 dribbles in. 3 curls around 4 for the possible lob pass and dunk. If 1 doesn't pass to 3, then he passes to 4 and 5 and 1 will double-down for 2.

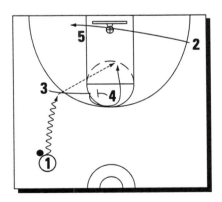

Diagram 31

Special Situations

(Diagram 1)   You must have a special play for the big possession. You can't just say run motion and get the best shot that you can get. "Pistol." Run this every day at the end of practice. This could be the last play of the game. 1 dribbles off 4's screen and it is a screen and roll. If X4 steps out to help, and 1 creates space with a back-off dribble, this is what we want. 1 passes to 4 who has the whole side of the floor. 3 and 5 will both cross to take away weakside help. 2 comes high. If X4 doesn't step out to help and X1 goes under it, 1 shoots a three-point shot.

Diagram 1

(Diagram 2)   Sideline out-of-bounds with from two to ten seconds remaining. 2 and 3 are shooters. 4 and 5 double-screen for 3. If the defense plays soft, make the direct pass to 2 in the corner for the three-point shot. If not, we want 4 to get the ball. 4 slips the screen and dives to the basket or else curls around 5.

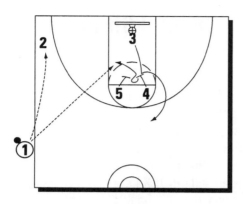

Diagram 2

(Diagram 3)   If X1 drops off, 4 will start to set the double-screen and come to the ball. 2 breaks high, 3 posts up. The ball goes from 1-4-2-3 or 1-2-3. This play needs about five seconds to run.

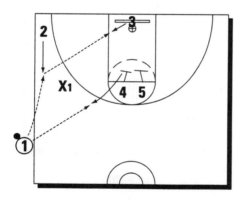

Diagram 3

(Diagram 4)   Length of the floor with from three to six seconds remaining. 2 cuts low and comes off of the double-screen of 1 and 5 to get the pass from 3. 2 takes the ball on the dribble to the basket and can pass ahead to 4 who has cut towards the ball and then went long.

(Diagram 5)   If 2 isn't open, 1 breaks off the double-screen for the pass from 3. 1 starts on the dribble and passes ahead to 4.

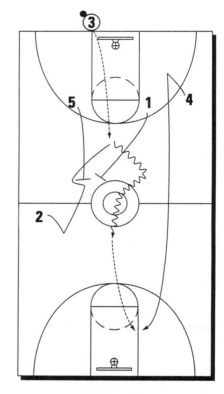

Diagram 4

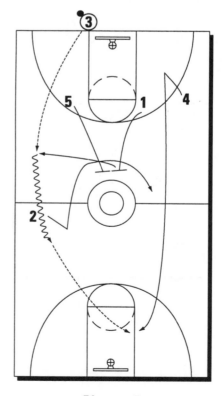

Diagram 5

(Diagram 6)   With one or two seconds remaining, 2 comes high as a decoy. 4 cuts to a spot on the floor as 3 passes to that spot. With one second left, 4 must shoot. With two or more seconds, 4 can volley the ball to either 1 or 5 for the shot.

(Diagram 7)   If you are on defense several points down with under 10 seconds remaining, deny everything. You have two options. You can play man-to-man or put two men on the inbounder, your two biggest men. You play a triangle zone trap with your remaining three men. Switch all screens. You have nothing to lose. With three minutes to go, the game changes. I think three minutes is the cutoff point. Run three-minute segments in practice with different point differentials.

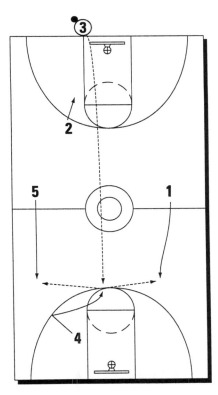

Diagram 6

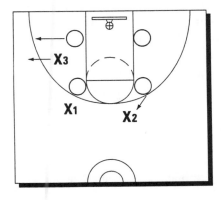

Diagram 7

Game Management

I want to start with the coach himself. Most of us love the creative aspects about coaching. What you are as a coach really depends on the good fortune and the education that you have. The things I have learned outside of coaching have helped me far more than anything in the X's and O's. It gets back to the creative ability we have and our ability to motivate people. If you are having a bad year, this is when you will find out how much you enjoy coaching. If it were easy, everybody would be doing it. Coaching is not easy, and it is getting harder. When it gets really hard, that is the time for you to grow as a person and as a coach. You have the opportunity to have an impact on young people. This is a tremendous responsibility.

Building a Snowman
This is about building your philosophy.

- What you really are:
  - Background—personality
  - Heroes/mentors—have the ability to look at the people you coach against and try to discern what makes them successful
  - Observation—what makes you tick
  - Other
- Don't use "yellow snow"
  - What you aren't—don't be somebody that you are not
  - Don't copy bad traits
  - Don't copy traits that don't matter. If you believe in what you are doing, you will make it come across to your players
- What are your best strengths?
  - In your personality
  - In your coaching style
  - In your emotional makeup
  - What needs improvement—now is the time for you to cover what you are going to be and do for the next year. This may be a little philosophical reinforcement. There are three things that you get out of clinics: (1) you get to see people you haven't seen in a long time; (2) you might get some new ideas; (3) it gets you thinking about things that you already knew. Just like what Hubie (Hubie Brown) did today. He gave you situations and said, "Tell me what you would do in these situations."
- Can all this be utilized in coaching?
  - At what level
  - Don't be in a hurry
  - Not everyone is a Dean Smith or Rick Pitino

Coach's Checklist
Chuck Fairbanks was a good football coach before I coached at Oklahoma. These are all football things that I adapted to basketball:

- Nothing takes the place of your team playing hard. Don't coach caution. I like technique, but playing hard is first. Coaches don't practice shooting enough, and they work on their man-to-man offense way too much.

- Avoid losing first. Your philosophy should include playing the percentages. If your transition defense isn't your best defense, it should be.

- Every coach knows more than he can teach—simplicity, consistency, repetition. This is the KISS Theory; (Keep It Simple, Stupid). Right now we can work on things with our players, three at a time.

- Encouragement and enthusiasm—create hope. If a person doesn't have hope when he wakes up in the morning, it's going to be a long day.

- Your players become what they believe you think they are (Joe Paterno). This is really important. Don't think for a moment that the way you treat your players isn't important. I rely on my assistants for this. They are younger and can relate to the players very well. If you treat them with respect, they will play a lot harder.

- Anger is a poor substitute for reason. Frustration is an enemy. Frustration usually emanates from two things. One is that you have too little time to prepare. Second, there are certain things our players must rely on. And if they aren't working hard enough, it can be frustrating.

- Some things are within your control, others are not. Know the difference and teach the difference.

- The game is usually not as important to them; this isn't always bad.

- Never second-guess yourself on decisions made with integrity, intelligence and the "team first" attitude.

- The most essential thing to teach in athletics is to never give up. Today, this is a challenge. By working hard, we can stay in the game and sometimes this gives the other team time to lose the game. Some games are lost, not won.

The Art of Solid Coaching

Our goal is to bring out the best in the players under our responsibility. It is not governed by technique. This is where our assistant coaches can really help. All of us heard that "People don't care how much you know until they know how much you care." We must listen to them, take an interest in them. We must be clear in what we want. You need to do a good job, in the spring, of explaining to each one of your players what you need from them. There are many things that they can work on to improve their ability.

Next Year's Wish List:
Defensive:
- Play hard VCR technique
- Block-out techniques
- Post defense—double vs. trap and rotate. We have some very good post players in our league, and we must decide how we are going to play them.
- Zone—especially baseline out of bounds
- Traps—very important in our league

Offensive:
- Post offense, hi—lo
- Offensive rebound philosophy
- Drive to pass—we come across the elbow and look to pass out. We think this is the best way to get a three-point shot. Anytime we are driving to the basket outside the three-point line, we are looking to pass. We don't shoot too many from the corner. The rebounds go off in the wrong direction.
- Pressure releases—back cuts, post flash
- Zone offense

Shot Selection
- Was the shot a shot that our team can afford?
- Was the shot taken in the flow of the offense?
- Are your teammates getting to touch the ball?
- Did you make enough passes to break the defense down?
- What did your conscience tell you about that shot?

Instead of calling it a bad shot, how about saying that it was too hard? That sits better with the players.

Grade Possessions

0 — turnovers	1 — too hard
2 — good shot	3 — paint basket

The shots that you are getting out of your offense are shots that your players can make. The last thing I want to tell a player to do is not to shoot.

Next Year I'm Going to Do It Differently

- Starting point for this year—recognize what you know about basketball and what you can communicate. We have job descriptions for the assistant coaches.

    — Reasons you lost last year

    — Areas you want to change

    — Do you fully understand your coaching philosophy?

    — How can you personally become more excited about next year? We must also keep our assistants excited about learning. If we are going to play badly, then the whole team is going to play. We don't want anyone on the bench saying he could do better.

- Preparing to be successful

    — Commitment—sense of urgency, priorities

    — Organized—not much time

    — Enthusiasm—every level, health—faith. Keep basketball a game.

    — Creativity—visit others

    — Know thyself and the team—strengths and weaknesses

    — Not afraid of failure

- Between now and the first practice

    — Create excitement— individual meetings, goals, booklets, include their ideas

    — Communication urgency now—leaders are developed, no long meetings

    — Coach confidence—know what you want, then repetition

    — Critique performances—your team will be satisfied with what you tolerate

    — Continue success—bounty hunter—gym rat—no garage/3 garage

- What coaches owe the players

    — Make them overachievers—this is very important. Have them feel a sense of pride in what they are doing more than they anticipated.

    — Develop talent within the team frame—if we don't do that, we are missing the boat.

    — Create atmosphere for individual growth

    — Be prepared

    — Create a good feeling—self-esteem

- What the players owe the team

    — No embarrassment, respect

    — Maximum effort—physical and mental

    — Sacrifice for the benefit of the team

- Areas to establish relationships

    — Discipline

    — Academic

    — Interpersonal

    — Demeanor off the court

    — Success/failure

    — Team reputation is determined by work ethic

Considerations for 1998–99

- Attrition basketball

    — Fatigue—lose breath

    — Fouls—lose players

    — Frustration—lose cool

- Aspects of winning team—We have a team camp and when the teams come in we talk to each team about what they want their reputation to be. We want each team to realize that they are in control of what other people will think about them. Make up the adjective you want for your team. Think of the things you are jealous of that people say about other people's teams. Incorporate that into your team.

- Teachable spirit

- Tough

- Chemistry

- Ownership

- Humility—hungry to succeed

- Depth—a happy bench wins games

- Make learning simpler—repetition is more important than variety

  - Switch 1-2-3 and 4-5. Switching is tough to play against. It takes away a lot of the screening game, so switch to increase pressure. Put down the three things that you don't like to play against. Then I ask you, why don't you do those three things?

  - Zone defense—offensive out of bounds. You don't have to spend practice time working against their out-of-bounds plays.

  - No point guard, 1 or 2 can run the offense.

  - Have an offense that:

    √ Plays vs. any defense

    √ Plays with five guards

    √ Is easy to enter at half-court. Have an offense you can enter at different spots.

    √ Your best defensive players can play

  - Fewer baseline out-of-bounds—change positions.

Statistics

Whatever you emphasize with your team, keep statistics. For example, if you want a team to play hard, keep track of the number of times they hit the floor.

Defense

- Deflections—important to a set defense.

- Hit the floor—which players are aggressive?

- Charges.

- Types of fouls, reach, shooter, rebounding, etc. 60% of the fouls are created with the hands and the arms. Demand that your players move their feet.

- Different defenses—press, trap, zones, etc.

Offense:
- Fast break from misses and turnovers

- Fast break from made field goals

- Offense from free throws

- Time-out offense

- Shot clock offense

- Post feeds, receivers and passers

- Fouls, charges, offensive rebounding

Situational
Make this a part of your game plan. Two things are baseline defense vs. out-of-bounds plays, theirs as opposed to yours, and free-throw block-outs, theirs as opposed to yours. Here's what happens. If the players know you are charting these, the players get pride in doing these things. We only run about three out-of-bounds plays, but we move all the players around, so it becomes a lot more.

- Free-throw offense and defense—give the players something to do—2nd and 3rd shots, fouls

- Baseline vs. defense, shots, fouls

Drills for Better Basketball
Catalog your drills—take all the drills you like and catalog them. Put them on a 5 x 7 card.

- Defensive   (a) team   (b) individual

- Offensive   (a) team   (b) individual

- Transition

- Tempo
- Preparation

5 x 7 Card

- Purpose
- Number of players
- Time
- Coaching point

Check up on your needs:
- Areas to improve
- Are your drills capable?
- Do you need new ones?
- Call other coaches

Background
- Purpose
- Types—vs. players—vs. clock—vs. number, familiarity and repetition
- Creative reflection of philosophy
- Remember—players will be satisfied with whatever the coaches tolerate.
- Guard against
  - Bad aspects competition—when a player is dominated by another
  - Drills that tire and don't condition
  - Running a drill too long
  - Worry about drill, not skill
  - Players' dislike for too many drills
  - Stubborn, not working, too long
  - At end of practice and season, evaluate the drills.

The best thing a head coach can do is to be an assistant coach for a month. You will be good to your assistants for the rest of your life. The head coach does the talking, but as an assistant, I could look and see how that talking was being received. I could tell when they didn't understand what was going on. If players are confused, they won't play hard. Give a title to your drills so they know what is coming.

Dribble Series
We start practice with this. Each skill we want to work on composes the first half hour of practice. The next half hour is transition time. Then the man-to-man defense, the special defense, the man-to-man offense, a scrimmage and then special situations. That's about two hours and 15 minutes.

- Straight in, right, left
- Crossover front
- Crossover between legs
- Hesitation
- Jump stop into power move—get your shoulders parallel to the board

Rhythm Shooting—Seven spots (two corners, two elbows, two blocks, top of circle). Work on your game shots, the shots you will get when you run your offense. If you have a series set up, you can say "dribble series" and your players know what to do.

Start straight in off Toss Back

- Three in a row—count number it takes to make three in a row
- Low game—how many to make one from each spot?
- High game—stay until you miss
- Plus/minus

Game Shot—Coach Pass—Follow All Shots
- V-cut to wing
- Fade to corner
- Curl to elbow
- Back-screen and pop back
- Flash to key

Transition Series

We don't do every one of these every day, but we will cover them in a period of about three days.

- Paired outlet—the man receiving the outlet pass has his back to the sideline. Cross over the mid-court line close to the middle of the floor.
  - layup
  - jump shot
  - free-throw jump shot (returned to the guard in the middle)

- Speed passing full-court

- 3/2 and 2/1

- Primary break
  - 1/1 layup or foul — if 1 man is back, go to the basket.
  - 2/1 layup or foul (2 passes)
  - 3/2 layup or short jump shot
  - 4/2 layup or short jump shot
  - 5/2 layup or short jump shot

Anytime more than three players back on defense, go to secondary break.

- Secondary break—run to left
  Fast-break drills for passing
  - Three lines straight
  - Weave down and back
  - NBA layups—120 in 3 minutes
  - NBA jumpers—(from the elbow)—70 in 3 minutes
  - NBA 3's—30 in 3 minutes

Start the NBA drills at each end, working against the clock. Have a series.

Game Management

This means changing defenses. If the offense can have a play, the defense can have a play. So, I want to show them something different and attack on defense. It makes your team become more aggressive. How would you like to have a box-and-one against your best player? How good would your box-and-one have to be? It would have to be better than your box-and-one offense. Maybe your zone isn't very good, but it might be better than the zone offense of your opponent. Be able to take advantage of the situation. With a prearranged game plan, you can do a better job of situational defensive changing.

(Diagram 1)   On an offensive out-of-bounds play, how many times does the opponent throw the ball into this area? If they do it 75% of the time, why don't we take advantage of that knowledge?

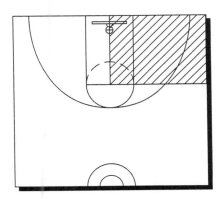

Diagram 1

(Diagram 2)   On a sideline out-of-bounds, what percentage of the time do they inbound to this area? We should be able to take advantage of that.

Something else I never understood is why people have to rush up to half-court to call time-out. I think that offenses run better from a 3/4 court set. Why rush up to half-court? Why not call it at 3/4 court? Many times the defense doesn't pressure you as much.

Game Autopsy

I took the tape from last year's Utah game and broke it down. Some of these possessions are covered by fast-break defense.

UNM missed FG	32
UNM missed FT, rebound by Utah	3
Utah steals	6
	41

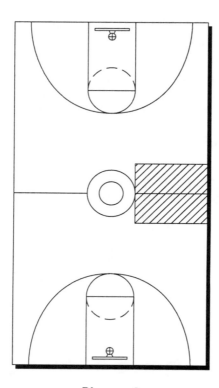

Diagram 2

This is 41 times we were in fast-break defense. If you have one defense that is your best defense, make it your fast-break defense.

UNM FG scored	21
UNM FT made	12
Dead balls	23
	56

(10 full-court, 1 3/4 court, 5 sideline, 7 baseline) Total of 56 chances where we can manage our defense. We had 21 opportunities after made field goals to make some type of defensive change, and 12 after free throws. After a made basket, there is a brief interruption in the play where you can take advantage of what you know about the other team. We had 56 chances in this game where there were interruptions in play to make changes.

We want to cause an empty possession. We want that trip down the floor to be wasted by you. We want your offense to be disrupted by what we did defensively. It might mean that the wrong player took the shot. It might mean that the player took a wrong shot. Early possessions show you what they are going to do against these changes. Early possessions are important. If we know what they are going to do, why do we let them do it? Is that overcoaching? No, if it is part of your defensive scheme. It is preparation that you can take charge of.

We are trying to take advantage of what we know about the other team. Here's what we do on defense. Whatever you do on defense, you must guard the basket. We want pressure on the ball. We try to be unique in our league. We try to give different looks. We want to infringe on your practice time. When the ball is in the middle of the floor, that's offense. When the ball is on the sideline, that's defense. Get the ball out of the middle. We stopped contesting. Why are we denying the ball to the wing when I want the ball on the wing? We want to pressure the ball and force the ball sideline and baseline. We want to spread the help.

Limit the reversals above the three-point line. Don't let them reverse it through the high post. Double all ball screens, double all post feeds and double all weakside drives and rotate. Here are the defenses that we play, with the transition defense being the most important. In our quarter-court we have man-to-man, a point zone, a trap with a 1-3-1, and the gimmicks. 3/4 court we play 2-2-1 back to a man-to-man. We do a man when we pick up the point guard after a free throw. We also face guard on dead balls. Full court, we play 1-2-1-1. We will change defenses according to what you run.

(Diagram 3)   We divide the floor into three parts. We keep the ball on the side and we make a box. All 5 players are within this box, no farther from the basket than the ball.

(Diagram 4)   If the ball is 3/4 court, then the box is larger.

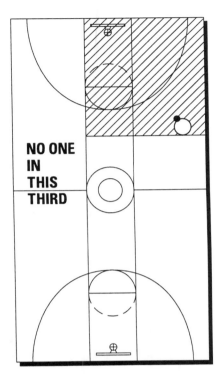

NO ONE IN THIS THIRD

Diagram 3

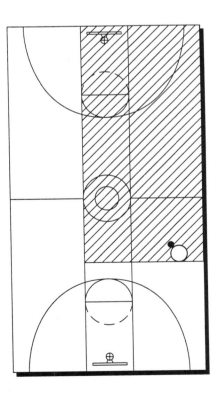

Diagram 4

(Diagram 5)   If the ball is passed from the top to the wing, the box gets correspondingly smaller.

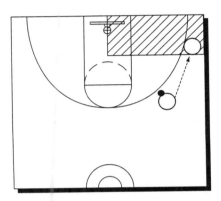

Diagram 5

(Diagram 6)   When the ball is at the wing, the box does not include the lane area.

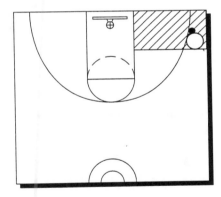

Diagram 6

(Diagram 7)   When the ball goes into the post, the box is very small.

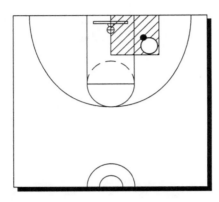

Diagram 7

Diagram 9

(Diagram 8)   This also occurs when the ball is dribbled toward the baseline.

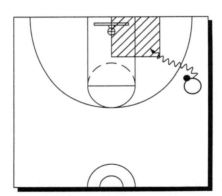

Diagram 8

Diagram 10

(Diagram 9)   When we bring the ball in after a basket and start our transition, the guard crosses to the left side of the floor.

(Diagram 10)   When 1 passes to a wing, he cuts through to the opposite corner.

(Diagram 11)   We have now formed a diamond, with the ball on the wing.

Diagram 11

(Diagram 12)   2 reverses the ball to the top to 5 who trailed the play after inbounding the ball. 5 reverses the ball to 3. 4 sets a back-screen for 2 and then 5 screens the screener by setting a down-screen for 4.

Diagram 14

(Diagram 15)   5 has the ball. 5 looks to 3, then passes to 2. 2 passes to 1. 5 goes off the screen set by 3, and 2 down-screens for 3 who breaks to the top of the key, and we are in a continuity.

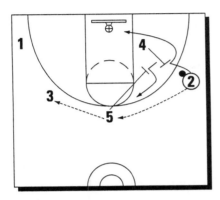

Diagram 12

(Diagram 13)   3 now has the ball and we are in this position.

Diagram 15

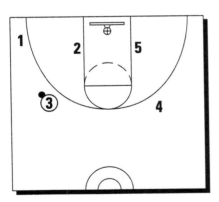

Diagram 13

(Diagram 14)   3 reverses the ball to 4 who passes to 5. 2 sets the back-screen for 3 who breaks to the opposite corner, and 4 down-screens for 2 who breaks to the top of the key. 4 then goes to the corner as 1 replaces 3.

(Diagram 16)   Drive and kick. Suppose that when we come down the floor, 1 dribbles toward 2. 2 crosses to the opposite corner. 4 is on the block. This is a great option because 4 is being guarded on the top. There are two options. The first is 1 driving to the baseline and passing to 2 in the corner. That pass is always open. The second is for 4 to spin out.

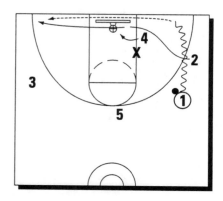

Diagram 16

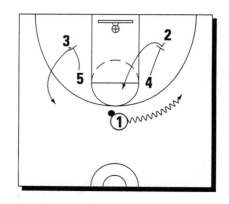

Diagram 18

(Diagram 17)   Suppose that 1 has dribbled to the wing. 1 reverses the ball to 5, then to 3. 4 steps out and back-screens for 1 who cuts low. 5 then down-screens for 4 who comes to the top of the circle.

(Diagram 19)   2 can make the call on this. It depends on how he is being defensed. If he would have trouble getting open, he lets 3 go first off the down-screen. 3 can curl, fade, or pop out. 2 then comes across the lane low and comes out on the other side.

Diagram 17

(Diagram 18)   The "A" set. We run this if we want a quick three-point shot. This is not a box; it is in the shape of an A. If 2 and 3 are wider than the lane, they are easy to screen for. 1 has the ball on the dribble and takes it to the side. 4 and 5 screen down. The low man on the ball side comes up the middle and the other man comes up outside.

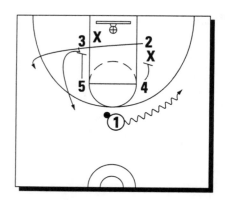

Diagram 19

(Diagram 20)   1 reverses the ball to 3, then to 2. 5 posts on the block. 4 sets a back-screen for 3. 3 can get the lob pass.

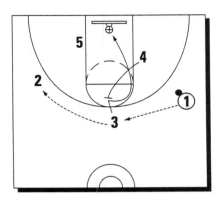

Diagram 20

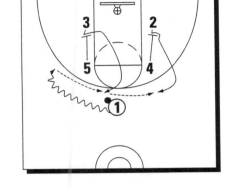

Diagram 22

(Diagram 21)   If 3 doesn't get it, he goes to the corner. The ball is reversed to 4, then to 1. 5 back-screens for 2, then 4 down-screens for 5. 5 comes to the top of the circle; 4 pops out to the wing.

(Diagram 23)   5 side-screens for 3, and 3 comes off the screen to receive the pass from 2 for the three-point shot.

Diagram 21

Diagram 23

(Diagram 22)   If you want to run this for a three-point shot, take the ball away from the side of the shot. 4 and 5 screen and 3 comes up the middle with 2 coming up the outside. 1 passes to 3, then to 2. 1 breaks to the opposite corner.

(Diagram 24)   Another variation. 4 sets the high-screen for 1 who dribbles off the screen. 5 then screens for 4 who pops out. 1 can pass to 4 for the three-point shot.

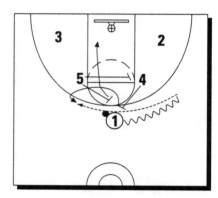

Diagram 24

other wing to open up the side of the floor. 5 rolls down the lane.

Diagram 25

(Diagram 25)   1 can get a three-point shot. 1 passes to 4. 5 sets the screen, and 1 comes off the screen and gets the pass from 4. 3 cleared to the

Motion Offense

Turning Losing into Winning

I inherited nine players. Four quit after the second team meeting. Then, we signed five junior college players who I had never seen play. We wound up this season with seven scholarship players. Our point guard broke his hand and missed eight games, and we played with a walk-on point guard. We had a shot to beat Kentucky with a walk-on point guard, a 6'6" post man, and the rest of the team under 6'5."

I'm going to talk about a system of play that can benefit you, providing you have the patience and want to teach it. There are some things you need to do to turn losing into winning. For any improvement to take place, the players must accept the responsibility that there is a problem. The coach is not the problem. The system of play is not the problem. The players are the problem. I tell my players they need to be humble before they can get better, and that they need to approach the game in that way.

Another thing in evaluating a player. Everyone can see the physical things, but one of the most important things that a player needs in order to be successful today is toughness. I label toughness as a talent. Regardless of his physical abilities, if he doesn't have a heart, I don't want him on my team. I would rather have a less talented player, because if he is tough and has a heart, he is going to be a winner. Also, to turn losing into winning, you must develop some attention to detail within your team. Winning teams, along with good players, have attention to detail in what they do. Not only in their play, but in their habits off the floor.

If you are going to have a good team, you must have players that take care of their business off the court. They must be on time in the classroom, going to the tutors, doing the things that are necessary.

The other thing you must develop is a sense of urgency within your team, and they must take care of what they are responsible for. If your team has no sense of urgency, and they don't have some type of fear of not doing what they are supposed to do, I don't think that progress can take place. There are many things that go into a coaching philosophy, but I do believe it is about responsibility plus accountability.

As the person in charge, you must tell your team what they are responsible for. That's the easy part. The hardest part is to hold your team accountable for what they are responsible for doing. If you don't have accountability, you cannot have growth and you cannot make progress. You must develop an identity of play with your team. When you think of great teams, you also think of how they play. This is what we tried to do at LSU this first season. We want people to know that LSU is a half-court motion team. We will run when it is to our advantage. When you have a better team than your opponent, you want to push the ball up the floor every time. We want to be known as a good half-court team that runs the motion offense and has the right player shooting the ball at the right time. We know who the best shooters are.

As a basketball coach, you build credibility with the play of your team. The team is an extension of the personality of the coach. You build credibility for your program when people actually see the team doing what the coach is saying. They see the coach talk about his team, then they go see them play and actually see it happening on the floor. We want to take advantage of a break situation if it is there. But if not, we want to run our half-court offense. On the other end of the floor, we want the LSU team to be known as a team that can play man-to-man half-court defense and finish the possession by rebounding the ball.

I'm going to speak on offense, but let me make this very clear. Successful teams think defensively. The cornerstone of any team is defense. Players, by nature, think of running offense and shooting the ball. Rarely do you ever walk into a gym and see a player working on his game in a defensive stance doing defensive slides. I have a saying. As a coach, you "criticize on defense and encourage on offense." You can criticize defensively because you are only worried about what is going to happen at the end; you aren't worried about the process. For effective offense, you must worry about the process of how you are going to get the shot. This is more sensitive.

Good Offense
- Ball movement.
- Player movement.
- Screening action.
- Opportunities to drive to the goal.
- Spacing.

If you can get an offense with these in it, you are on your way to having a good offense. You want to create some situation where high percentage shots are achieved by specific players at unpredictable times. We want to develop an offense that has a priority of shooters and a priority of screeners. As a coach, you sell that to your team. You want your best player shooting the ball. A good offense forces the defense to help. Any screening action or any dribble penetration action that forces the defender to help and you can throw the ball to the open man is good offense. A good offense exploits the help.

Why Run Motion?
- It's unpredictable. It's hard to have any secrets on offense with the scouting and TV of today. Motion offense is more unpredictable.

- Teaches players how to play, which makes them better players. They must read how they are being defended. They can run motion when they are in pick-up games.

- The passer, the cutter, the screener are all of equal importance.

- Makes better defenders. In practice, they are guarding unpredictable situations. If you run specific plays, what do they do in practice? They guard the play. They aren't guarding situations.

- Players feel better when they make the decisions.

- To be "shot specific." You have certain players shoot because they all agree who the best shooters are. With one team I had, we tried to get a three-point play every time down the floor. We wanted to shoot the 3, get the ball inside, score and be fouled, or drive to the basket and get fouled. We wanted to eliminate medium range jump shots. Why would you shoot at 17'9" when you could take one step back and shoot at 19'9"? One year, 51% of our shots were behind the arc. Sounds good, doesn't it?

Untrue Assumptions About Motion
- You don't know who is going to shoot. That's not true. Be shot specific.

- You don't know where they are going to shoot from. Yes, you can.

- You can tell them where they can shoot. You can be as loose or as tight as you want.

Suggestions for Teaching Motion
You must stay with it and be committed to it. When you first start it, it can look bad. Year after year, it gets better as the players understand it. You need to be patient. You need to expose your players to situations that may occur in a game.

There are different types of motion:

- 3 out, 2 in. I don't like that because you always have a post man standing on the block and you have a difficult time driving to the goal.

- 4 out, 1 in. I may use some this year. We have a big player coming in.

- 5-man motion, pass and catch people. This is my favorite. Restricted post players are much easier to guard. We did passing and catching drills to start practice. The receiver showed a target hand. When he caught the ball in his target hand, he would immediately transfer the ball to the other side of his body. If he caught the ball in his left hand, and transferred the ball to make a right-handed pass, he pivoted with his right foot, and he would pass the ball back to his partner. He would be in the receiving position, knees bent, hands up giving a target. Right-hand pass, right-foot pivot. Left-hand pass, left-foot pivot. It's always a step through.

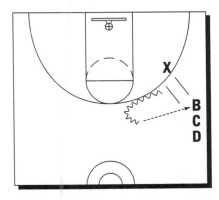

Diagram 1

We did ball spins daily. We would be on the arc with our backs to the basket. We would toss the ball out in front of us with a backspin. We would make a jump stop and catch it. We would then pivot on either the right or the left foot and face the basket, and then either sweep or swing the ball. When I sweep the ball, I bring the ball below the knee. When I swing the ball, I bring it above the shoulders. The worst thing a player can do is to catch the ball, turn and face the defender and let the defender create the action. Players need to learn to catch, pivot, and create space between themselves and the defenders. Keep the ball out of the middle third of your body. Don't expose it to the defender.

(NOTE—Coach Brady uses letters for offensive players.)

(Diagram 1)   Dribble back. The ball starts in the wing position with his back to the arc. There is a defender. We spin the ball to ourselves and do a jump stop creating space between us and the defender. Then, we drive the ball to the lane line extended area. We sweep or swing the ball while the defender is up on him, putting his hands on him and trying to shove him off the lane. The ball is passed to the next man in line and the drill is repeated. We are trying to learn how to protect the ball under pressure.

(Diagram 2)   Basic rules for our 5-man motion. We try to occupy certain spots on the floor: the point, two wings, and people in the corners. We will have players on the post positions, and also when we drive the ball from the wings, we will have players in what I call the near-guard spots.

Diagram 2

(Diagram 3)   Beyond the arc, the idea is to fill out—up—in. You want to fill and cut in a straight line. When A passes to B, A face cuts and goes to the open corner. A is going to fill a spot. If a spot above you is unoccupied, that is the spot that you want to fill next. On the wing, C will fill the open spot above, which is the point. You fill out, up, and in; out to the corner, up to the wing, and in to the middle of the floor.

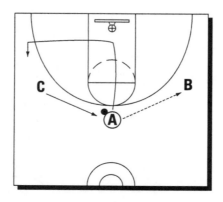

Diagram 3

immediately cut. Don't stand at the point. Face-cut through to the corner and fill up and in. In our sequence of teaching, the first thing we teach is cutting. With each pass they make, they should cut. We want the defender to respect the face-cut. If B passes to A, B cuts, and then empties out to the same side. A will face-cut. If he does that from the middle third of the floor, he can empty out to either corner. After B cuts, he will fill up because the space above him is unoccupied. Why do you cut? You cut to score. The second reason you cut is to create help.

(Diagram 4)   We divide the floor into three areas. The rule is that if you cut from the outer third of the floor, you must stay on that side of the floor. A passes to B and A cuts; he must stay on that side.

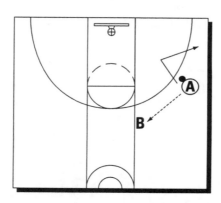

Diagram 4

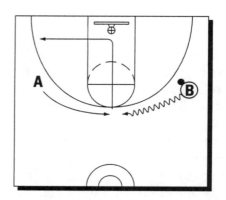

Diagram 5

(Diagram 5)   If a player is on the wing, and is filling the point, he should keep coming until the player with the ball dictates the action. Since B is dribbling at A, A should back-cut to the goal. Since he is not involved in a screen and he is coming from the outer third, he must stay in that third of the floor. (We will talk about how dribbling takes precedence over cutting in just a moment.)

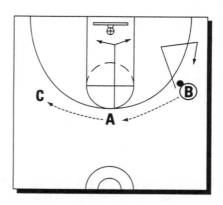

Diagram 6

(Diagram 6)   When you catch the ball in the middle third of the floor, you want to reverse the ball quickly with the pass first or the dribble second. If you fill the point and you do not catch the ball, you

(Diagram 7)   When A passes to B and cuts, and the cut is taken away, it sets up good screening angles.

Diagram 7

(Diagram 8)   The second part of teaching motion is dribbling. We have two types of dribble motion. One is the non-penetrating dribble used to change the floor. The non-penetrating dribble is when the ball is on the wing outside the arc, and the ball is dribbled in that area.

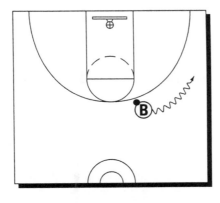

Diagram 8

(Diagram 9)   The penetrating dribble goes inside the arc. If a player is driving the ball, then B fills behind.

(Diagram 10)   Dribbling takes precedence over cutting. Suppose that the point position is open and B starts to cut to that area and A starts to dribble to that area. When B sees this, B immediately cuts to the basket because dribbling overrides cutting. B will empty out to the same third of the floor. C then fills up.

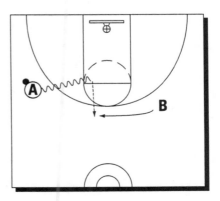

Diagram 9

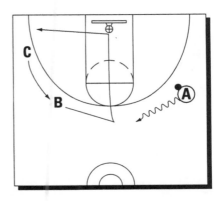

Diagram 10

(Diagram 11)   Dribble follow. Anytime there is a non-penetrating dribble, the person below the ball follows the dribble. A drives the ball to the point. C cuts to the basket and empties out on the same side of the floor because he was not involved in a screening action. B follows the dribble, fills up. D fills the corner position from the post position. This opens the way for a cut by A. A passes to B, and then A can face-cut. This gives you a cutting-dribbling game. We do this late in the game, an offense with no screens, and a dribble-follow rule.

(Diagram 12)   Another one. A is on the wing with the ball. (Don't worry about the post man.) C fills the point. A passes to C. A face-cuts from the outer third and empties to the same side. B fills up. D fills up behind C.

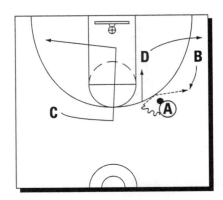

Diagram 11

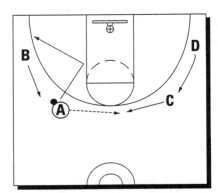

Diagram 12

(Diagram 14)   The third thing we teach is the screen. We teach proper screening techniques. A passes to B and tries to cut, and the defender takes away the cut. Then A must screen. The cutter needs to bury his defender behind the screen. The cutter needs to come off the screen shoulder to shoulder so there is no space between the cutter and the screener. That's critical. The defender cannot force the screener from where he wants to go. The back of the screener should tell the cutter where he should receive the ball. In theory, you want the cutter to catch the ball behind the screener's back. That's the widest point of the screen.

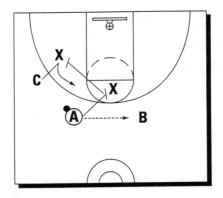

Diagram 14

(Diagram 13)   C has the ball; C wants to pass to D, but the defender is in the passing lane. C sweeps the ball and drives at the defender. D then cuts to the goal. D empties out on the same side. B fills behind, as does A.

(Diagram 15)   Suppose C's man sinks the screen. The cutter-screener relationship changes because the cutter should realize that the defender has sunk the screen. Therefore, the screener should turn his back again, and C should catch the ball away from his defensive man.

(Diagram 16)   Types of screens. Down-screen. A passes to B, and down-screens for C on the wing.

(Diagram 17)   Back-screen. B passes to C and A will step up and set a back-screen for B. D fills and the ball is reversed to D.

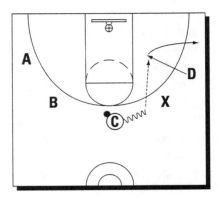

Diagram 13

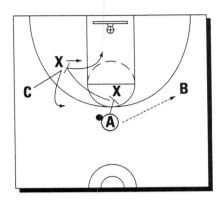

Diagram 15

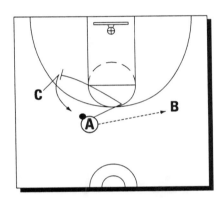

Diagram 16

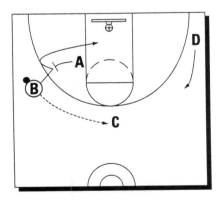

Diagram 17

(Diagram 18)   Up-screen. A is on the post. B passes to C who reverses the ball to D. A back-screens for B and then back-screens for C at the point. D will drive the ball and pass the ball back to C for the three-point shot.

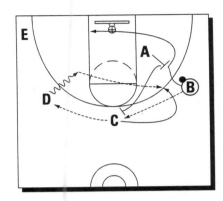

Diagram 18

(Diagram 19)   Slip-screen. A passes to B. If A can't cut, he goes to screen for C. If A loses sight of his defender, that tells him that the defense is going to switch, so A slips the screen and comes back ball side.

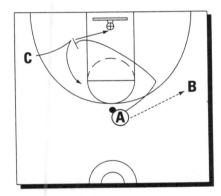

Diagram 19

(Diagram 20)   There are three different cutter-screener relationships. The first is the undercut. A passes to B and goes to screen for C. C buries his defender behind the screen, but the cutter's man beats him to the screen. C is the cutter. C undercuts the screen and occupies the post. A pops back to the ball to become the reversal man. If C isn't open, it is likely that A's defender dropped to help on the cut by C leaving A open.

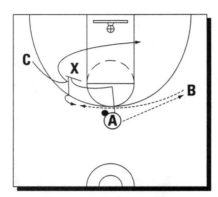

Diagram 20

(Diagram 21)   Curl cut. A passes to B. A tries to cut, can't and goes to screen. C buries his man on the screen. C loses sight of his defender, so he curls off of the down-screen. When the screener sees the curl, he pops back out.

Diagram 21

(Diagram 22)   Again. A passes to D and screens for B. B curls the screen and A pops back for the pass from D and the shot. C will fill up behind the cut.

(Diagram 23)   A then passes to C and you are running the offense.

(Diagram 24)   The "L" screen. When the defender sinks the screen, B starts to cut and A turns his back. B then makes an "L" cut away from the screen to get the pass from C.

Diagram 22

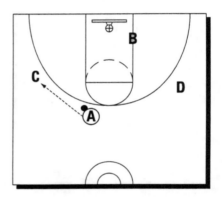

Diagram 23

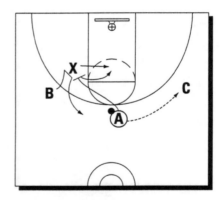

Diagram 24

(Diagram 25)   A good offense exploits the help. B has the ball and the ball is reversed to C to D. There are two ways you can get off the post in motion. You can screen your way out or you can follow the dribble out when the ball is dribbled out of the corner. A back-screens his way out of the post. B cuts off the screen to catch and score or to create help. B creates help from A's defender. When the ball is reversed, C screens down for A and A pops out.

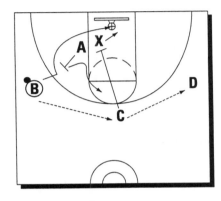

Diagram 25

(Diagram 26)   "Back-down." This is a back-screen followed by a down-screen. B is in the post, C has the ball on the wing. C reverses to A to E. B screens for C. C can stop on the post or continue to the open corner. A down-screens for B, and B will come to the point.

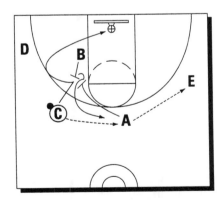

Diagram 26

(Diagram 27)   D fills up, and the ball is reversed from E to B to D.

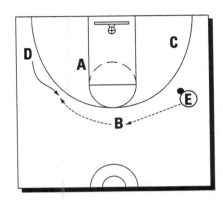

Diagram 27

(Diagram 28)   "Backup." B passes to A to D. C back-screens for B. C will turn and up-screen for A. A is the shooter.

(Diagram 29)   If D dribbles up, then E fills behind.

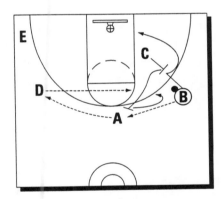

Diagram 28

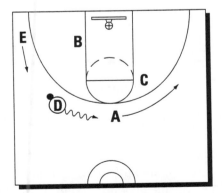

Diagram 29

(Diagram 30)   D can pass to A and then C rolls to the goal.

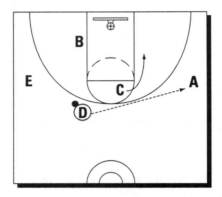

Diagram 30

(Diagram 31)   "Fill-up" or "Screen-up." When a player is in the corner, he can do two things. They can fill up from the corner or they can screen up from the corner. A passes to D and screens for B. B curls. C can either fill up or screen up. He knows that a shooter is above him so he comes up to screen for A. D drives to the middle. A comes off the screen by C, and C rolls to the goal. D passes to A in the corner.

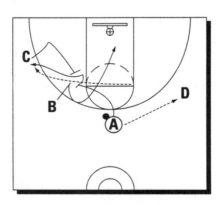

Diagram 31

(Diagram 32)   Accidental screens. This will happen. C reverses to A. B back-screens for C. A sees the defender and drives the ball toward the wing. D backcuts. D and C are both converging in the middle of the floor. The player who screens is the player who finds himself closest to the middle of the floor.

In this case it is C. When D empties out to the other side, he is looking to go out, up, and in. C is in the post. B is at the top.

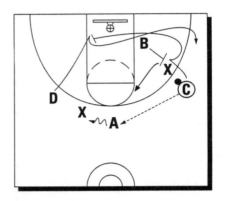

Diagram 32

(Diagram 33)   Late in the shot clock. We call this "shooter screen on the ball." A passes to B. A is the shooter and screens on the ball. B drives the ball off of our best shooter. C then screens for A. A flares and B passes back to A.

Diagram 33

(Diagram 34)   Anytime our best shooter (B) is on the wing with no one below him in the corner, he drives up and the post will automatically up-screen for B. A cuts away from the dribble and C fills up to get the pass from B. B then reverses off of the back-screen of D and goes to the corner for the shot.

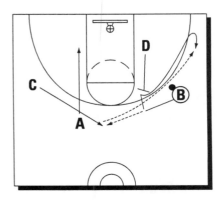

Diagram 34

(Diagram 35)   We really don't want to ever throw the ball to the corner, but if we have to, then A, who has passed to B, will cut through, and B will dribble the ball up.

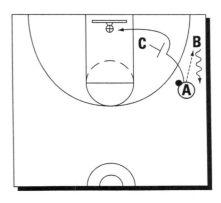

Diagram 35

(Diagram 36)   A can pass to the corner and ballscreen for B.

(Diagram 37)   This is the rule for a double-screen. B has the ball on the wing and reverses to D to E. How do you get out of the post? A must screen to get out. D is the shooter. A screens for B, then for D. C comes out of the corner and also screens for D. E drives the ball to the top and passes to D on the wing.

(Diagram 38)   If D doesn't shoot, A rolls to the goal, and C steps out for ball reversal.

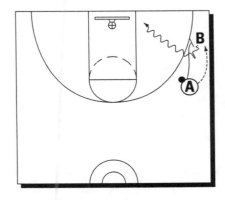

Diagram 36

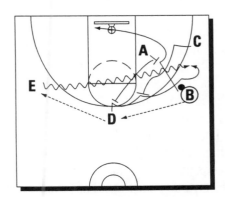

Diagram 37

Diagram 38

Game Preparation and Strategy

You never stop learning. We ran a UCLA cut with the Kentucky Colonels when I coached here (Louisville). My daughters were playing on a little grade school team and I went down to watch them play. The guy is running the UCLA cut and then doing several other things off of it. I took that and put it into our offense so that we had 5 options to the right and 4 to the left. Then when I went to Atlanta, I incorporated that into our fast break. So, the point is that you always listen for little things.

In 1986, I am doing a clinic with John Wooden. I did four hours and John Wooden, who at that time was 72, sat in the first row for 4 hours. When I finished, the clinic director opened it up for questions for Coach Wooden and myself. A young man asked, "Coach Wooden, what do you miss?" Some of you may not know who John Wooden is. He won 10 NCAA Championships. He would always sit there with his legs crossed. He never got out of his chair during the entire game. He just sat there with a rolled up program in his hands. Coach Wooden looked at this guy and said, "The smell of the gym." That's all he said. What did he mean? He missed the creating. He missed the practices. He didn't miss the games. He missed the developing of the talent, forcing guys who were selfish to play as a team, forcing guys who didn't want to be disciplined to play within the system. And every day on his 5 x 8 card, that practice session moved. Every single thing was done, 2 minutes, 3 minutes, 5 minutes, air horn. Next thing. Every day was prepared. Let me ask you. If I went into your gym on Monday and asked you to show me your daily practice card, what would you show me? It's interesting; it doesn't change. Because the great guys are organized. Bob Knight is so organized that it is frightening. Nothing goes undone.

Everything is done for you meticulously so that you teach.

(Diagram 1)   In that clinic, I was talking about defending the fast break. I say, we stop the ball like this. We stop the ball at the top of the circle, not at the foul line. If you stop it at the foul line, one pass is a layup. We always stop the ball at the top of the circle where you are unaccustomed to stopping, and then the next pass is into an area where guys are not accustomed to catching the pass. Little things. Then, when the pass is made to the right, we would come out and play that man with the deeper man, and the top man would drop down and be standing sideways. Now, if you have a player who doesn't want to do that, tell him to leave. Don't have him run suicides. Players hate you when you have them run suicides. Just tell him to leave.

Diagram 1

(Diagram 2)   Now, on the second pass, who has the second pass for you? We don't send the back guy up. If the ball comes back to the top and the man moves to the foul line extended and you step up, this is a short pass and this guy is getting a layup on that pass. Defensively, we always slide to the corner of the foul line. You also have second pass. So you have first pass, and then on the ball back, you have second pass. I can't stand it when you score a layup. Now get this. It's 11:35 p.m. and Coach Wooden and I are walking through the corridor and he says to me: "Hubie, I've never heard you say that about the ball back. Do you mind if we walk through that?" We are in the corridor of a Marriott Hotel. He's 72, in the Hall of Fame first as a player, then a coach. The only other guy in the history of basketball who is going to do this is Lenny Wilkins. Ever! We stop three young coaches. We don't have a ball so he rolls up a paper. He takes off his coat, hangs it on a doorknob, and we go through this. He says, "I like that. I've never heard that before." He asked, "Do you know what we used to do?" I said, "Why don't you just show me."

take away one of the two. We would rather take away the layup and force you to take the jumper. We hope that the third guy is coming and hope that he can pick up the guy at the line. We never stop learning little things.

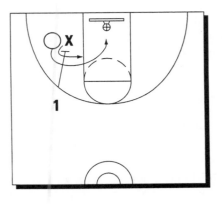

Diagram 3

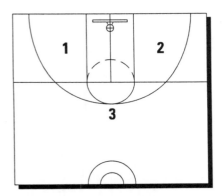

Diagram 2

(Diagram 3)   UCLA defense. If you think that your half-court defense wins your games, you don't understand the game. If you take film and break it down, you will find out that only 30% of your points are coming out of your set plays and the other 70% are coming in transition, second shots, and foul shots. So the transition game is what it is all about. Now I ask you, how much time are you putting into your transition game; 2/1, 3/2, 4/3? And your second shot game? So here is what Wooden does. When it is 3-on-2 against UCLA, UCLA is side by side. We feint at the ball and come back. As soon as you ball pick up, we drop back and play both wings. Wooden says, "Fake, fake, fake, make the ball pick up, and then come back and cut off the two layups." Really, his theory and my theory are the same thing, no layups. We will live with the jump shot. We can only

Here is a quick exam about the past year. If you are a new coach, this is a good thing to be thinking about. Give me the biggest game that you lost this year. In your offensive set, number one, the biggest things we always talk about is spacing - spacing - spacing. Because against the good defenses, if you don't have spacing, they will trap you and one defender will play two guys, because you have lousy spacing. But if you have good spacing, and they trap you, one defender cannot play two guys, and you are going to make them pay. In spacing, the first rule is when you leave an area, replace. Second, you must have a short and a long pass against great defenses. Third, can you reverse the ball? Good teams don't let you reverse the ball. Fourth, can you start with a pass or a dribble? If you play a good team that is quicker than yours, they will out-quick you on the wings. They will get up and deny and overpower you. How are you going to get into your offense if you can't make the first pass? So you must be able to open up your offense with the dribble. The last thing is do you have a backdoor game against overbearing pressure? I know what that's like. I've been there. You can't let your team lose confidence against better players. I found that these are the same things that work in college and really work in the NBA where you have the 24-second shot.

Now, about your offense. Last year, was your offense for you or was your offense for your players? Were the shots the ones that you wanted to take or were the shots for the players? Did you get high percentage shots for you or high percentage shots for your best kids?

(Diagram 4)   When you chart your shooting drills in area 1, 2, and 3, I will guarantee you right now that every kid on your team cannot shoot the same percentage in all three areas. What you will find out is that they are good in two of the three areas. Here you are setting up shots for a kid who is a hell of a player for you, but he is getting shots in an area where he can't make them. But the offense is getting him shots. Are you charting your shooting drills? If you did, you would know where your kids could shoot from. If I do that in the NBA, I certainly hope that you do it in high school. Now, when you broke down your shots, did the right two kids get the most shots and did they get them in their most productive areas? There are a lot of coaches who run beautiful offenses but the ball does not go in. And until they start giving out points for the degree of difficulty, you are screwed. This is the time of the year to admit your mistakes. And stop blaming the kids. Examine yourself and become a better coach.

Diagram 4

Let's talk about end of the game clock management. I am doing a game the other night (on TV). This is a big game, Miami at New York. New York is up 3, 19 seconds to go. Miami has the ball. Do you go for the 2 or the 3? Some guys say that they go for the open shot. That's great; it takes you off the hook. But what is your philosophy? I'm going for the 2 because the coach in the other huddle is saying "Don't give them the 3." But they will give you a quick 2. Don't tell me they won't. With 19 seconds, if you go for the quick 2, you will score somewhere between three and five seconds. You still have 14 seconds to go, and you are down one.

I know you. You are right into what you practice every day. As soon as you score, you are denying on the ball. You are overplaying the right hand by half a person and your arms are up and crossed so that he can't see. Whoever scores is the guy who is guarding the man taking it out. And we deny. We do this five minutes every week. Now, we go for the first steal. We never assume that they can pass it in. No steal, then foul. The game is a one point difference. Four seconds went off the clock and they must now hit both free throws to get it back to three. Now there are 10 to 11 seconds left. It is a lifetime if I think that it is a lifetime. If I practice it, it is a lifetime. But if I don't practice this, the kids think that the game is over. I even go for a quick two between 10 and 12 seconds. That's me. But what do you like to do? How many times have you seen this. A team is down three inside of 15 seconds. They come down and shoot the three. They miss, they foul, and now it's four- or five-point spread and the game is over. Always take the quick two with preparation with a play that you know is a quick hitter going to the rim. In the Miami game, they came down with five guys at the three-point circle, and all the Knicks did was switch on every pass. They never got off a shot.

Next one. Ten seconds left, other team scores and are ahead by either 1, 2, or 3. Do not call time-out. Because all great coaches will change the defense. If you call time-out, you now must go 84 feet. They will change the defense and get the ball out of the hands of the best person. When you get to half-court, they may be in a zone that they haven't played before in the game. And you gave them that chance by calling time-out. As soon as the ball goes through the basket, you practice your sideline. You should jump out of bounds with the ball, get it in, and get it up the court in three seconds. If you don't have any type of good shot, now you call time-out. And you might even catch them lackadaisically going back. The Celtics would do this. Bird would jump out-of-bounds. Danny Ainge going out for a 28-foot pass. Ainge would get it up ahead to Dennis Johnson and you would see McHale running down the floor. Then the Chief would come down the middle of the floor, boom, dunk. How did that happen? Because Sir Lancelot was taking it out. Bird jumps out of bounds and often passes directly to the Chief, or else Ainge to McHale. Then he shows you one of his six back-to-the basket moves. They are all great. Ask anybody who played in the NBA. They will all tell you that Kevin McHale had the greatest moves ever. You are going to catch your opponents cheering on the way back. So, we are not going to call time-out and let the team change defenses and make us fight 84 feet. We will take the shot if it is there. If not, we will call time-out and have the ball 28 feet from the basket.

Did you go the entire season before you did your shot distribution? Or did you understand that things change, things are different from year to year. We want to do it at $1/3$ of the season, $2/3$ of the season, and at the end of the season. In our sets, are we getting the ball to our best three people for high-percentage shots? You now know which sets are working and you are current. If you do this, you will not get to the end of the season before you realize that your first two shooters were low-percentage people. Every team that I took over in the pros, every team, the guy who led the team in shots attempted by 500 shots was never more than a 41% shooter. That's why the coach got fired. The wrong guy was shooting. Because in every team that I took over, their second and third best players were high-percentage shooters but they never got as many

shots. Interesting, it was always the point guard. Selfish.

What bothers you the most? Great pressure by the opposition bothers you the most. We spend 15 minutes every practice against traps. We go five minutes full-court. We might be in 1-2-1-1 full-court or our man-to-man run-and-jump. If they steal the ball, they are allowed to come down and take one shot. They also do this if the other side gets the ball down and misses a shot. While this is going on, the second unit is practicing the press. We let the defense fast break because if they score, they are then on offense. Always reward the defense. This helps you develop players eight, nine, and ten. You are letting your kids grow. Then we go five minutes 3/4 court with a 2-2-1, even on foul shots. We can get in it make or miss. Now, five minutes we go 1/2 court 1-3-1 half-court trap. This helps you to keep from being intimidated by the good teams with the better athletes. And, we got good at it defensively, and so we used it. Put in the whole 1-2-1-1 and walk them through it. Then each day emphasize certain parts. Teach backwards. Teach with the whole. Give the kids credit for their IQ. You'll be shocked. Put it in, and work on certain things each day so you will be ready. What is the message? Relieve the pressure by preparation. Have it in your game formula. Teach the whole and work backwards. Don't work parts up.

Offensive rebounding. When you dummy your offense, when the shot goes up, what happens in your gym?

(Diagram 5)   In our gym we rotate two guys back. If those two guys aren't standing in the center circle, it's $50. Because all of our transition defensive drills start from half-court. Who's on the offensive board? We call it "two and a half." The center is always on the board and a forward is always on the board. The two guards are always back, even if they drive and lay it up. Don't tell me that they can't. Here's where you get burned. Everybody loves to send three men to the board. But if you have a forward who takes a shot outside of the paint, the percentages are against him getting the rebound. If you take a jump shot outside the paint, go back. You are wasting your efforts going to the board because of the angle of the rebound.

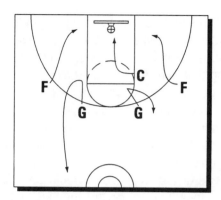

Diagram 6

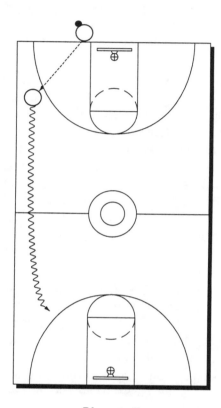

Diagram 5

(Diagram 6)   If the forward shoots the ball in the paint, he is on the board. You are shooting a softer shot and the ball will rebound somewhere in that area. If a guard shoots, naturally you have two forwards and the center on the glass. Your offensive sets will dictate to you when you force the two guys to come back, how far they must go. I never blame poor offensive rebounding on players. I look to see where the player is in the offensive set when the shot goes up. Do you give the forwards and the center a chance to get to the glass? I'm fanatical about offensive rebounding, because that is where you win. You are only going to get easy shots in a couple of places: turnover, fast break and second shots. And, you must get more shots than the opposition if you have less talent.

You are up 3, and here comes the last shot. You are on defense. Will you foul? This is a hard one. If you don't foul, they can tie the game. You can say that you are not going to foul, I am going to rely on my defense to put pressure on the shot and force a difficult shot. I see this all the time. Indiana is down six at Atlanta with 11 seconds to go. A loose ball in the right-hand corner, Mark Jackson runs over, picks it up, shoots it, good!! A three-point game, nine seconds to go. Atlanta calls time-out. They move the ball to half-court. They throw the ball inbounds, and it goes right through a player's hands. Travis Best dives on the floor. Time-out! Four seconds to go.

They throw the ball inbounds, and take it up the floor. They are still up 3. Now, they dribble the ball and Steve Smith reaches around and knocks the ball away from him. Reggie Miller picks it up, and shoots it from away out. He should have had a hernia operation after the game. Swish!! The buzzer goes off. Overtime. Indiana wins by five in overtime. After the game they are saying, we should have fouled. If we foul and we are up three, the guy fouled still must make the first foul shot to get the score within two, and then miss the second shot. Do you have a play for such a situation? Don't let the other team tie the game. I'm being forceful because I want you to have a philosophy. Foul, make them make a foul shot and then have a play. If I ask two coaches, one will say that he will foul, one won't. But you must know what you are going to do. This is a tough call, and an easy second-guess. What are we talking about today? We are talking about things that get you fired.

In the first half you need an alarm clock in your head. The opposition runs a 6-0 to a 10-0 on you. When do you call time-out? You can't go by the pros because they have more time-outs. When do you do this in the second half? If you have a big lead, you might get complacent. One of the best in the NBA is Pat Riley. You cannot run Miami a 6-0. When do you call time? What are you comfortable with? Remember, your AD is not going to give you a bonus for time-outs that you did not call.

(Diagram 7)   The ball is out-of-bounds, two seconds on the clock. The team with the ball is losing by one. 5 is the center. As soon as the ball is handed to 1, 3 broke to the corner. 2 comes down and screens the center. 4 comes off of 2 and goes to the elbow (leave an area and replace). Set the back-screen on the defender. 5 must roll to the outside and rolls in. If they switch, it is a lob from 1 to 5 with a smaller man guarding your center.

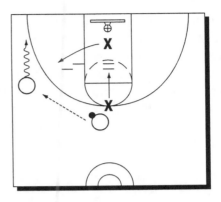

Diagram 8

(Diagram 9)   For the teams that are trapping you on the wing, by sending the player to the corner, the next person who can guard him is the one on the baseline. The rule is, when a person leaves you, go to the front of the rim. If they trap, take the trap towards mid-court one bounce. Go to the spot-up person in the corner at the mid-point. As they rotate, you now have a short and a long. Out of traps against good defenses, the first pass will not get you the open shot. The good teams will rotate. The second pass is the pass that will get you the high-percentage shot.

Diagram 7

(Diagram 8)   For all the teams that play screen and roll, please do this. Set the screen on the left side of the floor. As I come off the screen, I do not roll; I spot up near the corner. As the dribbler takes two dribbles, the low man always steps into the dotted line. Now you have the perfect triangle away. Why bring this up?

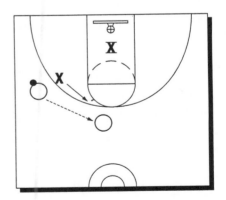

Diagram 9

(Diagram 10)   This is a great play; the Chicago Bulls could not defend it. And the Chicago Bulls can defend anything because they have three of the best defenders who ever played the game, Jordan, Pippen and Rodman. Jordan is on a par with Bill Russell.

That's a hell of a compliment. He is going to make the All-Defensive Team for the ninth time. But they couldn't stop this play. Put a good shooter in the right corner. Stockton comes off the screen. Karl Malone sets the screen. If Stockton comes off the screen, he goes all the way. Who will cheat to help? The guy in the corner. Pass to the shooter in the corner, and he has a wide-open shot.

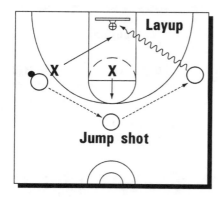

Diagram 10

(Diagram 11)   As soon as he starts off of the screen, bring another shooter, Hornacek, to the top. Leave an area and replace. They will sucker you into helping. If they play it man-to-man, Stockton turns the corner, who tries to help the center. Layup, 2-on-1.

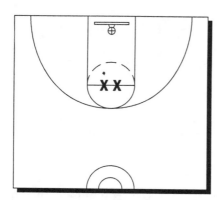

Diagram 11

(Diagram 12)   Now they trap Stockton. As soon as they trap, he steps back and Malone rolls. Here comes Hornacek and there goes the center.

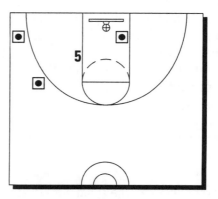

Diagram 12

(Diagram 13)   Then they switched, and the ball was passed to Hornacek for the shot.

Diagram 13

(Diagram 14)   On made foul shots, we like to take the ball out on the left side and blow it up the floor. We might pass ahead, or dribble it, but the ball will eventually be on the left. As soon as the ball goes into the post, nine out of ten post people are right-handed, so you must get them into the lane. So, backdoor the person out of the corner. That's an easy bounce pass.

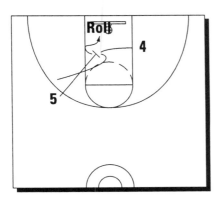

Diagram 14

(Diagram 15)   As soon as the catch is made in the post, the forward sets a back-screen for the shooter, right on the line. We are sending a shooter to the side to stretch the defense.

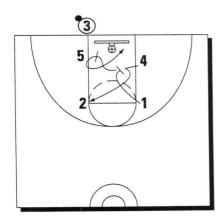

Diagram 15

(Diagram 16)   I think that this is an easy "three" area.

(Diagram 17)   After setting the backscreen, the forward comes right down the lane and screens for the person who made the backdoor cut. He curls off of the forward. But think about it. Come up the left side of the floor. Most teams are right-handed and come up the right side. Give them a different look.

(Diagram 18)   When you set a screen in a stack, anytime you have a screen down and the person curls, and the defensive person steps up on the screener or the top of the stack, the defense bangs the curl person. 4 is Parrish, 5 is Bird. We always played high on 4, and up against 5 so he can't go backdoor. 5 can then come around, and bump, or he is going to curl. You can do three things, but you can't take away all three.

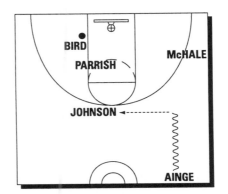

Diagram 16

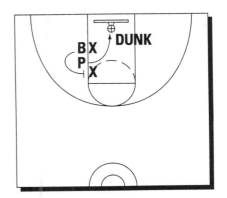

Diagram 17

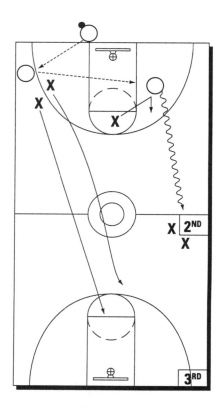

Diagram 18

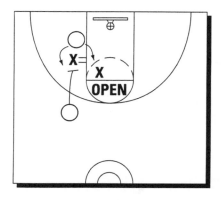

Diagram 19

outside the box. That eliminates the gray area for any kid who says he doesn't know where to go to rotate. If he is on the wing and coming to the middle, you rotate outside of where the foul line and the circle meet and you don't let him into the circle. If he comes down the middle, rotate to the dotted line in the lane. Stop the ball; make the ball change direction. You must stop the ball.

(Diagram 19)   How do we play screens? On the down-screen; you must use your forearm. You can't control him with your hands; you must use your forearm. Any time the offense screens down, the player on the box yells "open." The man defending the screener will allow his teammate to slide through and take away the curl if the offensive man has no range. When the top man spins, I am on his top foot. As he spins, I am in perfect position to close down on him from the front. The player coming on the trap is responsible for the shoulders turned. The player coming on the trap is not only responsible for the split, but he is responsible to turn the shoulders of the offensive man so he cannot see all the movement below the trap. It doesn't matter whether it is full-court, half-court, or the tops of the circle.

We had a rule. Anytime a man came into the middle and was a shoulder ahead of the defensive man, from the foul line down, we would fly at you and trap you. When you rotate across the lane, be

(Diagram 20)   On the screen, let the screener step to the rim if his man steps up and helps. As Bird curls, we stepped up to stop Bird; Parrish went to the front of the rim. Dunk. So, if you screen down in the stack, give the screener at the top of the stack the liberty to step to the front of the rim. Where did we break down? We did not jam the ball. Defenses can only take away two out of three things. If they follow, and you step up, you must punish them by stepping to the rim. He must know that he has that freedom. As soon as you pick the ball up above the letter, our defensive man is taught to jam and cross face. I don't care if he has the dribble left. He must be turned. Defense is not just two against two, it is the third guy guarding the passer. As the man with the ball lifts the ball, make him turn his shoulder. He can't dribble it. If he does, the curl is over, and get your arms up and crossed. He'll turn. I'm telling you that he will turn.

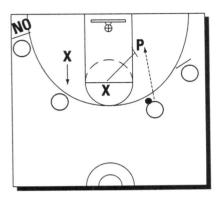

Diagram 20

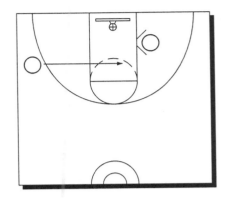

Diagram 21

You are down one, and you have the ball for the last shot. Do you hold the ball for the last shot, or do you shoot and play clock management? If it is your philosophy to hold, when do you go? Always go with at least six seconds. Because you will get a shot and a chance for one offensive rebound. Don't wait until the last second. You put incredible pressure on that kid. The best person to take this shot is not always your best scorer. A lot of the best scorers don't even want the ball at this time. Even in the NBA. I am never holding for the last shot. I am shooting, crashing, and if we miss, we are going for the steal and then the foul. I will make you shoot two foul shots at the other end. You don't have to feel like this, but the key is, how do you feel? What is your philosophy?

Anytime that you make the steal and come down the floor and lay it up, how about a press? Put one man on the ball and everybody fronts. You will be shocked how many times some of the players don't get across half-court. They may make a bad lob. Why? They are made because they just had a turnover.

(Diagram 21) You take the shot, and the person guarding you takes off. Will you take off? I don't know. If they don't run back with you, we have a potential easy basket. When two teams of equal talent play, it's the team that gets the most easy baskets that wins.

(Diagram 22) Homerun. We have been showing homerun since 1972. This is the length of the floor play for a last second shot. One man is at the opposite free-throw line, the other three are near mid-court. The rule is if you catch it in the paint, take one bounce and go for the score. No fade-away jump shots unless there is less than one second. If there is more than one second, drop-step and take it to the rim. You have a chance to win on the shot or the foul. If you take the fade-away jump shot, you can only win on the shot. The rule is that if you cannot catch it in the paint, you volleyball pass it because the wings are coming down to the foul line extended. The third man used to come down the middle.

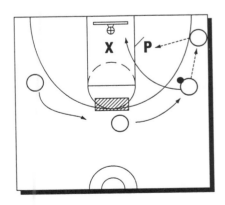

Diagram 22

(Diagram 23)   Some changed it. They took the middle man and put him at the other free-throw line and as the inbounder would run the baseline, he would set a screen and draw the charge. But you never get the call, and you won't get it in women's basketball either because last year, Tennessee lost a game running that play against Auburn. Pat Summit was out on the floor by the time her kid hit the floor yelling that she didn't get the call. So, I stopped teaching that part because you won't get the call.

Additional Thoughts
Defensively, when you press full-court, after you get the first trap, why take off the press? Why not match-up and get a second trap at mid-court? Then get a third trap in the corner. Stop taking the press off after one trap. There aren't that many good point guards. Everybody is playing the passing game. There aren't that many good passers.

If you are going to front the post, don't front the post back to chest. Face the post, and get your arm under the arm of the post.

Why do you follow on curls? If you do, the man is open. Do this. On all screen-downs, open up. We see ball and man. We step back and allow the defense through. Then we close back. Shoot the gap.

Anytime you throw the ball into the post, send a man to the dotted guy and replace.

Double the post and turn him so that he can't see the weak side.

If you send this guy, you replace behind. Don't leave a man on the other side where the post, being doubled-teamed, can't see him.

You are going to walk out of this clinic with a ton of notes. The factor is, take what is good for your philosophy. It might not be good next year or the year after, but keep it current on your files because your talent base might change and/or you might go to another level, and you have all of that philosophy there for you to continue to review. It was a tremendous pleasure to be here.

Individual Perimeter Play

One of the things we really believe in at Kansas is that you teach players how to play, instead of teaching plays. Control seems to be a big concern in most high schools where, if you have one player better than the rest, he will be double-teamed. One way to help that problem is to improve all of your players in the ability to handle, pass and shoot the ball. We will concentrate on this during the off-season, but we will also spend a great deal of attention to it during the season. Individuals need to improve their skill level so they feel comfortable wherever they catch the ball on the floor. When everyone on the floor must be guarded, your offense is going to go a little bit better. Most coaches will go into a situation where you are going to work a kid out, even if it is one-on-one. You have that kid working hard, running after all loose balls, etc., and you really lose focus on what you want to do. Let's say that it is a simple shooting drill. Remember what your goal is, what you are after.

The segment in which we want them to go hard is when they cut to receive the ball, and then go up hard. They are going to work for two or three seconds, then they rest, etc. What that will accomplish for you over a period of time is very good repetition as opposed to worrying about chasing a ball down and sprinting back. As you condition, you are going to get less good reps of what you are really after. We do everything game speed, and concentrate on a few things. No walks. Concentrate on the pivot foot and the beginning of the dribble. Have a quick release on all shots. Try to get as close to a game situation in these individual drills as you can.

Pet Peeves: Catch the ball with both hands. Any bobbled catch in a shooting drill, don't let them shoot the ball. If they want to shoot it, they must catch it. Their concentration will improve during the game, and their shot selection will improve. We want to finish each move, if it is a penetrating move, straight up and straight down. Get your kids to play under control, so they are not floating.

Typical Individual Workout: At Kansas, gym space and availability of coaches is not a problem. I understand this isn't the case at the high school level. At the high school level, you may not know which players are going to be the best. We do these drills with three players at a time, even during the season. This is a rule during the off-season, but we also do it this way during the season. This way we get maximum reps and we don't spend too much time on the floor with each. One of the first things we do is ballhandling drills. It doesn't matter who they are. They are going through stationary ballhandling drills. We don't necessarily tell them what to do. This goes back to teaching the players how to play. They can do figure eights, pounding the ball through the legs, over the head, etc. They get creative just watching each other. The bottom line is that they get more comfortable with the ball.

We then go to two-ball drills. In this, we want to accomplish the use of both hands. We do these about $3/4$ speed. First, we do the zigzag drill, alternating the bouncing of the balls. We then do it bouncing the balls at the same time. We do these across court. Then, we do the advance and retreat dribble. We attack a spot on the floor and then back up. We continue to do that first a little to the right, then a little to the left. Alternate dribbles and then dribble at the same time. Next, do change of pace, change of direction. Don't get discouraged when the balls start flying all over the place. Our best ball handlers are kicking them because of the speed of the drill. They are doing it faster than they would normally bring the ball up the floor in a game. The goal here is to push yourself to see what you can do. The goal in the game is to not lose the ball. You will learn your capabilities.

(Diagram 1)   Chair Drills. Chair at the top of the key. We will also do the same thing on each wing. We will do a series of four moves. The idea is to fake the defense without turning your back. Face the defense. The first thing is a change of direction move, between the legs, crossover, etc. When they make this move, they then go shoot a layup. You must score the layup. Catch your rebound, and then repeat the drill coming back and go to the end of the line. He must make two layups going right to left, two layups going left to right. That's four made baskets. By the time he finishes the four moves, he will have 16 made baskets, just on the layups.

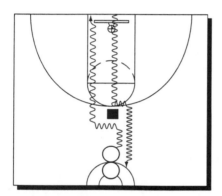

Diagram 1

(Diagram 2)   Attack and retreat. We don't particularly tell them how to do it. You push the defense, retreat, and then beat the defense to the basket.

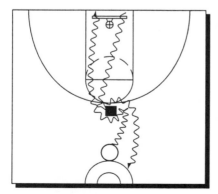

Diagram 2

(Diagram 3)   Inside-out move. No hesitation on this move. This is your fast-break type of move. The fourth move is a change of pace move where you slow, and they blow by the defense. Give them some freedom on this move to use what they feel comfortable with.

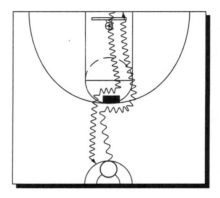

Diagram 3

(Diagram 4)   We do the same four moves for jump shots. Move the chair out. We want the shot taken in this area. They must follow their shots. We want them to make two of the four.

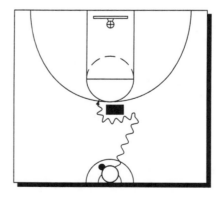

Diagram 4

Combination drills. You combine ballhandling as well as shooting. Try to keep in mind what you want to do, and minimize other things that will interfere with it. A stationary shooting drill is one where you are standing still, a coach passes you the ball, and you shoot it. The second I make you move and put the ball on the floor, you are in a combination drill. We try to set up a situation that you are going to see in a game. You are going to see situations where you catch the ball and you are guarded closely on the catch. You are going to see where you catch the ball and it is a close-out situation. You are working around screens so you can receive the ball. We try to focus on things they will see later on.

Spot and pump fake. We work both wings and the top of the key. This drill simulates when you receive the pass and you are going to try to get the defense out of their stance and take advantage of it. First of all, we want our players down when they catch the ball. On all pump fakes, the only thing we emphasize is that you stay down and the ball goes up. We want the ball to go all the way up to your eyes, and it looks just like your jump shot. We have them make five shots.

(Diagram 5)   Then we have them catch the ball and make one dribble either toward the baseline or toward the middle.

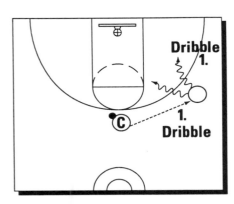

Diagram 5

(Diagram 6)   Now two dribbles, with sometimes changing direction on the second dribble. This is a big difference. When you go to a two-dribble move, you are actually reading the rest of the defense. On one dribble, you are just working on the man guarding

you. But with two dribbles, you must read the rest of the defense.

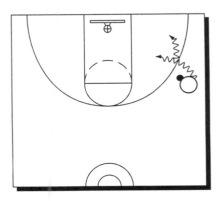

Diagram 6

(Diagram 7)   Live, one-on-one. Now add a defensive man in the middle and repeat the one-dribble and two-dribble drills. Don't let them force a shot.

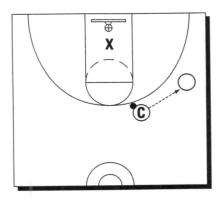

Diagram 7

(Diagram 8)   Drive series. The defense is there on the catch. You need to protect the ball. We teach our players to swing the ball across low. First, jab step and go. Make five layups. Then jab step and shoot. Freeze the defense and go up and shoot. Third, jab step, pump fake, and go. A coaching point is that when the player catches the ball and turns toward the basket, be sure that his lead foot is in the direction of the basket. Don't pivot in such a way that the lead foot goes too far and is pointing toward the baseline. Don't pivot in such a way that it takes you farther away from the basket. Make every player think aggressively.

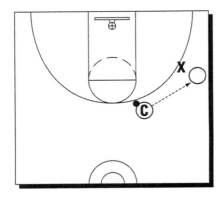

Diagram 8

(Diagram 9)   Step-to-side-and-back–type finishes. We use this move for those players who want to work with the idea of making the NBA. You may think that in a game situation that a player is working a little too hard to make a one-on-one move. But we are trying to meet the goals of our players as well as our team. Start the dribble and then dribble back for the shot. Step to the side quickly, get your space, and shoot. Everyone doesn't have this ability. Maybe you let them do it in practice, but not in a game. Our philosophy is that if you do it in practice, you can do it in a game.

(Diagram 10)   Cut, catch, and shoot off a down-screen. Coming off the down-screen, you can curl, fade and pop out. These are all reads according to what the defense does. So, cut, catch, and shoot. Coach at top of key. Shooter gets own rebound. Follow the shot. The shooter does not have to sprint after the ball. We are working on the cut and shot. Do this on both sides of the floor. Check the footwork; they must come off the screen very tight. We tell our players to grab the screener as they go by. That will keep the defense from following. It will emphasize the tightness of the screen. If you can get the ball where you want it, you are a good offensive player. Balance and square the shoulders for the shot. Don't be as concerned as to how they get into it as how they finish it. You must have a quick release, a two-second release.

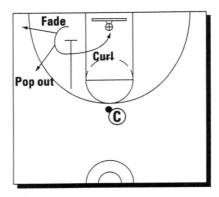

Diagram 10

(Diagram 11)   "Knockout." You have a passer, a screener, and a shooter and a defense. The passer must read the defense and deliver the ball. If the ball goes in the basket, then the shooter gets one point, the screener gets a half-point, the player that passes gets a half-point. First player to five wins. This gives the screener and passer credit. You can rotate this any way that you want. If the defender is scored on, he must leave the floor. If the offense scores, he stays on. You can also change the point of emphasis and give the shooter a half-point and the passer or the screener one point No rebound, no second shots.

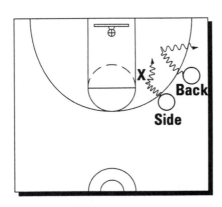

Diagram 9

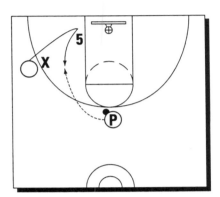

Diagram 11

the lane and can be screened in either direction. Player will probably go to the corner. We shadow all lateral-screens.

(Diagram 12)   "Flare-screens." On the flare-screen, the player sprints to the cut. We are big on these as these are difficult to guard. No defense is involved. Cut into the lane and then run away. Have the shoulders square to the basket as long as you can.

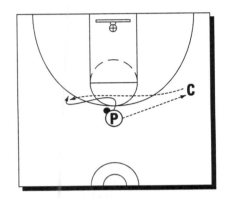

Diagram 13

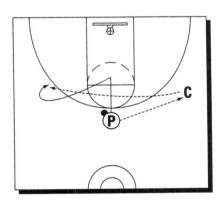

Diagram 12

(Diagram 13)   Do you want your players facing in all the time, or do you want them to backpedal? When you backpedal, your cut is much sharper.

(Diagram 14)   A counter to the flare-screen. Run the flare-screen and on the catch, push back one dribble toward the defense for the shot.

(Diagram 15)   Shallow cuts on the baseline. These are lateral-screen type situations. Player comes into

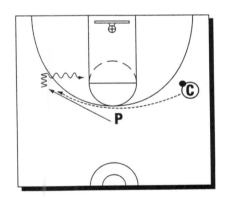

Diagram 14

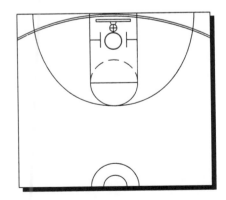

Diagram 15

(Diagram 16)   Catch the ball, pull the ball through, step in and shoot.

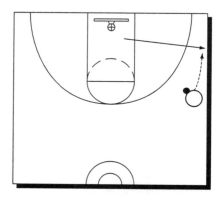

Diagram 16

(Diagram 17)   Fast break shooting drill. Sprint, catch, stop, go straight up and straight down.

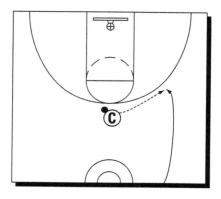

Diagram 17

(Diagram 18)   Getting into the lane. Offensively you want to get into this area. If you get the ball into this area, you have an opportunity to score or to pitch the ball to the open shooters, but most importantly, you have broken down the defense so that you have gained an advantage on the boards.

(Diagram 19)   These drills are set up from the wing area. Make one or two hard dribbles into the lane, get there, stop, elevate straight up, and shoot the ball.

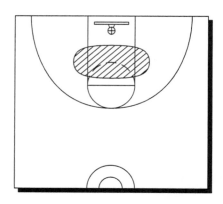

Diagram 18

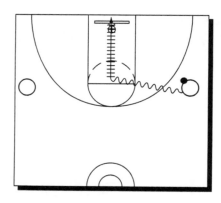

Diagram 19

(Diagram 20)   The second thing is to stop and fly by. As you get into the lane, stop, shot fake, and the defense will fly by. Lift is important to finish this play. Straight up, straight down.

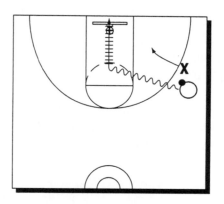

Diagram 20

(Diagram 21)   This is a stationary drill. Coach will hand the player a ball and smack the ball. The player must fight off the coach and go up into a shot. That's the kind of action that goes on in the lane. The lift is straight up. It's a difficult shot. You need touch and strength at the same time.

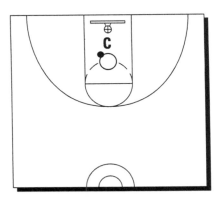

Diagram 21

(Diagram 22)   Shooting Drills. "Twenty-Five." Pick spots on the floor. You are going to combine twos and threes in the drill. Pass the ball for a three. The next time they receive the ball, they pump fake and take a dribble and take a two. Always return to the same spot, 3, 2, 3, 2 until they get to 25.

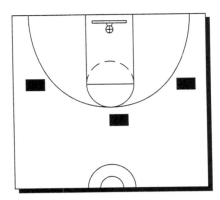

Diagram 22

(Diagram 23)   Three players, two balls. 1 and 2 have balls. 1 shoots and follows his shot. As he does so, 2 breaks out to the arc for a pass from 1. As this occurs, 2 shoots and follows his shot. As 2 shoots, 1 breaks out to a position on the arc. This is a continuous motion. You can run this against time, the number of makes, or you can change the type of shot.

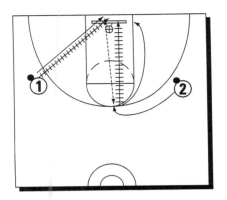

Diagram 23

The last thing we do is free-throw shooting. I try to create different situations. Some coaches don't want anyone talking while shooting free throws. They want the shooter concentrating on the free throw. But that's not how it is in a game; especially on the road. So, if you are duplicating game-like situations, even your teammates aren't quiet. They are communicating. Allow the players to talk, and make the shooter focus on shooting the ball.

Choosing a Zone Defense

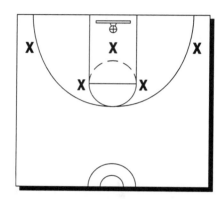

Diagram 1

We don't play zone much at Kansas. If you are going to choose a zone defense, the first question you must ask yourself is "why?" If you are like Temple, it will fit your philosophy. They probably play zone 95% of the time. Some other reasons could be that you have a lack of depth and you don't think you can make it through the whole game playing a man-to-man pressure defense. You may have a lack of quickness. You may play it when you are in foul trouble for a change of pace. You may have scouted an opponent and think they can't shoot the ball from the outside. Perhaps you use it against out-of-bounds plays.

The second thing you must ask yourself is what is the goal of the zone? Is it to trap? Do you want to protect the lane area? You can use a zone to speed up opponents. You can use a zone to slow down opponents. You can start a fast break out of the zone. You can run a numbered break. You know 2 will be on the right and 3 on the left.

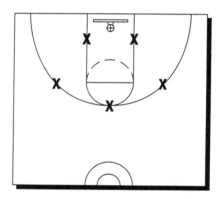

Diagram 2

A third thing you must consider is your personnel. What is the size and quickness of your team? You can do a lot of things with your zone.

(Diagram 1)   You can play a 2-3 zone that is strong in the middle. Your bigger players are closer to the basket for rebounding.

(Diagram 2)   You can play a 3-2 zone with the wings extended out to the three-point line and stop the perimeter shooting.

(Diagram 3)   You can bring the wings in a little and protect the lane a little better.

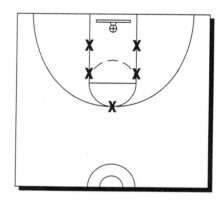

Diagram 3

(Diagram 4)   A different type of 3-2 zone is when you put a bigger man on the point and drop him to the block when the ball goes to the corner.

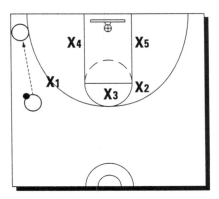

Diagram 4

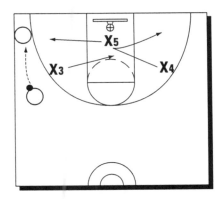

Diagram 6

(Diagram 5)   UNLV used to play the Amoeba. They had great talent. X3 would pressure the ball and on the pass to the corner, X5 would take the ball. X4 would take the low block on the ball side, and X3 would make the long slide across to the weak side. The movement would be on the pass.

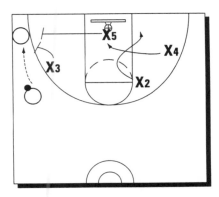

Diagram 7

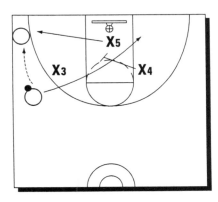

Diagram 5

(Diagram 6)   They also played it another way. On the pass to the corner, X3 would drop to the block, the short slide, and X4 would start into the lane and then cover the weak side. They did not worry about the skip-pass because X5 was quick enough to get to the corner.

(Diagram 7)   You can also trap out of this with X3 and X5. This is a very aggressive zone. You are trying to confuse them, you are trying to steal the ball and you are trying to throw them out of sync.

At Kansas, our primary defense is the man, and the goal of that defense is to steal the ball. When we went to a zone, we had decided several things. First, we decided what we could live with, and we decided how long we wanted to play it. We went to a zone just for a change, to give a different look, and also because of foul trouble. We might also play a zone because of our scouting report. We never enter a season thinking we will be a zone team, but we have control over that because we can recruit. In our man defense, we want to steal the ball. We don't even want a shot to go up when we play an extended zone. Our goal is to make a team take an outside shot over a hand, and a limit of only one shot. We will allow perimeter passes, but not penetrating passes. We will guard the ball, but we don't guard one or two passes away.

(Diagram 8)   Our zone is a 2-3 set that actually turns into a matchup. It is a partner situation. We have a simple set of rules. X1 and X4 are partners, X2 and X3 are partners.

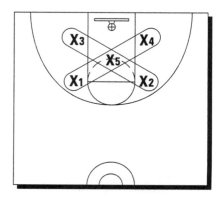

Diagram 8

(Diagram 9 and 10)   X5 stays between the ball and the basket.

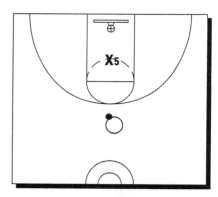

Diagram 9

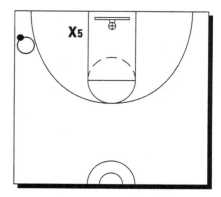

Diagram 10

Now, let's take X5 out of the diagram.

(Diagram 11)   If X1 is pressuring the ball. It's not a true matchup in that we don't follow the cutters through the zone, but X1 does guard the ball in this area. X4, his partner, is under the basket. X3 will rotate up; X2 will play the wing on the other side.

Diagram 11

(Diagram 12)   If the ball is passed to the corner, X3 takes the ball. X2 is X3's partner, and according to the rules, should be under the basket. But if that happens, that would put X4 off the court. So, X4 comes into the lane and X2 drops down in the lane and is aware of the weak side. X1 drops to the elbow. Picture this with X5 on the ball-side block. Remember, we are protecting the lane, and giving one shot over an outstretched hand. We have at least four people with one foot in the lane. We will adjust this if there is a very good shooter spotting up on the outside.

(Diagram 13)   If the offensive post would step out on the perimeter, we don't want X1 or X2 to guard him. We want X5 to guard him, but we don't want X5 to come out farther than the three-point line. Most of the times he is a passer. X2 will hedge if a shooter is on the wing.

(Diagram 14)   If 5 passes to the wing, X2 can guard the shooter. X3 is his partner and is under the basket with X1 and X4 adjusting. X5 drops back to his basic rule, between the ball and the basket.

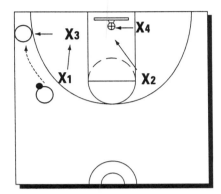

Diagram 12

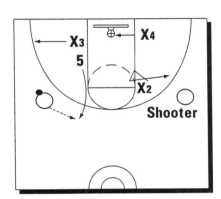

Diagram 13

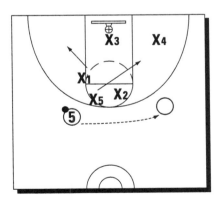

Diagram 14

(Diagram 15)   When the offensive center breaks out either to the top or the side, X5 will only follow as far as the three-point line. But it is his move.

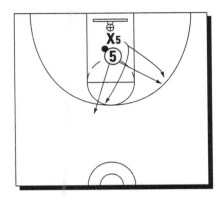

Diagram 15

(Diagram 16)   A four-out, one-in set puts this zone at a disadvantage. We don't have four people on the perimeter. We really want one person near the ball on the perimeter and four people touching the lane. Our goal is to protect the lane and a shot over a hand.

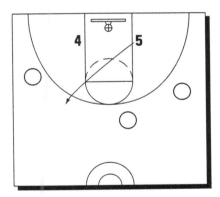

Diagram 16

(Diagram 17)   When teams have four players on the perimeter, X1 has the ball. X2 should be protecting the opposite elbow, but instead, he must cheat up. X4 should be under the basket inside the lane, but he must cheat a little to the outside, as does X3. So actually, we have given up our goal of protecting the lane. We have one man in the paint.

Diagram 17

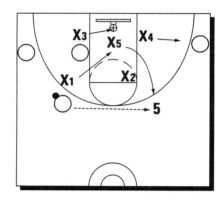

Diagram 18

(Diagram 18)   If X5 is on the perimeter and the ball is passed to 5, X2 will back off and X5 will come out as far as the arc to play him. If this happens too much, we then ask ourselves "why are we in it?" Because of the way that we play this zone, we cannot zone this team. Too many capable shooters are on the perimeter.

When you decide to go to zone, unless it is a pressure, trapping-type zone, I think that you must decide what you can live with. What will you allow? What is the goal of your zone? If the zone is your primary defense, you must learn how to work with that and adjust it to force some of the issues.

Drills for Post Play

You can add height to your pivot players. Height is the most overemphasized thing in the game. The high school coach must make a team out of whatever he or she has. You must adjust your thinking and work around what you have. Don't worry about height, and don't say that this is a rebuilding year. Your players read these things. Think about the opportunity that you give the players to lie down or to bail out. That's human nature. It can be a subconscious thing. Don't let them look for the easy way out. It can be a very subtle thing.

If you are not very tall around the basket, you can be quicker and you can learn to use the body. Teach kids to play laterally. If you can't play vertically, teach them to play laterally. If you are going to use your body, you must learn to shoot an extended arm shot. I can't bring the ball directly over my head to shoot inside if I am 6'2" against a 6'6" defender. The only way I can shoot such a shot is if I shoot a fallaway jump shot, and then that eliminates the second effort part of the offense. We don't win games on one effort alone. The best play in basketball is the three-point play, but it is the three-point play that occurs when you score on the inside shot and get fouled. For this to occur, your kids must know how to finish that shot.

You must practice finishing. Get a football air dummy, and make contact with your player as he is shooting. After you shoot, as soon as your feet hit the floor, you leap back into the air. You don't want to see where the ball is coming from. If you do that, the big player gets it. The extended arm shot is important. Not many people teach hook shots anymore. But if I take the shot with an extended arm away from my body it will make me taller. A hook shot is not shot from the eyebrow, but shoot it so that the upper arm, the biceps, hits your ear. Now I am as tall as I can possibly be inside. Most missed hook shots are short. When we teach hook shots, we emphasize

never to leave a hook shot short. Get that ball high and soft on the board and drop it through the basket.

Another thing is faking. There is too much ball in the fake. Don't fake the ball up over your head. Don't straighten your knees. I'm not going to beat him with size; I am going to beat him with quickness. If I straighten my knees, I am very slow because I must bend my knees to get into a basketball position before I can go back up to shoot. If you did get the man in the air, you aren't in a position to shoot. The fake should be, not to get him in the air, but fake to freeze him. To do that, the ball never leaves the basketball position. Keep the ball between the waist and the chin.

The best fake inside isn't the ball, it's the head and the eyes. If you look at the basket, you only need a small ball movement. Keep the ball close to the body. Keep the ball face high and start your shot from there. Catch it high; keep it high. The same thing is true on a rebound. Don't bring it down. Palms. I want to see your palms all night. I am controlling the defensive man from my elbow to elbow. Plus, you have your hands where you can be quick. I am now a target. You aren't going to outjump the opponent because he is taller, but you are quicker to the ball. Tell your shorter kids that we will not win the game if we rebound over our heads. I must rebound the ball in front of my face. First, I must find my man, make contact and keep him behind me, then I can rebound in front of my face.

(Diagram 1)　　Double bounce drill. How do you practice offensive rebounding? Your player must want to rebound offensively. Coach has the ball. 1 and 2 have their hands on their knees. We have two managers, each with a ball. Coach bounces the ball. 1 and 2 cannot take their hands off their knees until the ball bounces a second time. Then, they go for it, the one who gets it is on offense, the other one is on defense. The game is to three, no rules from then on. You must score. You soon see how important the jump shot is inside. I don't allow every player to shoot a jump shot in the paint. I want you to rebound and go to the basket with an extended arm shot. I want you going to the basket with a jump hook. If the ball happens to get knocked away, the manager tosses a ball to the closest man. This will teach them to protect the ball. This will teach them to finish.

Diagram 1

(Diagram 2) These two spots are paramount to any drive. If your player can get into this box area and he has a little jump hook, he can shoot this shot.

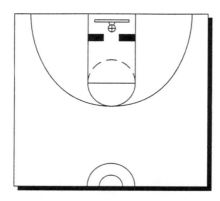

Diagram 2

(Diagram 3) Anytime your pivot man gets this pass with defensive pressure on the top, don't have him think basket. Have him think to drive to that spot. Make one dribble between the legs and look to

land on that spot with both feet. To do this, you must take the roundness out of the game. The game is angles. The dribble is making the game round.

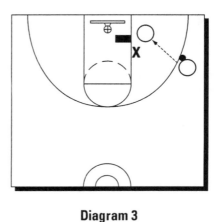

Diagram 3

(Diagram 4) Don't make an arc to the box. Footwork puts the execution back in the game.

Diagram 4

(Diagram 5) The same thing is true on the wing. You can't have a banana drive. You can't shy away from contact, or you can't control the ball when getting contact, or you have lousy feet, or any combination of the above. When I fake and go, I am thinking box, not basket. Drive with the inside leg first on a direct line to the box. Play the angle. Get some charging fouls. If I am going to drive, I must realize that I have a little advantage. On any drive, I must get a piece of the defensive man immediately. Now I am playing with angles, and it takes him out of the game. But if I banana drive, he has the angle to cut me off. If I have my back to the basket, drop-step and nail him behind me. And don't bounce the ball to the middle of the lane. If I catch my defensive man on the high side, I can bounce it toward the baseline because there is nobody there. But if you don't bounce it in the middle, you need to shoot the hook shot.

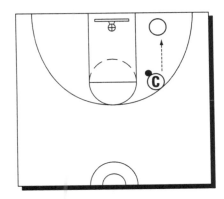

Diagram 6

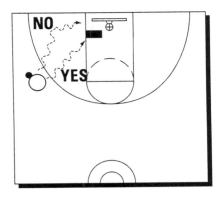

Diagram 5

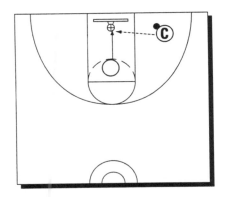

Diagram 7

(Diagram 6)   Start this drill with your pivot player with his back to the coach. Your pivot player is wearing gloves. Coach calls out the name of the player, and then the player spins to face the coach. Coach has thrown the ball, not always a good pass. It may be a chest pass, or a bounce pass. This helps the pivot player to catch the ball.

(Diagram 7)   The coach has the ball and lobs the ball into the lane. The player must catch the ball one-handed, control it and shoot it. Make them have their hands ready. If your post has a problem catching the ball, don't allow bounce passes to the post. Where does the big kid have the problem? With the low pass. Pass the ball in at eye level. Fake down and throw up.

(Diagram 8)   Positioning. If I am going to be a target, I must demand the ball. Make your guards pass the ball inside, and give them credit when they do. Keep track of pivot feeds in practice and in games. Sometimes when you are playing 5-on-5, nobody can shoot until your post has touched the ball three times. Your post must demand the ball. In order to do this, the post must control a certain area of the court. I must control this arc area, which is on a direct line between the ball and the basket. If I am higher than the direct line, I am susceptible to the low front. If I am lower, then the defense can front me on the high side.

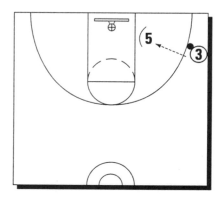

Diagram 8

(Diagram 9)   This could be in the center of the lane for a count or two if I catch the ball in the arc area. The shot is made by pointing the foot and the toe in the direction you are going. The foot of the offensive man controls the top foot of the defensive man. Don't let pressure from the defense move you up the lane. You must resist that pressure. I take a washable mark and make a half moon on the floor. Get your heels on that half moon, as wide as you can. Show your palms. Be a target. If I get pressure to the top, don't let your legs go together. Keep a wide stance. And use a stutter step to keep the defense sealed. Then you must go to meet the pass.

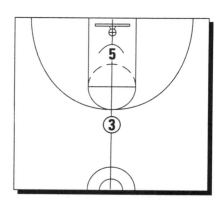

Diagram 9

(Diagram 10)   If I am overplayed on the high side, I am not in a good position to receive the ball.

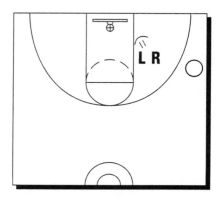

Diagram 10

(Diagram 11)   But if I move my feet in his direction, then I open up a passing lane. The weight must be over the balls of the feet. Don't fight with the shoulder blades, use your butt and hips.

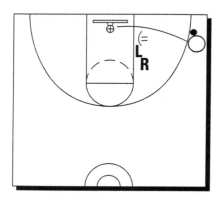

Diagram 11

(Diagram 12)   Second feeder. If the post is being played on the low side, the entry pass can be made by 1 passing to 2, and then the pass is made inside.

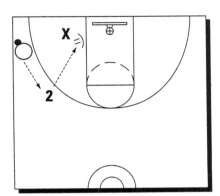

Diagram 12

Match-Up Zone

First, let's talk about attacking any zone. Then we will get into the match-up.

(Diagram 1)   Do not pass the ball in the direction of the dribble. If you want to pass to 3, take the ball away first on the dribble, then make the pass to 3. If you dribble in the direction of the dribble, the entire zone moves in that direction. Don't throw the ball into the corner unless you have a shot. Fill the short corners.

(Diagram 13)   Or 2 can dribble the ball toward the baseline to improve the angle of the pass. This is one bounce, two at the very most.

Diagram 13

Diagram 1

(Diagram 2)   Put men in the short corners behind the zone. Just occupying that area keeps the back line of the zone from coming high. You must emphasize the pass fake. The defense is attuned to your face, and the ball. By faking the pass, some zones will move five feet.

(Diagram 3)   The zone wants to keep C, D, and E back, and never move. If you allow A and B to cover the rest of the area, you will never get an offensive rebound. If the ball is passed to 3, A will take the ball and B will drop into the middle. To be successful, you must attack the area between B and C.

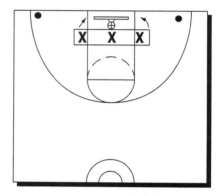

Diagram 2

Diagram 4

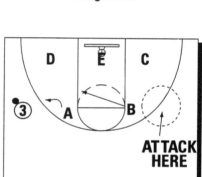

Diagram 3

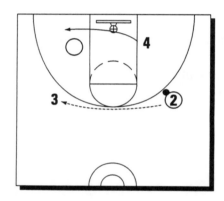

Diagram 5

(Diagram 4)   Penetration. You can't beat zones by just shooting threes, you must penetrate into the gaps. 1 passes to 3, A comes over, B drops back. 1 steps in and gets the return pass from 3. If he doesn't step in prior to receiving the pass, 1 is two dribbles away. We don't want that. We want to pass and step in and penetrate. The dribbler will point his hip toward the closest defensive man and will bounce the ball near the center of the body.

(Diagram 5)   If at all possible against a zone, reverse to three people. Show the ball to one side with the idea of attacking the other. We want to catch the ball in the shot position. Make your players catch the ball with their knees bent. Catch the ball with the shooting foot back. As they step into the shot, the elbow is over the knee; we call it "the gather position."

(Diagram 6)   Against the match-up. Anytime there is a switch, someone is not guarded.

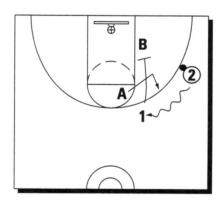

Diagram 6

(Diagram 7)   If 2 cuts against a match-up, D will take him until 2 gets into E's territory. E then takes 2 and D comes back.

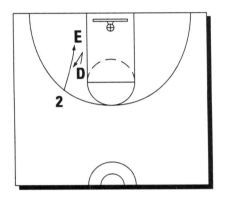

Diagram 7

(Diagram 8)   By the way, if you are playing against a man-to-man switching defense and you know they are going to switch, don't cut over the top.

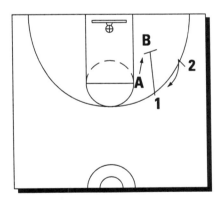

Diagram 8

(Diagram 9)   Come up, then go below.

(Diagram 10)   In a match-up zone, there are two basic lines of defense. We are going to cut through those lines and drive these lines. We want to split

two people with a cut. 3 can split D and A. 1 can split A and D or A and B. That moves you into an open spot. That cut is not any more than three or four steps. Then, I change directions, and V-cut into an open spot.

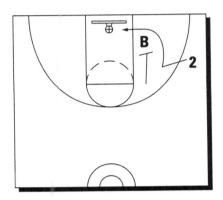

Diagram 9

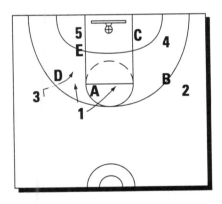

Diagram 10

(Diagram 11)   1 cuts by A. A follows him for about three steps and gives him to E. Just then, 1 will change directions and go to the open spot. The rule is that you never cut into an occupied area. Find an open spot.

(Diagram 12)   2 goes down, B stays with him for several steps and comes back and C takes 2. Then, 2 can cut in either direction.

Diagram 11

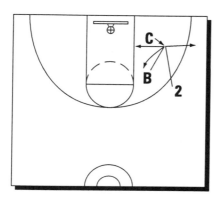

Diagram 12

(Diagram 13)   Never do this. Never run 2 completely through. That's something the zone practices. You must attack the seams of the zone. Don't attack the floor with positions of players; you attack the seams.

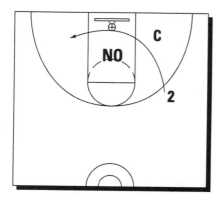

Diagram 13

(Diagram 14)   You must also cut from the rear and fill the short corner.

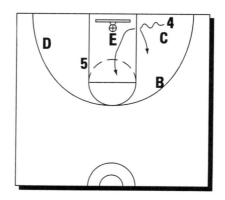

Diagram 14

(Diagram 15)   Drill. Put two players in the short corners, and you can use managers. Make the zone move as the managers pass the ball back and forth. Make the offensive players find the cracks in the zone.

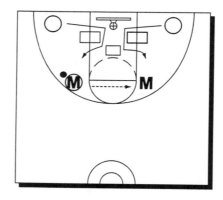

Diagram 15

(Diagram 16)   4 starts in with D on him. 4 steps out to the top. Who takes him? A and B are matched up with 1 and 2. Anytime you cut into a position, you occupy it for two seconds. Read the defense. Don't hurry. Find two people, split two steps and cut into an open spot. The man in the short corner is in the

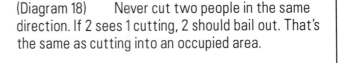
gathered position, ready to shoot. If you have the ball on the left side of the floor for three seconds, you should change sides. Three seconds is long enough. Make the zone move.

Diagram 16

(Diagram 17)   It is easy to rebound because you have all five men moving. If you have a little guard, keep him in that area. Put your big man in the area from short corner to short corner. Modify that to fit your personnel.

Diagram 17

(Diagram 18)   Never cut two people in the same direction. If 2 sees 1 cutting, 2 should bail out. That's the same as cutting into an occupied area.

Diagram 18

(Diagram 19)   Back to penetration. 1 has the ball and passes to 2. 2 dribbles into the gap favoring A. When stopped, 2 can pass back to 1 who has stepped in as B sagged into the middle.

Diagram 19

Pressure Defense

Pressure defense is used to control tempo. When they press, they don't go for the steal, as they want turnovers. Don't run at people. We used different calls depending on scenarios (time, score, who's inbounding).

"121" Alignment and Roles

(Diagrams 1 and 2)   Alignment: If 4 keeps his dribble, X2 contains his man. X3 picks up 4 and X1 traps from behind. X4 and X5 are back.

Don't deny 3 and 4.

Push 1 and 2 toward the corners.

X3 is on the ball.

If 4 inbounds the ball, they will let it go back to him.

Don't let guards handle the ball. Instead, keep it in the big men's hands.

The trap comes from behind.

(Diagrams 3 and 4)   The ball goes to the corner and then comes back to the inbounder. X2 fakes and recovers, X3 takes the ball, and X1 blocks the corner man.

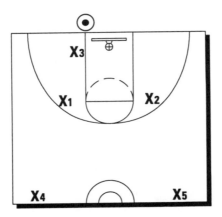

Diagram 1

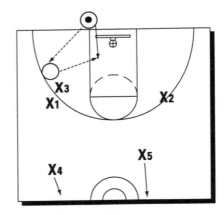

Diagram 3

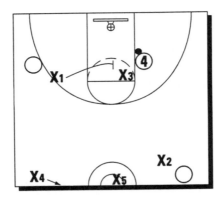

Diagram 2

Diagram 4

"Hard" (Point guard inbounding the ball)

(Diagram 5)   X1 and X3 trap. X2 takes away the pass back to the point guard. X5 must slide into the play. X4 covers up. They will give up the long diagonal pass because they'll run it down.

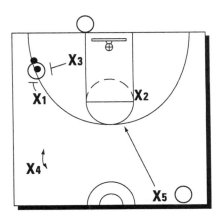

Diagram 5

(Diagram 6)   If the ball does get back to the point guard, X2 fakes and recovers, X3 picks up 1 and they'll trap from behind.

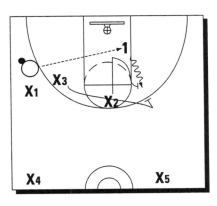

Diagram 6

We only try to get two traps; then we run to the land and match down.

The ideal trap area is just over half-court because you can't pass back.

"Stay"

(Diagram 7)   X1 picks up the ball and tries to entice it up the sideline hard. We want to trap from behind.

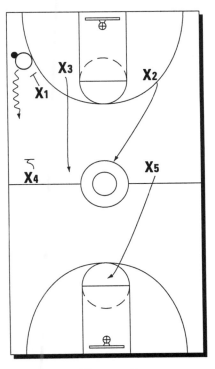

Diagram 7

(Diagram 8)   Once the ball is trapped, X2 has 2 helpers, X4 or X5 can take the cutter, but they must talk. X2 fakes and recovers.

Here we are letting you get the ball in.

This is used as a controlled press to make you work in your half-court "D."

What if a team uses a 4-across set?

(Diagram 9)   They will match up. X1 and X2 deny. Let the ball come in to 4 or 5. Don't make a trap. Let them make a play.

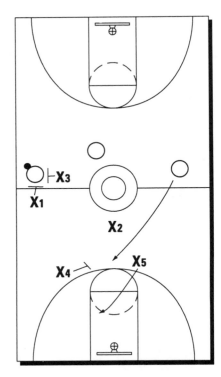

Diagram 8

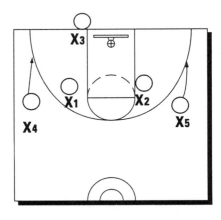

Diagram 9

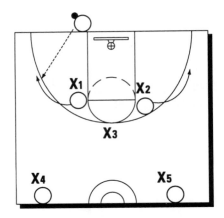

Diagram 10

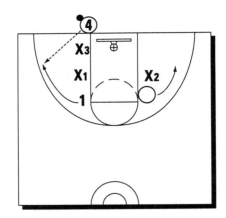

Diagram 11

(Diagram 12)   X3 then goes and traps with X2. They will let it be reversed back.

Diagram 12

"Dead Ball Situations"
Centerfield and shortstop

(Diagram 10)   Centerfield. X1 and X2 face guard and X3 roams wherever it goes. X3 and that man will trap.

(Diagram 11)   Shortstop. X3 is on the ball and then gets the best ballhandler so he can't get it.

Don't let the point guard get the ball. Make it go to the other side of the floor, but still let it come back.

Tips

Pick a spot in front of the man with the ball to cut him off because the trap is coming from behind.

If the trap gets beat, they hustle back to the lane and match down.

It is a conservative press. They let you catch it for the most part and they don't give up the easy hoop.

See your defensive man's back.

Never put 4 or 5 on the ball because a big player ends up playing a 1 or 2.

By trapping a big player, you're forcing the ball into a ballhandler's hands.

Drills

Knick Drill:

(Diagram 13)   4-on-4 continuous. X has the ball going at O. The O's on the sideline must get a foot in the circle before they can get into play. If X scores, they are on defense and O tries to inbounds up the floor against them until half-court where next group is waiting for them (Z).

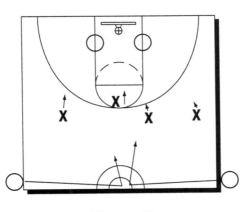

Diagram 13

(Diagram 14)   After X scores. Once O gets over half-court, Z is on defense and two Z's must get a foot in half-court circle.

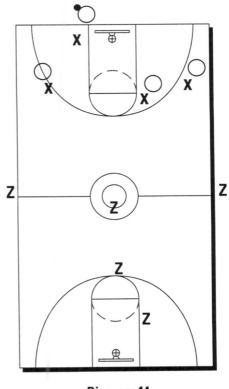

Diagram 14

Zigzag Drill: Covers three things in one: sliding, flicking, closing out.

(Diagram 15)   Zigzag to half-court. O throws the ball to the coach on sideline. Manager with a ball runs and O must flick from behind. O then turns and must close out X who got the ball from the coach.

(Diagram 16)   Press Drill (4-on-4 or 5-on-5)

The coach throws the ball over X's head, and they go down the floor. O is on defense and must get in the play.

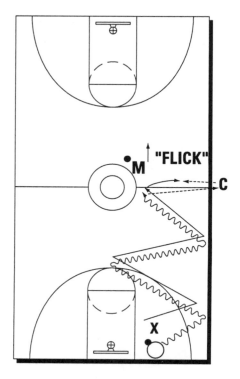

Diagram 15

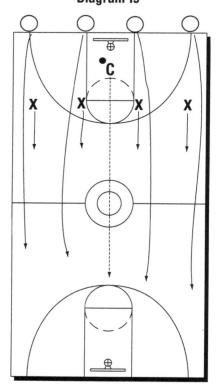

Diagram 16

(Diagram 17)   If, when X scores, they get into the press and O goes up the floor.

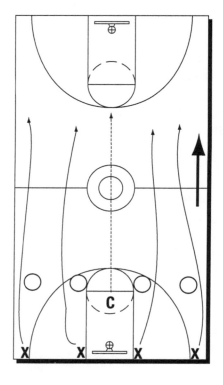

Diagram 17

Do lots of full-court drills because it enhances conditioning.

20/20 Hindsight

I have been working mostly with the Big Twelve Conference as the liaison between the coaches and the Commissioner and the officials and the Commissioner, and I work with game management. I was fortunate that when I finished coaching, I became the interim AD at Northwestern University, and I saw basketball from a little different perspective, just as I do in my present job. I am allowed to do what I think we need to do to have a presence for Big Twelve basketball. I have had a chance to see what the NBA is doing in promotion and marketing. I was at the NBA camp with college seniors and will be in Chicago for the International camp where players come to try out in front of 30 or 40 foreign coaches. I help run the conference tournament in Kansas City. We run the men's and the women's tournaments at the same time, alternating throughout the week.

I see many games each year. We want to do everything we can to improve basketball and basketball relations, marketing, etc., in the Big Twelve. I got out of being an Athletic Director because I saw myself getting further and further away from basketball, which has been my whole life. When I went to Duke, they had been losing and I had to do many things marketing-wise to promote the program. Today, you must be very cognizant of the marketing of your program. I've seen coaches lose their jobs simply because the seats weren't being filled. If the attendance goes down, they don't get rid of the players, they get rid of the coach. It's really getting tougher and tougher to coach today. You had a player trying to choke a coach; another player threw somebody out the window. They are really great role models. If you want to impress your kids about how to dress, you can talk about Dennis Rodman. It used to be that more and more people looked to Washington for leadership. Unfortunately, Washington died in 1799.

The profession is really getting more fragile. This is a profession of decreasing opportunities. When you get a coaching position opening in our league, you can't believe the number of requests to be an assistant coach at that level. When I was at Northwestern, I had at least 100 applications for an assistant position. How are you going to select? As you move up the ladder, it is a profession of decreasing opportunity. I think there are some opportunities at the lower levels. In looking at the upward mobility, one of the most important things is your networking and your preparation. Preparation includes working camps, attending clinics, and meeting with other coaches. I've been trying to sell an idea to a company nationally that would help coaches where they would just sponsor little workshops where players could get together and share ideas. Not a speaker, but each coach offer some ideas. Preparation is so important. Here is a saying: "Good things come to a person who waiteth, if he works like hell while he waiteth." That applies to the coaching profession and officiating.

In our conference we are trying to bring in new, young officials. From a defensive standpoint, we say to make something happen, don't wait for something to happen. That's applied to our basic development. The things we expect our players to do, we must do ourselves. We must lead. I sometimes wonder about coaches having players coming out at 6 a.m. to run, and the head coach doesn't show. I think the head coach must be involved. The players are smart in their perception of you. If you are demanding something of them, you certainly must be the example for them because they are going to follow along in a much better fashion if you are involved.

Another thing is, make your own job better. Some coaches want to coach at the college level and spend all their time preparing for that and let some things go unturned, and they could be doing a better job at their current level. "If you aren't excited to be where you are, and you don't put all your energy and enthusiasm in the job, you aren't helping anybody."

You aren't helping yourself, you aren't helping your players, you aren't helping your school. That's what happened to me when I was interim AD. I couldn't get excited about seeing all the other sports contests. I didn't have the passion for the other sports that I did for basketball. I think basketball is one great sport, an unbelievable sport, but from the coaching standpoint, it is getting tougher and tougher and the word I use is that it is becoming very "fragile." Think about what a coach has to be and what he has to do. He must be a master of the X's and the O's. He must be a master of psychology, a psychiatrist and a motivator. When you talk about motivation, you start at the top with self-motivation and then your staff. There's the periphery, the cheerleaders, the band, etc. You need a pep band. Then, you must motivate the fans. You must be able to market your program. "If you don't promote it, a terrible thing happens—nothing!" Today, one of my biggest fears I see is the decreasing attendance. If you want to be big time, look around at the big-time programs and see what they're doing.

"Success comes in cans, not cannots." I know you are limited, especially in high school, but you must continue to chip away, and improve something in your program for the coming year. At the end of your year, write down the number one thing that you need to improve your program for next year. Then, put down how you are going to attain it. Make a list of several things in order of importance. It's frustrating, but you must be able to pay for it. More and more budgets are being cut and you are going to have to raise the money outside the budget. Look at the amount of games that some teams play on the road to get the guaranteed gate, and get beat. That's a tough way to coach. Right now there are 307 Division I head coaching jobs. How many really good jobs came open this year? When someone takes a job, he or she is confident that it can be done. You are always building your reputation. Wins and losses is where it starts.

I'm involved in game management. When I was a high school coach, I knew nothing about game management. If something happens at one of your home games, guess who's held responsible? We make a game management tape and send it to our schools. We talk about how the officials should be greeted when they come in, food for after the game, what they will have before the game, security for officials, security for the visiting team, security for the home team, parking places, etc. We have a game management manual, but we also put out a videotape. We have the supervisor of officials come in and go over rules, rules interpretation, new rules and experimental rules. This will go to the schools, and the coach can use it with his team. We also give our guidelines for a game being called because of inclement weather, etc.

Also, a coach is wise if he makes friends with the head of the business department. Maybe he can get some student help with correspondence, etc. Another is the art department for posters, etc. This will help you build interest in the program. Building interest is not seasonal. Your season is 12 months of the year. Maybe your school has a printing shop. I always sent my players a newsletter every month. I send things to the coaches of our league. I had a coach leave our conference, she went into the pros, and she asked to remain on the mailing list. Coaching demands constant attention; you really must work at it. Not only do I go to clinics, seminars, etc., but I send my secretary to seminars. It recharges them; gives them new ideas.

One thing about attending clinics. When my assistants attended clinics, I wanted them to give me notes when they returned, particularly on how our program could be improved. I wanted them typed and given to me, and I wanted copies of all other notes given to our staff. One of the easiest things to do in this profession is to forget. You must invest in your future. One way is to buy the materials that will be helpful to you. Organization, loyalty, communicating to your boss. That is key. Lack of communication in the athletic department is leading to the downfall of a lot of people. What great teaching aids videos are; you can do so much with them. We would make a videotape on the expectations for our program so the new players coming in would know what to expect. Sit down with your players and watch it. Remember, you must promote your program all 12 months out of the year.

You can't just play in a summer league, you must learn the game. We would assign videos for our players to watch. We would always have something on shooting. We would have a tape on defensive expectations. Our league is advocating being able to work with four players at a time instead of three. In that way, there can be an offense and a defense. We have some legislation going on that. We had a video on dress codes. We had an A, B, and C dress code. A was coat and tie, B was sweater with shirt with a collar, C was sweats. If we were just riding to an away game on a bus, we would just wear sweats. But with the video, the new players coming in would know what A, B, and C dress codes were. We had a video on principles of offensive movement. If you get the ball, your share of the time you will be on offense, 80% of the time without the ball. You must sell your players on that concept, and you can get this across with the use of the video. We had our players sign in when they watched.

The ultimate responsibility of you as a coach is to get your players to overachieve. Give them lessons on the court and off the court. Of course, you are always working with behavior, with drugs, and with alcohol abuse. The NCAA has a seven-minute tape; all the schools in the tournament had to look at it. We must address this problem. I sent out the article in the New York Times concerning the betting scandals. With the game management, you need to have a manager to greet the visiting team when they come in the night before; you must be organized. The more you write it down, the more you become known as a better organizer. That helps you in your professional growth. How about your filing system?

At a clinic like this, I would take notes on everything. I would add on the side with a red pen the things that will help our program.

You need to assign summer projects for your staff. You also must assign responsibilities. The delegation of responsibility is very important. I have been involved in the hiring of some coaches. It is really important that your reputation is one where you are really going to follow the rules, not take the shortcuts. The expectations of the athletic departments are high and they are trying to find someone to fit those expectations. The one thing that is so important today is people skills. You must be able to be interviewed. Some coaches have the reputation of being a recruiter, some have the reputation of being a teacher. I spent a half a game sitting with Pete Newell recently. Some of you younger people don't know who he is. He is the man who runs the big-man camp for the NBA. Sitting with him and talking about the players on the floor was very interesting. He has a video coming out about big-man play (available through USA Coaches Clinics). He is a great teacher of the game. This type of tape would be invaluable to a young player. Look at it with the player, and have some notes to go with it.

In hiring a staff, you must be able to get along and trust one another. In upward mobility, it is not who you know as much as who knows you and your personal reputation. If you are interested in moving up in this profession, you must have a game plan.

Why should someone hire you? How good is your resume? How is yours going to be a little different? You should read a book on hiring. Here's another saying: "At first you inherit millions—not dollars, but hours. It's how you invest those hours that counts." I really believe that, and it can be related to players. If they will spend time on their game, you will see improvement. If I am going to give you a recommendation for a job, I must know you. But it is still better if I know the person at the other end where they are applying. Networking is also staying in touch.

Here are some things I see happening on the court today. I see teams running their out-of-bounds plays too slow. I always put something new in about January, just to stimulate interest, an out-of-bounds play for example. This is good, particularly the second time around the league. I like what I see offensively with misdirection. Offensively, the more you are in the middle of the floor, the harder you are to guard. You must keep the ball in the middle and you must have offensive sets for different situations today. And you must really look at your spacing.

(Diagram 1)   I think this out-of-bounds set is easily played because there is no spacing. You need to be spread out on an inbounds play either at the end or on the side.

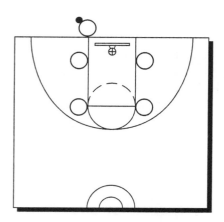

Diagram 1

if the ball came out of the trap until X5 could recover back.

Diagram 2

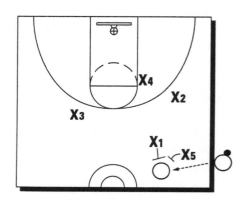

Diagram 3

(Diagram 2)   I haven't seen many people do this. We ran a 1-3-1 half-court trap. We would hold X4 near the elbow and then come over for the second trap on the short pass, and if it is the long pass to the corner, we had the X move where X4 comes down and fronts on the block. X3 was responsible for everything on the weak side as far as rebounding was concerned. X1 had to protect the high-post area. This is a great chance for a steal. You try to sell the fact that the high post is open, but it really isn't.

(Diagram 3)   This is a "one and done" trap on the sideline out-of-bounds. Again, we put our big man on the ball. X5 plays between the inbounder and the basket. X4 had deep responsibility. X5 and X1 would trap, X2 takes the ball side and X3 would slide back

At our staff seminars, we would go over staff responsibilities and make some changes. I don't want the same coach to be in charge of scouting for five straight years. I felt that changing duties would also help to develop my staff so that when they had an opportunity for a head coaching job, I could say they had these various responsibilities. So, we would switch responsibilities. We would have someone in charge of academics and someone in charge of housing. I wanted to know where they lived. I also had a job description for my secretary so that my staff knew her duties. Make your own situation better. What does your locker room look like; what does your office look like? Step back, look, analyze and don't get too impatient. Work at building this program one brick at a time so that it is solid. Go over with your AD what you need to make your program better, but be able to show how you are going to finance it. The best time to get this is when you are signing your contract. After you sign your contract, you are on your own. I've told coaches that one of the things they should have in their contract is that the school should hire a very good marketing person and give that person a budget. You have a great opportunity to improve your players. Your plan has to be how each player has the opportunity to improve. Correct practice makes perfect, not practice makes perfect. Give instruction out of season with your videos.

Meetings with the parents are important, and an out-of-season improvement plan is important. At the end of the season, each of our staff would put down two or three things each player could do well. Plus areas to work on out of season to make themselves better. We gave out notebooks to our players. One thing was the player questionnaire; this gives you a little more insight on the team. Have your team fill this out and return without names. Have them list the first and second player for each of the following:

- Which players have the best "team" attitude on our squad?
- Who are the most popular players on the squad?
- Which players spend the most time reviewing videotapes on themselves and the team?
- Who are the strongest players on our team?
- Who are the most dedicated and disciplined players on our team?
- Our team is behind one point with eight seconds remaining in the game. If you could pass to anyone on the squad, to whom would you pass?
- Of all the players on our team, who exhibits the most poise on the floor during crucial parts of the game?
- Who are the "take charge" players on our team?
- Who are the most consistent ballhandlers on our squad?

- Who are the most consistent shooters on our squad?
- Who are the most valuable players on our squad?
- Which players are the most unselfish, most interested in the team as a whole and play most "for the team"?
- Which players on our squad have the most overall ability?
- Who are the most "disciplined" players on the squad (and off the court)?
- Which players on our team are in the best physical condition?
- Which players have actually helped you or influenced you the most?
- Who are the best students on the team?
- To which players do you look most often for leadership?
- Who are the hardest workers on our squad?
- Who has improved the most over the past six months?
- Who are the best defensive players (stoppers!) on our squad?
- Your vote for captain (co-captain) for next season.
- Which players are most likely to "give up their bodies" and dive on the floor or draw a charge?
- Which players are the most "vocal" on the floor?
- Who are our biggest basketball "junkies"?

They fill these out and they turn them in without putting their name on it. You can learn a lot. Also, in the notebook there were tips on shooting, and on various offensive and defensive techniques of our team. There were some running drills included also. We must give our players positive reinforcement because we are living in a world that has a lot of negativity in it. You can't do it alone, so you better learn how to delegate. You must be creative to get the seats filled. I hope I have helped you to understand just how important the areas are that I have mentioned.

Post Play

I was fortunate to work the Pete Newell at his Big Man Camp in Hawaii with the pros. People told me that the pros would not be that receptive, but I found it just the opposite. We have 25 players each session. They are tremendous; they thirst for knowledge. They have a great work ethic. The game is different for big players. They have to run the court further than the perimeter players; they get banged every time they go to the basket. There is a myriad of things that happen to post players that other players on the team really don't understand. I have coached at all levels; the important thing on all levels is that you never stop learning. When you get tall players, many times they become a project. You need to work on their agility to get them to become coordinated so that they can become a player. Some coaches forget that. They spend time with the other players. We want to make players better, whether they are All-Americans or role players.

As an assistant coach, I must ask myself after practice if my players have improved. Am I using the right drills; do we need new drills? To me that is the fun part of coaching, to come up with some new drills, to elaborate on some drills, to extend some drills that we already have. You can't give them the same drills day after day, year after year. You must come up with some drills that change a little bit. And your drills must be challenging. Sometimes it is just the particular number of exercises that have to be done which makes the drill really good. We do this in all our shooting drills. We end with a buzzer shot. They must make the last shot. They become more intense. We want to make the drills game-like. Think of that when you prepare drills. If they aren't, I don't think they will be as effective.

We want to have a ball in the players' hands. The kids like to have the ball in their hands when they do the drills. Be careful that you don't work too much on

making your plays better rather than making your players better. I'd rather have the better players. You are high school coaches and most don't have the luxury of assistant coaches where you can break up your team into small and big players. But you can bring in groups for pre-practice or post-practice or on Saturdays and work with them. It really pays off. When you start devising drills for player improvement, it becomes coach improvement.

One last point. I can't overemphasize the idea of game play. Your reward in coaching comes from the fact that you see them use these skills, moves, in a game. Don't forget to work with your perimeter players; teach them passing angles, teach them to pass away from the defense or your post players aren't going to reach their potential. You can't just work on post moves. They must get the ball in the post in the game or they will stop working. They must touch the ball in the half-court offense.

(Diagram 1)   "8 Across." I like multipurpose drills that include conditioning while getting the players to do the fundamental skills. This is a good drill to end practice. It gets players to make the power layup as opposed to a shot in and around the basket. The power layup is when a player squares to the glass and knifes to the basket. I like that term; you are a blade of the knife. The inside elbow is up, looking for the foul and protecting the ball. This is a power move. On the run, it is a jump stop power layup. You can add a 4" to 6" shot fake to it. Start the player out of bounds. Coach is in the lane and a manager is under the basket with a ball. A player starts with a ball, and passes it to the coach and sprints to the basket. Coach passes back to the player. As he gets the ball on the run, he must catch, square, and make a power move to the basket. A favorite phrase of mine is to tell them to have a confrontation at the basket. They must take the ball strong to the hoop. He runs and touches the other sideline. By that time the manager has passed the other ball to the coach. The coach makes a bounce pass so that as the player turns at the sideline, he has the ball in his hands. He catches it, passes it back to the coach, who returns it to the player. The player should catch this pass at the lane where he will square his shoulders and take it up strong. Do this eight times. Maybe you want them to make eight, or eight in a row. At the end of any drill like this, he goes to the free-throw line to make one-and-one. If he makes the first one, it gives him another 10 seconds to rest while he is shooting the second. If he doesn't make the first one, we go on to the next drill.

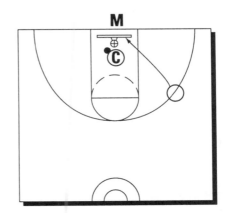

Diagram 2

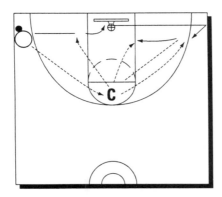

Diagram 1

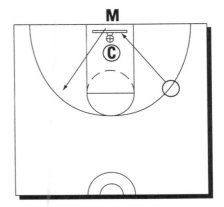

Diagram 3

(Diagram 2)   "Attack the Rim." You may not want to do this with junior high kids. This could be a dunk drill. This is a good drill to get your perimeter kids to come to the board. This is an extension of the "8 across" drill. Coach has a ball, bounces the ball hard so that it goes next to the basket. On the bounce, the player attacks to the ball. He gets the ball at the peak of his jump and puts the ball in. I'm not a big one for players trying to finesse the ball and tip it in while they are in the air.

(Diagram 3)   Now the player sprints to the other side of the floor and the ball is again bounced up near the rim. Bounce and go get it. When the player sprints to the three-point line, we get the other ball from the manager. We do this eight times; he makes eight touches of the circle.

(Diagram 4)   Coach will shoot from the side and the offensive player must go around a screen to get the power layup.

Diagram 4

How do you make a big man tougher? That's your job. I'm not a psychologist, so I don't know whether these drills will make your big man tougher. You can define their limits, but I don't know when you give them unrealistic contact drills that knock them around that it will make them tougher. Some of these drills will help and test your players as to whether or not they are going to be tough players. There is room here for verbal feedback and rewards. You can critique their performance and their moves. You can say that a move was soft. I use this football dummy pad. One of the things it does is to keep the coach from getting injured. Make your player fight through the contact. If you don't do contact drills, your players won't get used to it. One thing you can do is to pass them a medicine ball. This doesn't necessarily make them stronger, but it makes them aware that if they can move the medicine ball around, they can do it with a basketball. Work with the medicine ball with three players passing and catching. It makes them stronger.

(Diagram 5)   We have a ball on each block. Pick up the ball, and knife to the basket. Go to the other side, pick up the ball and knife to the basket. Keep the inside elbow up. While they are doing that, use the football dummy and make contact, especially with the inside arm.

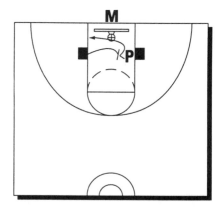

Diagram 5

(Diagram 6)   Post players are in a line up the lane. We want the first player to "bar his arms." (This means that the upper arms are horizontal, level with the shoulders and the forearms are vertical with the fingers pointing upward.) A manager with the dummy is under the basket. The coach shoots the ball. The player knocks the dummy out of the way and gets the rebound. Finish with a power layup, square to the basket, or you will get your shot blocked. You must get the inside position, get the rebound, and knife back up. Protect the shot with the inside arm and elbow. Keep the dummy away from the ball.

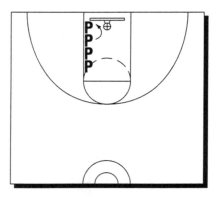

Diagram 6

(Diagram 7)   Deny flash cut. I worked with a coach who had a grading system for defense. If you could defend the ball, you got a 1. If you could defend the ball and help another player, it was a 2. If you could play your man, help, and also recover, you got a 3. If you could play your man, help, recover, and did other things, you got a 4. In this drill, we have two offensive post players and one defensive man in the middle. We want to deny the flash cut which means playing the man before he gets the ball. Therefore, the post must know man-to-man defense. Coach has a ball. Manager is ready with another ball. Another offensive player is on the opposite wing. The drill starts with the off-side offensive post making a flash cut. The defense must deny the flash cut. He must get his body in the way. He is not allowed to move in a straight line. There will be contact. The defensive man rides him off of his spot. Coach makes the pass, but the defense should knock it away.

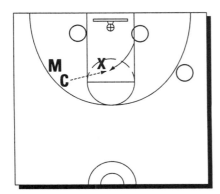

Diagram 7

(Diagram 8) The manager hands the coach another ball, and the coach makes a pass to the other offensive player in the low post. The defensive man must recover and go down the lane and defend the low post. Get behind the post; don't get caught on the high side. Have a wide base.

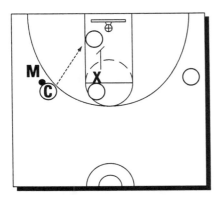

Diagram 8

(Diagram 9) Meanwhile, the first ball has been retrieved. The high post has it. After the low post has been played, coach passes the ball back to the high post, the defender must attack the ball at the high post and trace the ball.

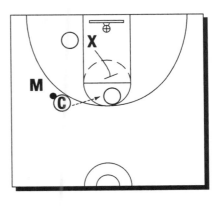

Diagram 9

(Diagram 10) The ball is passed to the offensive player on the other wing. The wing stays on the three-point line until he catches the ball and then drives the ball to the basket with one or two hard dribbles. On the flight of the ball, the defensive player must get into position and take the charge. In this drill, the defensive man denied the flash cut, played defense on the low post, charged to the high post and got all over the ball, and then dropped back down and took the charge.

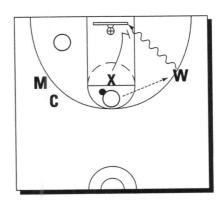

Diagram 10

(Diagram 11) Offensive drill that involves the perimeter players. Start with two double stacks. There are several options. First, 1 can come off of the double-screen of 2 and 4. 2 can then come off of the single-screen of 3. 3 can duck in the lane and get the pass from the top. Stacks work for several reasons, one because there are a cluster of players. Getting free off the stack is based on making a read.

the ball. It is a game-like shooting drill and it involves post play. 1 gets eight shots. First thing is that he comes off the double stack either in a curl, or he can fade for a three.

Diagram 11

(Diagram 12)   Keep two things in mind when running off the stack. You want to change direction and you want to change speeds. Start out slowly as if you aren't in the play and then explode. Or start out as if you are coming off of the screen and then break to the ball.

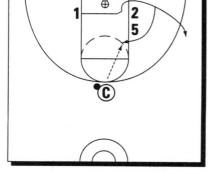

Diagram 13

(Diagram 14)   If he fades for a three, I want him ready to shoot when I pass him the ball. I want him giving me a target. 2 crosses the lane and 5, the post player, stays on the ball side.

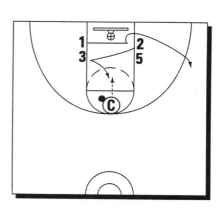

Diagram 12

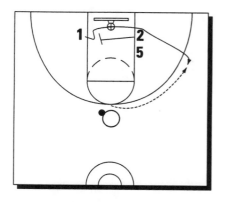

Diagram 14

(Diagram 13)   Stack drill. We do this with one post and two perimeter players. This teaches kids how to play, how to move in the offense. Coach has

(Diagram 15)   The coach has another ball. 1 comes off of the screen set by 5 and 2 and curls into the lane for a jump shot.

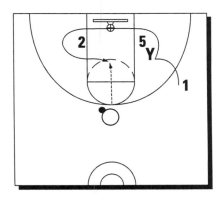

Diagram 15

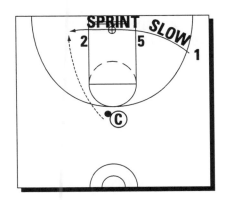

Diagram 17

(Diagram 16)   1 curls around 5 and gets his third shot. Eventually 1 will curl around 5, pass to the post and move to get the return pass, and shoot.

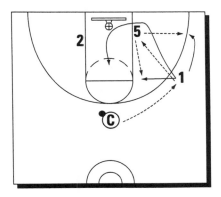

Diagram 16

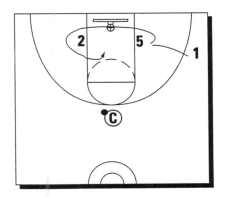

Diagram 18

(Diagram 17)   1 then starts slowly toward 5 and then sprints off of the screen to the other side where he gets another shot.

(Diagram 18)   Sometimes I start a countdown, and 1 can curl around 2 for the shot with about two seconds on the clock. Don't shoot too soon; time your move.

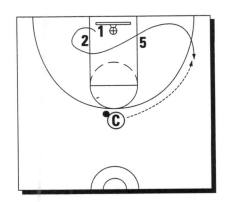

Diagram 19

(Diagram 19)   1 replaces at the low post and 2 comes off of 5, and we have the same drill with the next shooter.

(Diagram 20)   How far out do you let your big man go? You need to make your big men versatile. I don't just mean using either hand. I want them to be able to hit the short corner jump shot and to have a foul-line game. If your big players don't have a foul-line jump shot, your post game is going to suffer. Here is where we want our post man. We don't want him on the block. We call it "getting a piece of the paint."

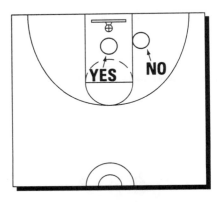

Diagram 20

(Diagram 21)   We want our big men fed from the hi-lo, then they can make a move either way. When someone doubles down quickly, feed the post from the top. The best place to feed the low post is from the high post.

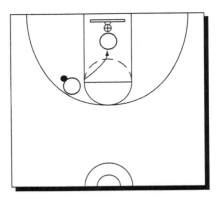

Diagram 21

(Diagram 22)   Drill. Coach passes the ball to the high post. He takes a jump shot, then a shot fake and takes it to the basket with one dribble. He can do spin moves off of this. The post then rebounds, and

flashes to the coach for the second pass and the post up. Each player shoots 20 shots. On the last rotation, he must make every shot. Make your jump shot, then go to the shot fake. If you miss it, take another one. Then take it to the basket and then post up.

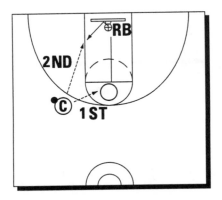

Diagram 22

(Diagram 23)   Guard drill, called the Circle Shooting Drill. Drive the ball as hard as you can as if you are in a fast break. Then jump stop, jump shot. Jog back, get another ball, and do it six times.

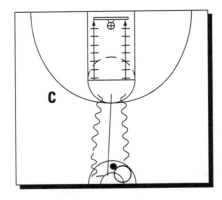

Diagram 23

(Diagram 24)   Change the drill. Have a defensive man near the foul line. He must take the ball down, create space, possibly with a crossover dribble, and then shoot the jump shot. Do this pull-back dribble three times.

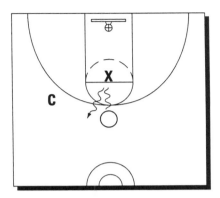

Diagram 24

(Diagram 25)   Next, break the defensive man down. I protect the ball and make contact with the defensive man, retreat back and shoot. Do this once.

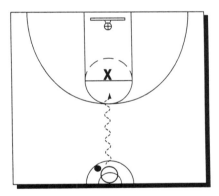

Diagram 25

(Diagram 26)   Now the hesitation. Drives to near the foul line, hesitation, and then explodes to the basket for the layup. As he makes that shot, the coach starts counting down—6, 5, 4, etc. The player runs to half-court and comes back for a pass from the coach for the game-ending shot. He must hit a buzzer shot to end the drill. If he misses, he then runs to $^3/_4$ court and comes back. If he misses it again, then he runs full-court and comes back for the buzzer shot. If you shoot enough buzzer shots, someday when that comes in a game, you will be ready.

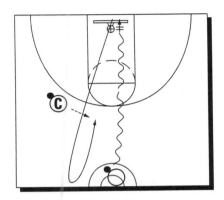

Diagram 26

(Diagram 27)   Post Trailer Drill. Coach has a rack of balls. Guard is near the top of the circle. Post comes down and the ball is passed from coach to guard to the post. He gets five three-point shots on each side.

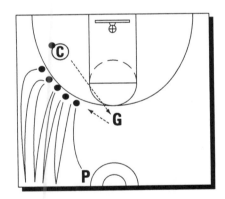

Diagram 27

Question—What type of agility drills do you do?

Answer—We use the Toss Back, line jumping and rope jumping. We do the Mikan Drill, the short left- and right-handed hooks from under the basket. They must do the crab dribble. They have the ball low between their legs and they pound it on the floor, just about six inches. They bring the ball from their hip across their body and then pivot. The more you can do with pivoting, the better.

You must give plenty of encouragement, positive feedback. We are going to take several days this summer and cover things for the big players. Height is relative. At the high school level, a big girl may be 6'1". I want someone in this camp to address self-esteem. I want someone to talk about buying clothes, how to shake hands, to walk tall and don't slouch. I want someone to speak to them about nutrition. I want them to try at least five different foods they haven't tried before. I want to cover weight lifting.

There are seven things that begin with the letter "R" that are really important for post play:

- **Run**. You need to have big kids who can run the court. When we recruit, this is the first thing we look for.

- **Root out in the post**. This means having a wide stance, asking for the ball and ready for the rebound. If the ball changes sides of the court, I can seal my man and move with the ball.

- **Rebound**. Along with the rebounding, you need the shot fake at the offensive end. Guys with a good shot fake get fouled more.

- **Reject shots**.

- **Rotate**. Rotate over and help with active hands.

- **Recovery**. Get back to your man.

- **Relocate**. Must see the perimeter players and pass back to the perimeter and relocate deeper in the lane.

Organizing Your Program

I was at UCLA for seven years where I learned a lot from Jim Harrick. But I also learned a lot from Coach John Wooden. It was great to be able to be around Coach Wooden. He probably shaped my philosophy more than anybody. One of the first things that he told me was "Teach what you know, know what you teach." Wherever I coach, I will use the high-post offense because that's what I know, and what I can teach. I can break it down and teach it. I believe in it.

Another thing Coach Wooden emphasized was to develop a philosophy and stay with it. If you stick with your philosophy, the players in your program will benefit from it and you increase your chances for success. I believe there are five things that are the most important in developing a successful program:

- Organization. If you can be unorganized, your staff is unorganized and you are successful, you will be one of the first. You must be organized in your practice plans, your daily plans, your year-round schedule. Your people must know what you expect every month. If you aren't good at it, get an assistant to help you who is organized.

- Develop your philosophy. I mentioned that previously. This includes your style of play and the things that you do in your community. Develop a philosophy and stick with it.

- Discipline. Coach Wooden said, "Discipline is getting your players to do what you want them to do and there are a lot of ways to do it." I don't like it when coaches get on their players, yelling all the time. "It's amazing how a player's hearing improves when he hears praise." Again, that's from Coach Wooden. Reprimand, yes, but follow it with praise.

- Surround yourself with good people. This is probably the most important thing you will ever do. This includes your players, managers, staff and coaches. If you have assistant coaches who aren't loyal, they can kill you.

- Put your ego on the shelf and work extremely hard. It's amazing what can be accomplished if no one cares who gets the credit. I try to treat my assistant coaches equally well. When I go out to speak, I bring my staff with me. I don't have an associate head coach. Both of my assistant coaches are equally valuable. When I took the job at Alabama, I insisted that both of my assistants got the same-size offices. This was a big thing to me. I didn't want anyone looking at the size of the offices and assuming that one was more important than the other.

I don't know if this can be taught, but you must be able to make good long-term decisions as opposed to short-term decisions. You must consider how your decisions will affect your program down the road, not just at the present. What is the long-term effect?

Before the First Game Checklist

Man-to-man offense	Zone offense
vs. pressure	vs. 2-3
vs. sagging	vs. 1-3-1
vs. full-court situations	vs. 1-2-2
vs. half-court situations	vs. box and I

Man-to-man defense, half-court, full-court. I believe the defensive field goal percentage is the most important statistic that you have.

Zone defense, you need some. At times, I thought your zone defense wasn't very good, but it was better than your bad zone offense.

Presses and press attack.

Free throws, both offensive and defensive alignments.

Out-of-bounds vs. man and zone—under the basket, on the side of the floor, from half-court, and full-court.

Delay game.

Fast-break offense.

Secondary break.

How to defend when you must get the ball, and how to foul.

Jump balls.

Last-shot situations vs. man and zone, full-court, half-court, and side out.

Offense vs. box and 1, or triangle and 2. We don't spend a lot of time on this, but it must be covered. We don't have a different structured offense for each defense. You can overcoach your team. Sometimes you can have paralysis by analysis. We just want our players to play.

Rules. Go over the new rules. Have your players know what you want concerning when you want them to call a time-out and more importantly when you don't want them to call time.

We also go over special situations. We put different amounts of time on the clock covering as much of these as we can.

I want to give your some out-of-bounds plays. One more statement from Coach Wooden. He said, "Coaching is your ability to put the right players in the right positions on the court." I want to score off of our out-of-bounds plays. We have the same player take the ball out every time.

(Diagram 1)   2 is your best shooter. 1 breaks out to the corner and gets the pass from 3. 4 and 5 set a double-screen for 2 who comes to the top of the circle. 3 goes opposite.

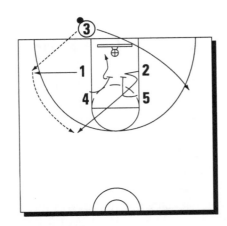

Diagram 1

(Diagram 2)   If 2 doesn't get the shot, then we are in this lineup and go right into our continuity.

Diagram 2

(Diagram 3)   Another play. 4, 5 and 2 are in a stack. Again, 2 is your best shooter. 2 comes off the stack either way and goes under the basket. 4 and 5 are shoulder to shoulder and 1 comes off the double-screen. 4 and 5 then turn and screen down for 2 coming to the top of the key. 3 goes opposite. The ball goes from 3-1-2.

(Diagram 4)   This is good if you have an athletic 3. 2 breaks to the corner; 4 flashes low across the lane.

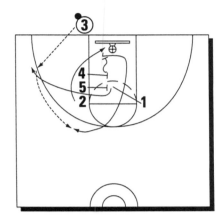

Diagram 3

Diagram 4

(Diagram 5)   5 sets a down-screen for 3. The ball goes from 3-2-1-3.

Diagram 5

(Diagram 6)   Side out-of-bounds. 4 and 5 stack along the lane. 2 comes off the double-screen of 4 and 5 to the corner. 3 can pass to 2. If not, 5 screens for 4 who goes to the elbow and gets the pass from 3. 4 is your best one-on-one player. This is your first option. He has the whole side of the floor.

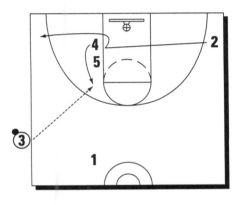

Diagram 6

(Diagram 7)   5 seals in the lane after setting the screen, and 4 can make the hi-lo pass to 5. 5 has his man one-on-one.

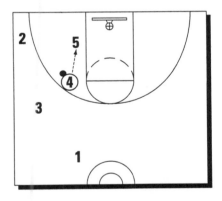

Diagram 7

(Diagram 8)   Sometimes 3 can make the pass directly to 2 or to 5.

(Diagram 9)   When you teach your players to defend the under out-of-bounds, make sure that your player guarding the inbounder shades far under the basket. Take away the under-the-basket move. Force everything outside.

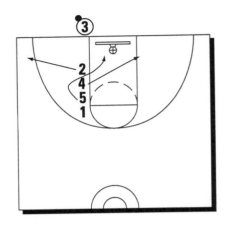

Diagram 10

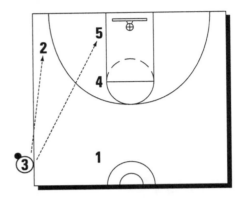

Diagram 8

(Diagram 11)   Another zone play. 4 breaks to the corner and gets the pass from 3. The ball is passed from 4 to 2 to 1 as 5 follows the ball. 3 steps in and sets a back-screen for 4 who could get a lob pass from 1.

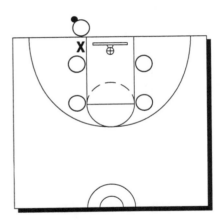

Diagram 9

(Diagram 10)   Against a zone. 2 breaks to the corner, 4 crosses the lane, 5 hesitates and breaks down to the open spot. 1 is for floor balance.

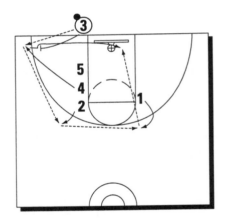

Diagram 11

Balanced Court Offense

This is a great way to play. Without changing my structure, if I have a great guard, I can make sure that I feature the guard. Same thing for any position. All I will do is emphasize different plays in different years. This can be run out of a one-guard front or a traditional two-guard front with a high post. The man in the high-post position must be able to pass the ball. He doesn't have to be a great scorer, but he needs to be a great passer. He is the hub of the wheel.

(Diagram 1)   When Coach Wooden had Kareem Abdul-Jabbar and played him here. This formation has balanced, consistent rebounding.

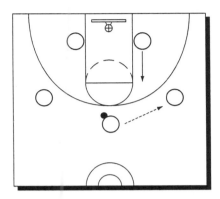

Diagram 2

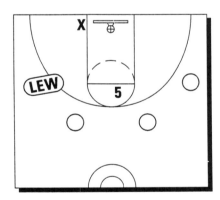

Diagram 1

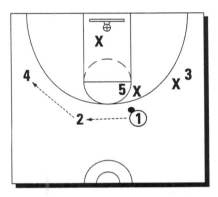

Diagram 3

(Diagram 2)   This is the one-guard front. In a one-guard front, you enter to the wing and either post man must come up. In a one-guard front, you have two post players.

(Diagram 3)   This is the basic series, the guard cut series. We will run it out of a two-guard front. The good thing about a two-guard front is that if they are overplaying the ball side, the ball can be reversed and the same play can be run from the other side.

(Diagram 4)   If 1 passes to 3, he cuts off the screen of 5. 5 is ball side at the elbow. (If the ball is passed from guard to guard, he must get to the other elbow. He cannot stay in the middle). You can have 5 screen several ways. Coach Wooden had him turn and put his back to the guard. He feared an offensive foul because of the way he would set the screen, but I like to keep his back to the baseline. We try to score on the guard cut.

(Diagram 5)   If 1 doesn't get the pass by the mid-post, he must get to the short corner. He cannot stay on the block. He must not stay in the lane because 4 is coming into that area. 2 moves to the middle of the floor. 3 has three options. The beauty of the offense is that I am going to take what you give me. What we run is going to be predicated on where we throw the ball.

Diagram 4

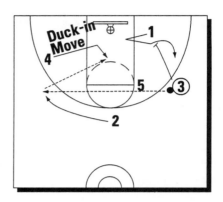

Diagram 6

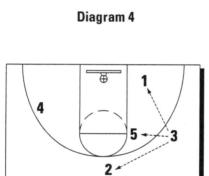

Diagram 5

Diagram 7

(Diagram 6)   If 3 passes to the high post, 2 goes away. 1 sets up the single down action (screen) of 3 and breaks to the wing. 4 does the forward duck-in move. He takes his man under the basket, seals him and comes into the lane. 5 takes one dribble to improve the passing angle and passes to 4.

(Diagram 7)   If 4's defender is playing him high and denying him the ball, 5 passes to 2 and then to 4. That is the basic guard-cut series.

(Diagram 8)   If 3 passes to 2 instead of 5, 5 and 3 set a double-screen or a staggered-screen for 1. (2 must be in the middle of the floor.) 1 breaks up for the pass.

Diagram 8

(Diagram 9)   If 2 cannot hit 1, then 4 V-cuts and comes to the other elbow. 4 is in a position so that he is facing the point where the sideline and the midcourt lines meet. He is posting at an angle. This is called the side-post series. When 2 determines that he cannot pass to 1, he passes to 4 at the elbow. We teach three things off of this.

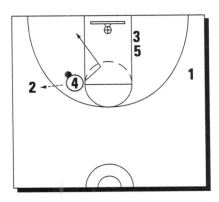

Diagram 11

(Diagram 12)   The second thing we teach is the screen and roll. 2 dribbles off of the screen set by 4 and they run the screen and roll.

Diagram 9

(Diagram 10)   First, 2 breaks off of 4 and can get the ball back and get the layup. That's the first option. Second option is that he doesn't get the ball and he cuts out to the wing.

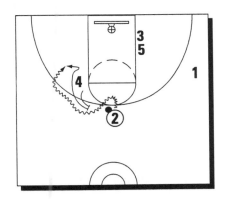

Diagram 12

(Diagram 13)   Third thing. 2 passes to 4 at the elbow and then sets a side-screen for 4. 4 would take one dribble and get a jump shot. This is the side-post series and this happens when the guard catches the ball at the top of the circle. We run the guard-cut series when the ball is passed from the wing to the post.

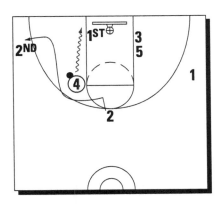

Diagram 10

(Diagram 11)   4 can pass to 2 on the wing and 4 then cuts to the low post.

(Diagram 14)   If 3 cannot pass to 5 or to 2, he makes the pass to 1 in the short corner. This is the third option. 3 then sets a side-screen for 5 who breaks to the wing. 3 then rolls to the basket.

Diagram 13

Diagram 14

(Diagram 15)   Rhode Island did this. 3 passed to 1, and cut through. 5 set a ball-screen for 1 who dribbled off for the screen-and-roll.

Diagram 15

(Diagram 16)   What happens if 1 cannot pass to 3? 3 goes backdoor for the bank shot. One of the good things about this offense is that when we start, we do not have anyone in the low post. The floor is open.

Diagram 16

If the guard-to-guard pass is taken away, 2 will cut to the basket and 4 V-cuts and comes to the elbow on the weakside. The ball can go from 1 to 4 to 2. 4 comes up with his knees bent. He catches the ball with his knees bent and drops a bounce pass for 2.

(Diagram 17)   If 2 does not get the pass from 4 on the cut, 3 and 5 set a down-screen double for 2 as he comes across the lane. 1 will cut off of 4 and go to the opposite wing. 4 can pass to 2 coming off of the double-screen.

Diagram 17

(Diagram 18)   Anytime a forward sees the guards being pressured at the half-court line, the opposite forward is coming up to relieve pressure. 1 can go backdoor.

Diagram 18

(Diagram 19)   Another way to relieve the pressure is to make a dribble entry. 1 dribbles to the wing and 3 goes away. 3 will screen in the lane for 4, and then 5 down-screens for 3. 5 rolls to the block.

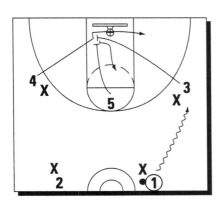

Diagram 19

(Diagram 20)   Another way to relieve pressure is to split the post. 5 steps out for the pass.

Diagram 20

(Diagram 21)   If 2 hits 5 and goes away, 4 and 3 go backdoor. If they don't get the pass, 5 passes to 1 and down-screens opposite. 3 posts up hard on the block. So, to relieve pressure, you have backdoor, guard dribble and hit the post.

-Diagram 21

(Diagram 22)   Louisville runs this. 1 passes to 3 and 5 rolls to the low post. 4 V-cuts and replaces 5 at the elbow.

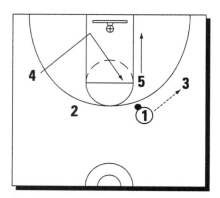

Diagram 22

(Diagram 24)   If 1 can't make the pass to 3, 5 screens down for 4 and 2 down-screens for 3. 1 dribbles into the middle to improve the passing angle.

Diagram 24

(Diagram 23)   This is called Guard Follow. 1 passes to 3 and follows the pass and gets the ball back from 3. 5 sets a side-screen and 3 comes off of the screen for the lob. 4 goes low and crosses the lane. 1 can pass to 4 or to 3. The beauty of the play is that everyone is above the foul line and 4 is going one-on-one.

This offense provides any one of your players the opportunity to score. It provides you the chance to have a balanced attack. It gives you balance on the floor so you can rebound well. It also provides you balance so your defensive transition is balanced going back. You can feature your better players in this offense.

Diagram 23

Special Scoring Plays

weakest defensive player. We will adjust to run that man off the screen set by 4.

We run a lot of special sets at Kentucky Wesleyan. You must determine what is best for you. Perhaps you want to run special plays only after dead-ball situations. Actually, we have cut back a little on running special plays this year because we wanted to push the ball after all made baskets.

(Diagram 1)   Play #1. This is for the three-point shooter (2). 2 breaks to the wing. Notice that we have overloaded the right side. This takes away all weakside help.

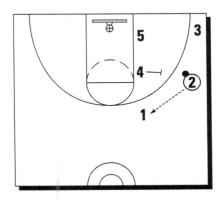

Diagram 2

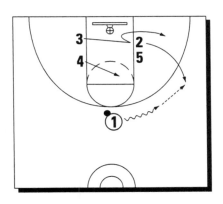

Diagram 1

Diagram 3

(Diagram 2)   When 1 enters the ball to 2, he immediately goes and gets it back. When 1 gets the ball back, his first option is to 5. 4 sets a side-screen.

(Diagram 3)   2 cuts off the screen and 70% of the time the defensive man will go under the screen. If he does, then 4 turns and seals and 1 passes the 2 for the three-point shot.

(Diagram 4)   If the defensive man goes over the top, 2 curls into the lane. When that happens, 1 and 4 will screen and roll as 5 sets a screen for 3. When we scout, we really look to find our opponent's

Diagram 4

(Diagram 5)   Play #2. 2 is the best shooter. 2 cuts down the lane and breaks to either side. If 2 goes out the single-screen side, 4 will screen and then post. 3 pops out and 5 goes to the mid-post.

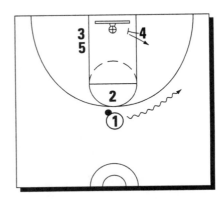

Diagram 5

(Diagram 6)   If 2 cuts out the side of the double stack, 2 will break to the corner and 4 will come off the double-screen set by 3 and 5.

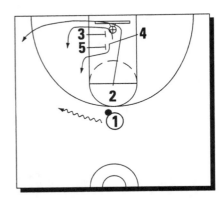

Diagram 6

(Diagram 7)   Play #3. 1 dribbles away from 2, your best shooter. 3 screens across for 2 who breaks off of the screen and posts on the block for about 1 and 1/2 seconds. (You may want to put your post in the 2 position.) 4 and 5 will double-screen down, and 3 will come off the double-screen for the shot. 2 continues on to the corner. 1 can pass to 2 or to 3.

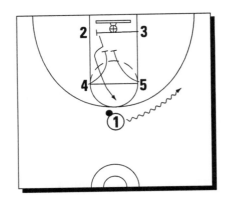

Diagram 7

(Diagram 8)   As soon as 3 clears the double-screen, 5 sets a screen for 4 who curls tight to the basket. 5 steps out to the mid-post. We set a goal to score from 16 to 18 points per game out of our special sets. If we do that, we feel we can win the game.

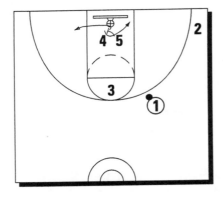

Diagram 8

(Diagram 9)   Play #4. Play #4 starts just like #3. 1 dribbles to the side away from 2. (But, these plays can be run to either side.) We set a double-screen up the lane for the post player, 2 and 3 for 4. The inside player of the double-screen will pop to the high post, the other breaks to the wing opposite. 5 will screen for 3 who is coming to the top of the circle.

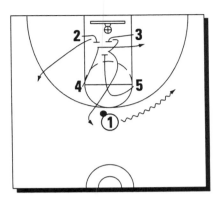

Diagram 9

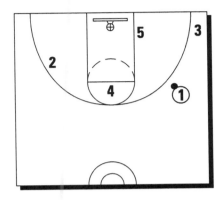

Diagram 11

(Diagram 10) Play #5. This is the set we use when we want to get the ball inside. This is a set call. You need to indicate which player is to get the ball. Let's say that we want 5 to get the ball. 3 breaks to the corner. Since the five-second count is in again, we allow 1 to pass to 3 in the corner. As soon as 3 clears, 2 and 4 will set a double-screen for 5. We want the screen to be set in the middle of the lane. We want 5 to go baseline. 2 breaks to the opposite wing; 4 opens up and comes high.

(Diagram 12) Play #6. 2 starts on the wing. 3 can take one step off the block to set the screen. We don't want 3 moving up the lane. 4 and 5 then set a double-screen for 2. We want 4 and 5 shoulder to shoulder. 2 must run his man into the double-screen. We don't want 4 and 5 moving to find 2.

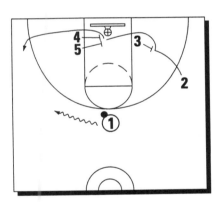

Diagram 12

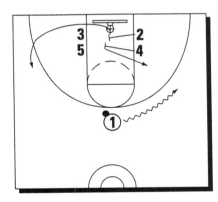

Diagram 10

(Diagram 11) What happens is that teams start to switch. When this happens, 1 passes to 4, then down to 5, a high-low action.

(Diagram 13) We never want the dribbler to go farther than the lane line extended.

(Diagram 14) As soon as 2 clears the double-screen, 1 must know whether 2 is open or not open. If not, 5 sets a screen down for 4 who curls over 5. 1 can pass to 2 or to 5.

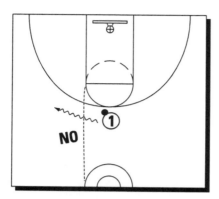

Diagram 13

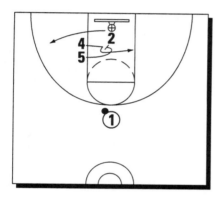

Diagram 14

(Diagram 15)   Play #7. After Play #6 is run several times, the defensive man on 3 will come off and try to bump 2 as 2 is cutting. So, 2 sends 3 instead of 2. We call this "Push."

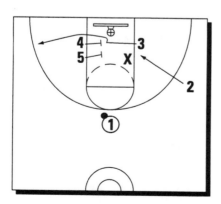

Diagram 15

(Diagram 16)   Play #8. 2 goes over the top of the screen set by 3, and we are looking to post 3. 2 doesn't run into the defensive man, but he does make a brush pick as he goes by. 3 comes off of 2.

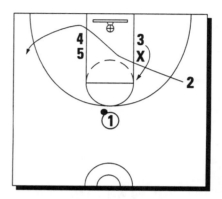

Diagram 16

(Diagram 17)   Play #9. This play begins the same way with 2 coming off of 3 and crossing under the basket. 3 immediately screens away for the bottom post man, 4. 4 cuts off low, and 5 then screens for 3 who cuts up the middle of the lane.

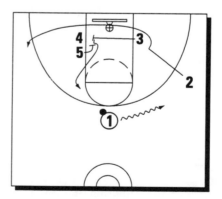

Diagram 17

(Diagram 18)   Play #10. Now instead of 3 screening, 4 and 5 will double-screen for 3 with 1 taking the ball to the left.

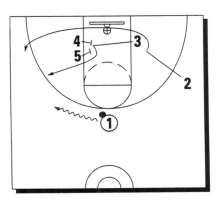

Diagram 18

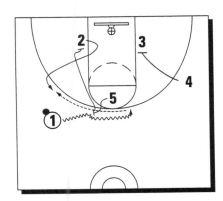

Diagram 20

(Diagram 19)   Play #11. "Alley Oop." 1 can enter with the pass or the dribble. Suppose he dribbles and 2 goes to the corner. 4 immediately flashes high. 5 V-cuts and then goes. 1 makes the lob to 5.

(Diagram 21)   If 2 has a shot, fine. If not, catch and make a maximum of two dribbles toward the baseline. Where is the defense going to get caught on 5? On the high side. A good post player will keep him there.

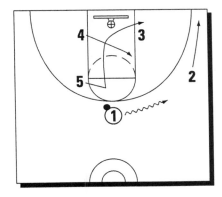

Diagram 19

Diagram 21

If the lob is not open, 5 continues to the block. That is what will be open. 1 passes to 5. That's what will be open the most.

(Diagram 20)   Play #12. We run several plays where we use the high-post screen for the guard. This will help the guard deal with pressure. 2 and 3 are on the blocks, 4 on the wing, and 5 at the top. As 1 comes off the screen of 5, 5 goes low and screens for 2 who breaks to the wing. 4 is screening 3 to occupy the defense on the weak side. 1 passes to 2.

(Diagram 22)   Play #13. This is the same except that 2 will upscreen for 5 and then step out and set up for the three-point shot.

(Diagram 23)   Play #14. As the season went on, teams started to trap the high screen. We sent 2 off the staggered-screens of 3 and 4, 5 rolled down the lane and 1 can pass to 2 or to 5. When 2 came across, it took away all weakside help.

Diagram 22

Diagram 23

(Diagram 24)   Play #15. 5 screens on the ball as 2 screens for 4 coming out of the corner. The first option is for 4 to post. If 4 is not open, 5 down-screens for 2. We want our little men to screen for big men to get the switch and the mismatch.

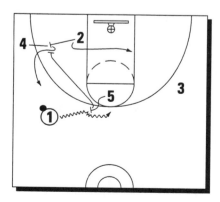

Diagram 24

(Diagram 25)   Play #16. We have a 1-4 set. This is about as basic as it gets, but we get a lot out of it. 4 and 5 screen for 1. 1 can go either side. If 1 comes off of 4, 3 slides to the corner. 5 turns and down-screens for 2 who breaks high. 2 will usually get the shot. After the screen, 4 rolls to the basket.

Diagram 25

(Diagram 26)   Play #17. 4 and 5 start low and both will break up the lane. 1 can pass to either side. The wing on the ball side, 2, goes backdoor.

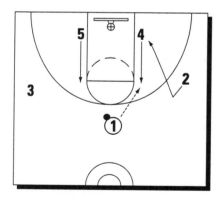

Diagram 26

(Diagram 27)   If 2 isn't open, 2 continues through the lane and gets a staggered-screen from 5 and 3. 1 runs a curl cut to the basket.

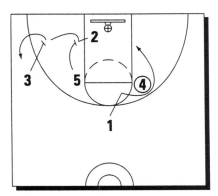

Diagram 27

(Diagram 28)   Play #18. "40 Series." 1 passes to 2 and makes a UCLA cut. If 1 does not get the ball, he cuts away from the ball and gets a staggered-screen from 3 and 4.

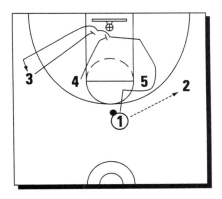

Diagram 28

(Diagram 29)   As soon as 5 screens for 1, he steps out to the top of the circle. The ball is reversed from 2 to 5 to 1. This is a great play if you have a point guard who can score.

(Diagram 30)   Play #19. 1 passes to 2 and cuts through and 1 screens for 3. 4 and 5 set a staggered-screen for 1 who pops back high. 3 goes across the lane low. 2 can pass to 3 or to 1.

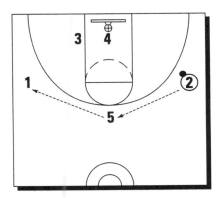

Diagram 29

Diagram 30

(Diagram 31)   Play #20. This starts the same way with 1 passing to 2 and making the UCLA cut. But 1 curls and screens for 5 who breaks low. 4 then screens for 1 who comes back to the top of the circle.

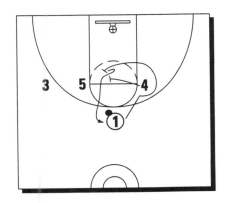

Diagram 31

(Diagram 32)   Play #21. 1 passes to 2 and makes a UCLA cut. As 1 comes off 5, 5 screens for 2. 2 and 5 can run the screen and roll. After 1 clears 5, 1 gets a staggered-screen from 4 and 3. 1 needs to come out a little slower for better timing. He needs to be coming off of the staggered pick about the time 2 is clearing 5.

(Diagram 34)   Play #23. This is good against a zone. 4 and 5 are on the blocks. If we want to run this for 3, we make the initial pass to 3 so that the zone will shift. 3 passes back to 1. 1 immediately passes to 2, and 3 walks to the corner. As soon as 2 catches the ball, 5 flashes hard bringing the middle defender with him. 4 screens across on the baseline so that the defensive man must go over the top as 3 runs the baseline. The ball goes from 1-3-1-2-3.

Diagram 32

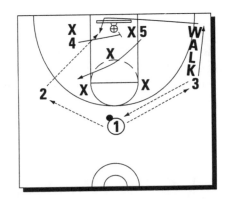

Diagram 34

(Diagram 33)   Play #22. This time 1 dribbles toward the wing, and 2 goes away and comes off the staggered-screen of 4 and 3. 5 and 1 will run the screen-and-roll.

Diagram 33

Balanced High-Post Offense

Basketball is a simple game; coaches make it complex. The court is an extension of the classroom. You are a teacher of basketball. Everything you do in practice is carried over to the game. How much slippage you have between practice and the game is the difference in how good you will play. Know your personnel. Pass to the right person. Basketball is made up of decisions and opportunities. As you practice, your players will have many decisions to make, and in a game, they will have the opportunity to make those decisions. How you teach them will determine what kind of opportunity they have. Are you going to shoot the air ball or shoot it off the glass? If you are a guard, you must make the right pass at the right time at the right spot to the right player. I want you to throw the ball to the target hand, not the pin hand. The pin hand is where the defensive player is.

Many coaches talk too much in practice. When we go on the floor, we have a 30-minute individual attention period, where we walk through some things. It is light, it is teaching, it is technique. But, once we start up for two hours, we never stop practice. If I talk to a player, it is after practice or I'll pull him aside. We run for two straight hours and we are off the floor. I want my players to be quick, but never hurry. We don't want to foul on the twenty footer and we don't want to foul in the last minute of the period. I want to be a balanced coach, score $1/3$ on the half-court offense, $1/3$ on the fast break, and $1/3$ off the defense, free throws, etc. Then, I become hard to guard. Our program is predicated on three things: fundamentals, conditioning, and team play.

The Big Five
- Stance. Feet are as wide as the shoulders, pointed straight ahead. Always bend at the knees and never at the waist. Have the chest up, back straight, chin up. Put your hands with the fingers up. Never play defense with the hands down.

- Concentration. I need your undivided attention. To make the same mistake over again is embarrassing.

- Quickness. The two most important things in basketball are quickness and balance.

- Balance. Balance means that the head is at the mid-point between the two feet in everything you do. The head is at the mid-point whether you are dribbling, rebounding, shooting, or playing defense. Coach says, "Don't reach." That means don't take the head out of the mid-point.

- Hard. You must play hard.

The Seven Areas for Daily Improvement
We teach everything from the part to the whole. We start with 1-on-1, 2-on-2 on up to 5-on-5. I believe you must run. John Wooden is my mentor and I teach his system of basketball. To be successful, you must have a system. I hear a lot of coaches yell, "Play defense, or get open." Have you ever taught them how? Do you teach the V-cut, the jump stop, the front pivot, the reverse pivot?

(Diagram 1)   If he can't get open doing that, come up the lane and break out to the wing.

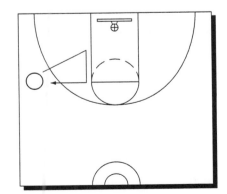

Diagram 1

(Diagram 2)   The center is in the high-post area. When the ball is passed to the wing, the center turns and makes a back pivot and then makes a V-cut to get open. He can't play there if he can't get open. The beauty of this offense is that you can design plays to fit the personnel you have.

them to be able to make their foul shots because at the end of the game, I want to put the ball in their hands.

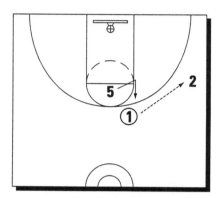

Diagram 2

(Diagram 3)   The guards are one step out from the lane and one step from the top of the key.

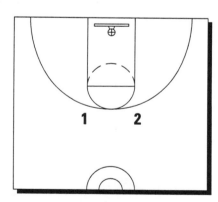

Diagram 3

(Diagram 4)   We dribble into the operational area. I want them to make the right pass to the right player to the right spot at the right time. I want them to get the ball into the operational area with as few turnovers as possible. I want my guards to be the best-conditioned athletes on the team. I want

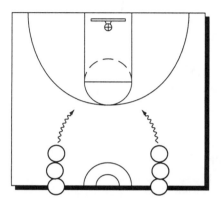

Diagram 4

(Diagram 5)   The left guard sprints down and cuts back. The right guard dribbles in and makes a two-foot jump stop. That's part of the seven fundamentals. I think your team will be better if they do these seven basic fundamentals:

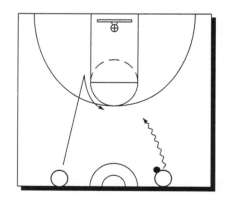

Diagram 5

- Acknowledge a good pass. If you pass to me, I want to thank you. If you pass to me, then I'll pass to you.

- Ball on chest, touching under the chin with the elbows out. Keep it close to the body.

- We jump stop on everything that we do with the head in the middle of the mid-point, under control. We make two-handed passes. Fake a pass, make a pass.

- V-Cut. You must make a V-cut and then ask for the ball.

- Step back—cross over when you dribble. I don't want the reverse pivot. They come from the weak side and steal the ball.

- Hands up on all shots. When the ball goes up, the hands go up. Hands are by the ears, fingers to the sky. If you do this, your team will improve so much that you won't believe it.

- Follow the shot with the hands up.

We talk about getting open at the forward, guard and center positions, and we talk about posting up.

(Diagram 6)   I like to post up one foot above the block and want to signal to pass me the ball. If he doesn't ask for the ball, don't give it to him.

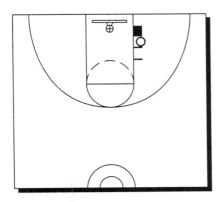

Diagram 6

I want to teach the post basic moves: turn and bank; drop-step and shoot a power layup; turn to the middle, pump fake, one-bounce layup; and I want to teach five power moves. They are: power layup straight up; pump fake power layup; pump fake one-bounce to the other side power layup; pogo when you catch it up high, keep it up high and shoot it; and then the two-hand follow shot. A one-handed catch is a 5% shot; a two-hand follow shot is a 95% shot.

(Diagram 7)   We have three or four players on each side of the basket. Throw the ball off the board to the other side. Catch, power it back up. The side post. Part of the offense is on the weak side.

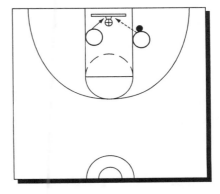

Diagram 7

(Diagram 8)   Pass, screen-and-roll. The guard passes to the post, cuts and gets the ball back and the post screens and rolls.

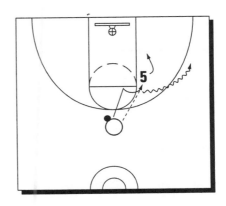

Diagram 8

(Diagram 9)   Dribble, screen-and-roll. The guard dribbles off the screen set by the post, he pivots and rolls to the basket.

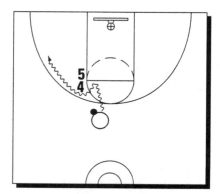

Diagram 9

(Diagram 10)   Inside screen. Pass to the post and set an inside screen. The post dribbles off of the screen; the guard flashes to the wing. The post makes one dribble and takes a jump shot.

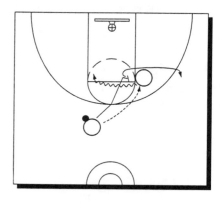

Diagram 10

(Diagram 11)   Side post delay. The guard passes to the post, cuts but doesn't get the ball, so he V-cuts and comes back and gets the return pass from the post while on the wing. The post then makes an inside pivot and rolls to the basket.

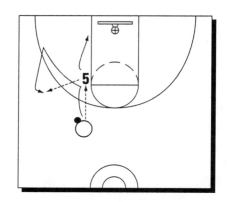

Diagram 11

(Diagram 12)   We add the double-screen to this. We want them to be shoulder to shoulder so no one can get through. 2 cuts off the double-screen. If 2 gets the ball, the top man screens down for the bottom man of the double-screen and he comes up the lane.

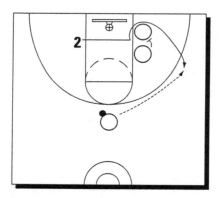

Diagram 12

(Diagram 13)   Now you have a three-man game. There are a lot of options.

(Diagram 14)   If 2 doesn't get the ball, we run the side-post action, perhaps the side-post delay.

(Diagram 15)   The high post passes to wing and rolls to the basket. We pop the stack on the double-screen side, and the low man can come to the high post. A good player can see what is happening on the court. You must be able to read the defense.

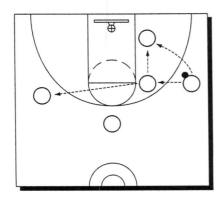

Diagram 13

Diagram 14

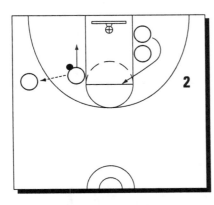

Diagram 15

(Diagram 16)   If your man follows you around the screen, you curl. If he chooses to go over the top of the screen, you flatten out. Teach your players how to read what the defense is trying to do to you.

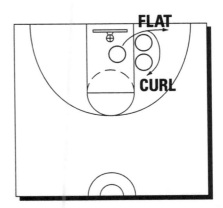

Diagram 16

(Diagram 17)   This is a two-guard, balanced offense. I like to start my forwards one step up and one step off the blocks, but they end up on the wings. We always start our offense with a guard-to-guard pass. 1 to 2, 2 to 3. 5 sets the screen for 2 who can go either side.

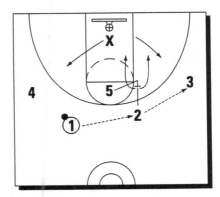

Diagram 17

(Diagram 18)   If 2 gets the ball, he shoots a layup or passes to 4 on the weak side.

(Diagram 19)   If 2 does not get the ball, he goes to the short corner. 3 has the ball. 1 V-cuts and comes head up. 5 V-cuts and steps to the ball. 4 drops low off the block.

(Diagram 20)   If you turn this court sideways, you are in a 1-3-1.

Diagram 18

Diagram 19

Diagram 20

(Diagram 21)   This play is called "guard cut." This is the bread and butter of it. 3 passes to 5 at the elbow. 4 ducks into the lane. 1 goes away. 3

screens down for 2 who goes under the basket and then comes off the screen to the wing.

Diagram 21

(Diagram 22)   5 pivots and looks to 4, 2, 3, or 1. 3 steps up in the lane. 5 can see all these things develop. 1 is his last choice.

Diagram 22

(Diagram 23)   Let's talk about continuity. If 5 hits 4, he screens down for 3.

(Diagram 24)   If 5 hits 2, he screens for 4 who comes up.

Diagram 23

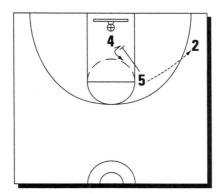

Diagram 24

(Diagram 25)   This is the way every play ends. It is an offense within itself. You can give the ball to 2 and screen down for 4 while 2 and 3 screen and roll. You can pass the ball to 2, and 4 can back-screen and 5 can go for the lob. You can pass to 2 and screen for 1, and 1 goes for the backdoor lob.

Diagram 25

(Diagram 26)   I like to send 5 down to screen for 4. 2 should try to get the ball into 3.

Diagram 26

(Diagram 27)   If not, pass to 4 and then to 1. 4 screens down for 3 who flashes into the lane.

Diagram 27

(Diagram 28)   Let's get back to the basic set, the guard cut (see Diagram 22). 3 has the ball on the wing. 3 reverses the ball back to 1. 3 and 5 set a double-screen for 2. 2 puts his head under the basket and comes off the double and comes high. 4 comes up the lane, and 1 has the option of hitting 2 or running any of the four side-post plays.

Diagram 28

(Diagram 29)   If 1 hits 2, we pop the stack while 4 goes down.

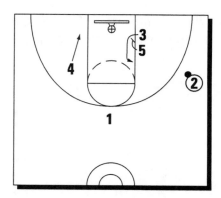

Diagram 29

(Diagram 30)   If 3 comes high and doesn't get the ball, he pivots and sets a down-screen for 5 who comes high.

(Diagram 31)   3 can pass to 2 and cut through to the short corner. 2 can dribble out and use the screen set by 5, and 2 and 5 can run the screen and roll. 1 goes away to take defensive man with him.

(Diagram 32)   3 can pass down to 2 and screen in for 5. 5 can come off the screen for the jump shot on the pass from 2.

Diagram 30

Diagram 31

Diagram 32

(Diagram 33)   3 passes to 2 in the corner; 4 sets a back-screen for 5. 5 comes off down the lane and 4 rolls low.

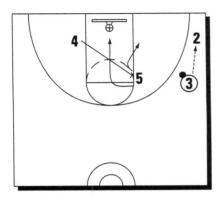

Diagram 33

Let's talk about the pressure release. The notoriety of the coach is dictated by how well his team performs while under pressure. The first pressure release is backdoor. It is a simple play. Anytime there is space between the guard and the top of the key, the forward, 3, takes two steps low and then breaks to the top. 5 and 4 set a double-screen. 2 comes off the double for the shot.

(Diagram 34)   If 3 can't make the pass to 2, 1 comes off of 3. Never give the ball to the second player through on a backdoor play. They never square their shoulders to shoot.

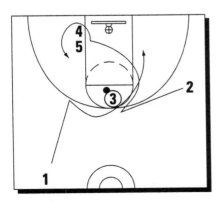

Diagram 34

(Diagram 35)   1 breaks out to the wing, and it is exactly like side-post delay. 4 and 5 pop the stack, 3 can pass to 1 who can skip-pass to 2.

Diagram 35

(Diagram 36)   The second pressure release is to hit the post, and the wings go backdoor. They can cross underneath if you so desire. We go right into continuity off of this play.

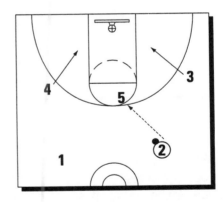

Diagram 36

(Diagram 37)   5 steps out and gets the ball. 5 can pass to 2 and screen down for 4. 2 can pass to 4, flashing into the lane.

Diagram 37

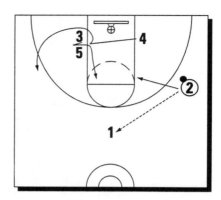

Diagram 39

(Diagram 38)   The last pressure release is called guard dribble. Dribble the ball right at 3, and 3 goes backdoor. If 3 is not open, he screens for 4. 5 stays high.

Diagram 40

Diagram 38

(Diagram 39)   Guard dribble. 2 has the ball, 3 and 5 set the double, 4 comes off the double and 3 and 5 pop the stack. 2 can run side post or 2 can pos up. You can do all kinds of things. You figure out what you want to do.

(Diagram 40)   2 gets the pass from 1 as 5 sets a down-screen for 4. 2 can pass to 4.

Diagram 41

(Diagram 41)   Guard screen. 1 passes to 3 and sets a side-screen for 2 who comes off the staggered-screen set by 1 and 5.

(Diagram 42)   3 and 4 both screen down for 2, and 2 can use either screen and come off to the wing. 5 screens down for 3, and they pop the stack.

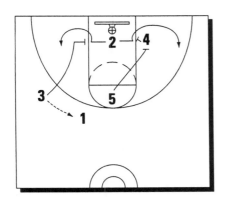

Diagram 42

one direction at the same time that 3 is coming off in the other.

Diagram 44

(Diagram 43)   Guard follow. 1 passes to 3 and follows the pass and gets the ball back from 3. 5 sets a side-screen, and 3 comes off the screen and goes down the lane. 4 comes across low.

Diagram 43

Diagram 45

(Diagram 44)   1 takes three dribbles and goes off the screen set by 5. 5 rolls down and screens for 4. 2 screens down the other side for 3.

(Diagram 45)   Guard around. 1 passes to 3 and makes an outside cut to the basket. If he doesn't get the ball, 5 drops down the lane and sets a double-screen with 1.

(Diagram 46)   4 comes off the double-screen and if he doesn't get the ball, 3 passes to 2 and breaks off the top of the double-screen. 4 is coming off in

Diagram 46

(Diagram 47)   You can use a one-guard front. 1 to 3, and 1 comes off the screen of 5 and goes to the short corner. 2 comes high.

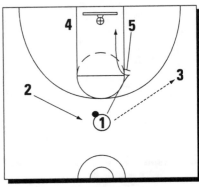

Diagram 47

(Diagram 48)   Now, we are actually in the same thing as the two-guard front with our sideways 1-3-1 alignment. You can run anything you want to run out of it.

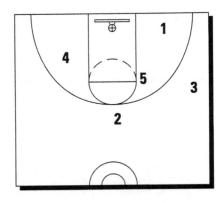

Diagram 48

(Diagram 49)   We can run the two-guard front with a low post. 2 passes to 4 and cuts. 3 comes across to the high-post area.

(Diagram 50)   Now you have a 1-3-1; the same thing as before.

(Diagram 50)   The UCLA Cut is Guard Cut. 1 passes to 2, and 5 sets a back-screen for 1.

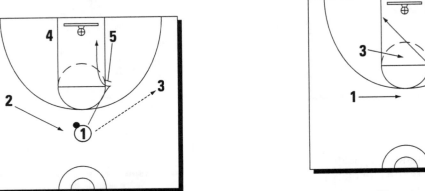

Diagram 49

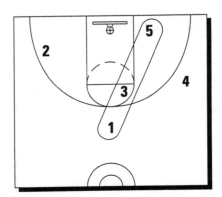

Diagram 50

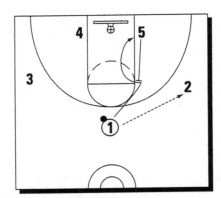

Diagram 51

Philosophy

I run my program like many of you run your high school programs. What I mean is that I don't have high school All-Americans. When we recruit, we must project what he will be like two or three years down the road. We don't get the kid who will have an immediate impact on our program. I need kids who play hard, who have the intangibles, kids who have a work ethic, kids who want to get better over a four-year period. The hardest thing for a college going out to recruit and evaluating kids, it's easy to see talent. The hardest thing to evaluate is the heart, the work ethic, the attitude.

How good do they want to be? Your kids must play hard. You must convince your kids to compete and play hard every single day. There is no magic formula. My style might be totally different from yours. I learned a lesson this year with my young team. We went through a stretch of games where we lost our confidence as a team. I did a poor job of handling this. My style is aggressive, intense, hands on. I try to get things intense in every single drill. When we started to lose, and to lose our confidence as a team, I didn't know enough to back off the pedal. I should have stroked them a little, but I came on harder. I had a lot of freshmen, and it is amazing when you get kids from high school, many of them don't know much about the game of basketball, especially with the ability to compete. We did get it back over the last weeks of the season.

Get your teams to play hard. Times have changed and players have changed. We run a lot of 4 out 1 in motion. I want my post player to be able to step out and shoot the "3." We had such a player, but he had slow feet. He certainly couldn't guard a perimeter player on the defensive end of the floor, and he wasn't that good defensively. This is one of the biggest differences for kids coming out of high school. So, we had to play post defense. We had a Saturday morning practice and the father picked him up after practice. My assistant coach came along and said hello. The father is telling my assistant coach that his son shouldn't be playing post defense. That's what is happening today. With the AAU programs, etc., a lot of people are telling them a lot of things.

Kids don't want to hear that they should do whatever we need for them to do. They all want to be shooters. It is very important that you need to get them to understand their roles on the team. You need to tell them what they do well, but I think we make a mistake when we don't tell them what they don't do well. They should be told what areas they are deficient in, what areas they must work on to help the team. They must accept their roles. Make your practices as competitive and game-like as possible. Your team will play in games the way that you practice. Every drill we do, we try to make it as competitive and game-like as possible. We don't always run the first string as a unit. We mix them. I really like doing this. We determine playing time by how you practice. Defense wins championships. At any level of sport, the teams that win are the teams that play good defense.

Convince your teams to do the little things. This is underrated. Loose balls, charges, 50-50 rebounds. One of the hardest things is getting a player to take a charge. Play as a team. We have a motto. We take the word "team"; Together Everyone Achieves More. Share the ball. Preparation. This is so important. At the college level, we have a greater opportunity to scout. We play what we call a scouting report defense. We will take the opponent's personnel, and we will defend you according to our scouting report.

Man-to-Man Defense

Our defense is very basic. We try to break down the individual part of the defense first, and then we build it up to the team level. Our primary teaching drill in our man defense is our 4-on-4 half-court shell, but we will not get to that for about two weeks into practice.

(Diagram 1)   The first drill we use on the first day of practice is the "Command Drill." We are teaching footwork, movement, stance. There are eight commands. When I give them a command, they must verbally give it back to me. What we are starting to incorporate from day one is communication. When I clap my hands, they will all get down and slap the floor and come up and get in a good defense stance and say "defense." I will walk around and check the stance. We are going to change the position of the hands next year. Watching Utah play, their hands were always up above the shoulders. I like that. We are going to be more active on the ball.

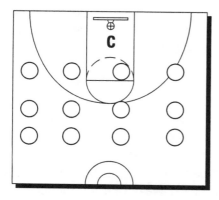

Diagram 1

The next command is "fire." That means that they are doing a foot-fire on the balls of their feet.

The third command is when I point. If I point left, the team calls "left" and steps in the direction that we want to go, and then slide. We do not bring our feet together, and we do not cross the foot. I then point the other way, and they call "right" and do the same thing in the other direction. Then I point "back." Now this is as if you are guarding the ball, and it is being advanced up the floor on you. When we go back, we step with our back foot and push off the front foot. As they go back, I will point diagonally. Now we incorporate the drop-step. Pivot off the back foot, swing the front foot, keep my base, and then change direction. As they are going back, I bring my hands toward my shoulders, which is "up." When we come "up," we want them to make believe they are closing out on the shooter so that they will step with the front foot and push off the back. The left hand must be up to contest.

The last command is "fire." I have a ball and move the ball, and they will trace the ball with their hands. We repeat the call of "five, five, etc." This is hard because it is tedious. It must be broken down, but as coaches, we must take the time to break it down. If you want to be good, it starts now. We do this for two or three minutes; stance, movement, position. This is a good workout.

(Diagram 2)   Zigzag Drill. This is the second thing we teach. We teach how to guard the ball in a full-court situation. We do three things in our zigzag drill. We put the perimeter players together at one end, and the post players at the other end. We use the foul lane extended and the sideline as the width of the drill. We use two words: pressure and contain. You must pressure the ball if you want a good defense. But your kids must understand that pressuring the ball is different for everybody. Pressure is predicated on your speed and quickness, or lack thereof, and the speed and quickness of the player that you are playing against. If you have a man who can penetrate against my man if he plays close, it does us no good to allow that to happen.

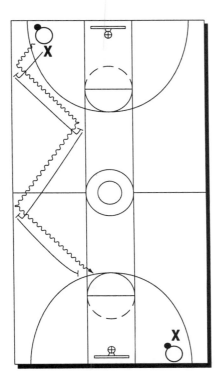

Diagram 2

The first time through this drill we go hands, half-speed. We work on the footwork. The man with the ball starts with his back to the defender. He must square up and get in the triple threat position, and the defender will get into position on the ball. I'm not really a big technique coach. The final analysis is that you must do what you must do to get into him and play. I don't care where your feet are. Just stay between your man and the basket, pressure and contain. First, the man with the ball goes half-speed. Our rule in the back-court is that we try to turn the ball as much as he can. We don't run and jump; we don't trap. Once the offensive player crosses half-court, our rule is just don't get beat. We don't force sideline, we don't force baseline. Just stay between him and the basket; don't let him get by you. Remember, the first time is half-speed. The offense is not trying to beat the defense. When I blow the whistle, the offensive player immediately picks up his dribble.

Offensively, we teach our kids to pivot, protect the ball, and get away from the pressure. Defensively, we go body up, trace the ball, and call "five, five." When I blow the whistle the second time, we will continue the drill. When we get to the other end of the floor, offense goes to defense and we come back. Next we go hands full-speed. This is primarily a defensive drill, but it is also an offensive drill. Your kids must understand their weaknesses. Sometimes your big player will be losing the ball. If he loses the ball, I'll have him go again suggesting he slow down and control the ball. I don't care how we get the ball up the court, but I want to have the ball. Here is the rule when we go full-speed. Any time we get beat, especially in the back-court, you get out of your stance, turn and sprint and reposition between the ball and the basket. In a real game, you are going to have some help at the other end of the floor.

(Diagram 3)   The third part is what we call "Zigzag and return." We are only going one group at a time. Full-speed. When I blow the whistle, the offensive player immediately reverses direction and attacks the basket he came from, trying to score in the open court. This teaches them to attack the basket from the open floor. Many will go too fast and miss the layup. I tell my kids, the closer you get to the basket, shorten your steps, get your body under control and we often use the two-foot jump stop. Defensively, we teach how to track the ball down from behind in an open court situation. The defense should chase it on the inside part of the floor. If you can tip it from behind, great. If you are quick enough to reposition between the ball and the basket, great. Then you will play one-on-one live. If not, don't allow any layups. There is a way to foul hard, not dirty, not cheap. Get on his arms and don't let him get it to the rim. Make him go to the line and earn it. The drill is live until the offense scores, the defense breaks it up, or the offense misses and the defense gets the rebound. We usually do this early in practice.

BILL HERRION

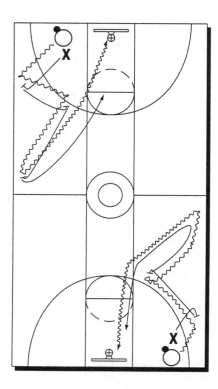

Diagram 3

(Diagram 4)   "One-on-one, roll it out." We go from three spots: wing, top, opposite wing. The offensive player starts outside the three-point line. The defensive player starts in the lane with the ball. We want our right-handed shooters with the right foot back ready to catch and step in to the shot. The defender will roll out the ball. We are teaching close-out. We don't have a lot of rules, just do whatever you have to do to get there. It depends on who you are playing against. Is he a driver or a set shooter? The closer you get to the offense, get your butt down and shorten your steps. This is primarily a defensive drill, but you are also working with the offense. As the offensive player picks up the ball, he steps into his shot. He squares up. The offensive player waits until he is touched by the defense. Now they play one-on-one. The rule has a two-dribble maximum. The closer the offensive player gets to the basket, the more you must get a body on him. If he shoots, the defense contests. We call "shot," turn and box, release and get the ball. The drill is not

over until the defense gets the ball. Then offense becomes defense. We go a minute from each position.

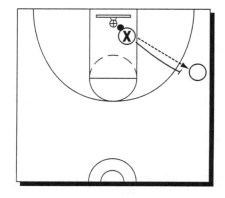

Diagram 4

(Diagram 5)   "One-on-one Attack." We use the same three spots. The offense starts at the hash mark; defense starts at the three-point line. The defense must play the live dribble in the open floor. The offense must make some type of dribble move to break down the defense. We teach five dribble moves: hesitation, inside-out, crossover, stutter, stutter-cross. I don't want the dribbler to turn his back. The worst thing the defense can do is to get back on his heels. Keep your feet moving, use the forearm and try to ride him to one side or the other.

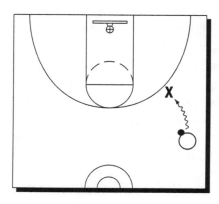

Diagram 5

(Diagram 6)   "Deny." We do not deny all over the court. We basically play the three-point line hard. The only passes we contest are penetrating passes toward the basket. Point to wing, we deny. Wing to post, we deny. Wing to high post, we deny. We don't deny ball reversal in our straight man. We have a lot of help and recover. We try to stop penetration. Why? We don't have great athletes.

Coach has the ball. The front foot of the defensive man splits the body of the offense. I don't want our body in the passing lane. If we get beat backdoor, we don't have shot blockers back there. We can't recover. We want our hand and arm in the passing lane, not our body. The key is our back foot. It is always between the offensive man and the basket. If he cuts, this will enable us to stay close. The drill starts with a V-cut by the offensive player and breaks the three-point line. The defense denies. Coach makes the pass. The defense must touch the ball. If not, he goes again. Reset.

Diagram 7

(Diagram 8)   The coach takes the ball to the wing. Now this is help defense. Once he crosses the front of the rim, the defense opens and finds the ball. The defense is touching the offense with fingertips. The hand and foot closest to the ball are always up.

Diagram 6

(Diagram 7)   Now the offensive player does the same thing and we again deny. Our rule is that if you cut away from the basket and break the three-point line and you are denied, you automatically back-cut. The defense does two things on the backdoor cut. Turn your head and look over the other shoulder and extend the opposite arm down because it will usually be a bounce pass. Once the man goes backdoor, he continues across the lane and goes to the opposite block.

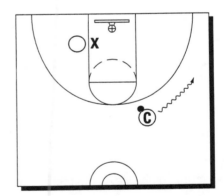

Diagram 8

(Diagram 9)   The offense runs a flash-cut. In our defense, that is a penetrating pass and is denied. The defense bumps with the forearm. Don't lose sight of the man and the ball.

(Diagram 10)   If he cuts to the basket, our rule is that no one cuts over the top of you. Make him go behind.

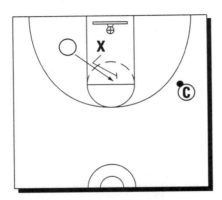

Diagram 9

Diagram 11

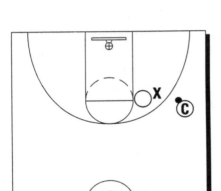

Diagram 10

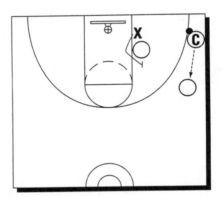

Diagram 12

(Diagram 11)   If the ball goes to the corner, the defense must work his way over the top of the post and play on the low side. If the ball is above the post, play on the high side. If the ball is below, play on the low side.

(Diagram 12)   If the ball comes out of the corner, you can't step over the top again. You must go behind.

(Diagram 13)   If the ball is passed from the wing to the top and the post crosses the lane, the defense will open as he crosses the lane.

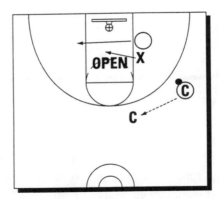

Diagram 13

(Diagram 14)   The offensive player breaks out to the wing, we close out defensively and we are one-on-one live from the wing position. Offense gets no more than two dribbles.

Diagram 14

(Diagram 15)   One-on-one feed the post. Offensively, we are teaching the wing to feed the post. The post player is on opposite block with the defender in help position. The offensive player has a live dribble, defense is pressuring. The defensive man bumps the cutter. On the pass into the post, the defense must get between the post and the basket. We try to favor the baseline side. We don't want to get beat baseline. On the pass, we get off of the wing to help with the hand and foot on the inside part of the floor extended.

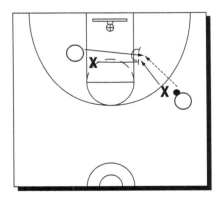

Diagram 15

(Diagram 16)   If the perimeter man is a good shooter, our defensive man will be "close enough to touch." He has no help responsibilities. We will designate one man to be the man who will double down on the post. We call that "red." This is predicated on scouting reports.

Diagram 16

(Diagram 17)   Defending screens on the ball, in the scoring area. We do a lot of screening on the ball with our post. The first thing we teach is "hedge over the top." The ball is on the wing, post at the elbow. The post will just step out. Whoever is defending the ball, the only responsibility is pressure-contain. The man defending the screener must communicate and alert his teammate. Once the dribble commences, we are going to hedge and get over the top. First, I want to hit the screen with my forearm. I can't hit it with the body, I will get hung up, but with my arm, I can get over the top. The key is the man defending the screener. He must get into the lane of the dribbler. He must show up in the lane. This forces the player to do one of several things. First, he might pick up his dribble. Second, he may go wider. Third, you may get a charge. The other man must step over the screen, and my teammate will pull me through.

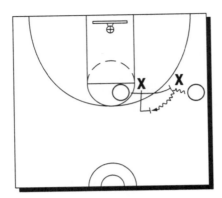

Diagram 17

Diagram 18

half-court, my assistant coach will take the defense. We may have them take five passes before a shot, we may designate a certain person to shoot, etc. This teaches shot selection and discipline. Defensively, we will play it differently. When I yell "change," the offense will drop the ball and become the defense, and the defense will pick up the ball and become the offense. In transition, all we tell our players is to run as fast and as hard as you can. I want all five defensive men ahead of the ball. Sprint! Get ahead of the ball, no matter where your man is. Somebody must stop the ball. This is where communication comes in. Protect the basket, and stay with the person you are guarding until you can change.

Diagram 19

(Diagram 18)   Slide, in the scoring area. From the scouting report, we know we can slide through. The man with the ball isn't that good a shot. The player defending the screener will step back so his teammate can slide between.

(Diagram 19)   Switch, in the scoring area. If size doesn't matter, we can switch.

(Diagram 20)   "Black," in the scoring area. If the man with the ball is extremely dangerous, we will double him. We try to get the ball out of his hands.

We work on transition defense every day. We do two drills. In practice, anytime we are working on 5-on-5, we will always try to convert at the other end. The first is the "change" drill. I will huddle the offense at

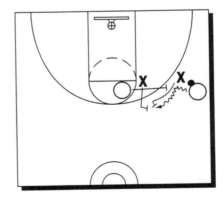

Diagram 20

(Diagram 21)   "Circle Rebounding." This is the second drill. Ten players are rotating counterclockwise. Coach has the ball. Coach misses the shot and all 10 players rebound. Whichever team gets the ball is on offense; the other is in defensive transition.

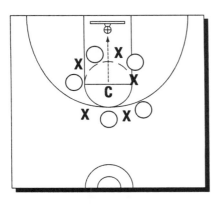

Diagram 21

(Diagram 22)   4/4 Half-Court Shell. This is our primary teaching drill. We make it as competitive as we possibly can. Offensively, we run motion. If you run motion, every conceivable situation that can happen will happen. We sub on each possession, but the four defenders stay. After some time, the defense can get off if they make three stops in a row. During the season, when we have scouting reports, we will incorporate what our next opponent does into this drill.

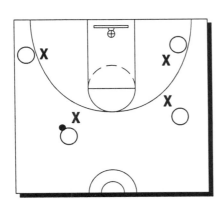

Diagram 22

Out-of-Bounds Plays

(Diagram 23)   "One." 2 screens for 3 who breaks to the corner. 4 and 5 double-screen for 2 who gets pass from 1.

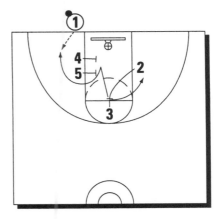

Diagram 23

(Diagram 24)   2 and 3 can switch positions. The defense will start to switch this play. 3 starts up as if he is to back-screen, but fakes that and then goes to the basket. 4 and 5 double-screen for 2, and 2 comes off of the screen.

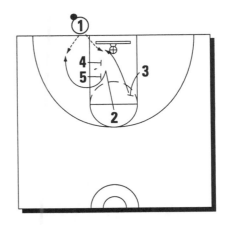

Diagram 24

(Diagram 25)   "Two." This is run against man or zone. 2 is our best perimeter shooter. Against a man, defense 5 breaks to the corner as 4 down-screens for 1. 2 inbounds to 5 who reverses to 1.

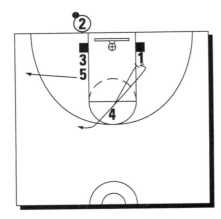

Diagram 25

(Diagram 26)   2 steps into the middle of the lane. 2 can break to either side, either off of the single screen of 4, or the staggered-screen of 3 and 5.

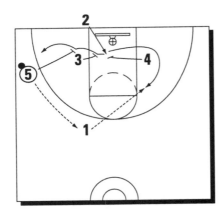

Diagram 26

(Diagram 27)   Against a zone, the play starts the same but 1 must take the ball on the dribble to get the zone to shift. 3 screens the middle of the zone, and 5 screens the back man. 2 comes off of the screen for the pass from 1. 3 or 5 are open after setting the screen and slipping to the ball.

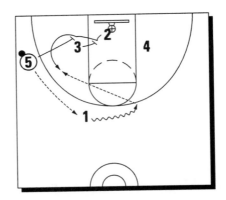

Diagram 27

(Diagram 28)   2 can also use the screen set by 4 and 4 will then slip to the ball.

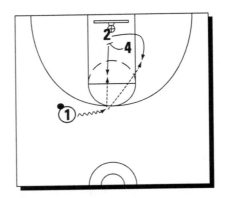

Diagram 28

(Diagram 29)   "Colgate." Box set against a man defense. 4 screens across for 2 and 5 also screens for 2, our best shooter. 3 holds for a half count, and then sets a back-screen for 4. 5 and 4 roll to the basket.

(Diagram 30)   "Stanford." This is a good continuity play. 2 is your best shooter. 1 loops under 3 and rubs his man off and releases out to the opposite wing. 4 turns outside to screen. 3 comes off of 4. 2 passes to 3.

(Diagram 31)   4 releases out for ball reversal. 5 cuts across the lane to the 3/4 post area. 3 passes to 4.

Diagram 29

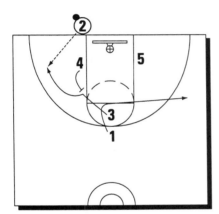

Diagram 30

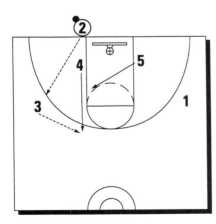

Diagram 31

(Diagram 32)   4 passes to 1. If 4 can't pass to 1, 4 dribbles toward 1 and 1 back-cuts to the basket because that half of the floor is open. But, let's say that 4 can pass to 1. On the flight of the pass, 5 steps out and back-screens for 3 who goes to the block. 5 then turns and screens for 2.

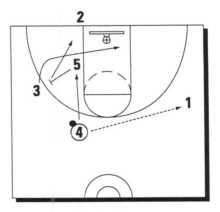

Diagram 32

(Diagram 33)   4 also screens for 2. 2 comes off of the staggered-screen set by 5 and 4.

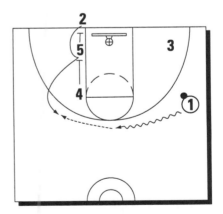

Diagram 33

Planning Your Practice Sessions

Drills for Daily Improvement

The main thing I want to emphasize is that at Kansas, we get a plan and stick with it. Our staff goes somewhere for about three days to discuss plans for the coming season, comes up with some ideas and goals and how we are going to reach them. We then stay with it. Assistant coaches make suggestions, but the head coach makes the decisions. We always want to change around more than Coach Williams, but he will not do that. So, we have a plan for individual improvement.

Individual Work, First Week of Practice

Perimeter Defense—1-on-1, control the dribbler. That's the hardest thing in basketball. Close-outs, denying inbounds sideline, forming double-teams.

Perimeter Offense—Begin the dribble without walking, feeding the post, ball lobs. I'm just showing you these things as an example of what we will do before practice for 10 minutes.

Defensive Plan for 1997-1998

What do we want to do? This was our plan for the year. We want to create turnovers, contest shots, get rebounds, force tempo, disrupt offense, bother the scorers. How do we do this? Keep the ball in front of you, stop the dribble penetration, deny one pass away, sideline position, form double-teams, etc.

Areas that need to change from one opponent to the next.

- How do we defend their favorite plays? In the past we didn't worry about that. We have a short scouting report. Our players get one sheet; personnel, and their three favorite plays.

Basically, we work all year long in getting our team better. We don't worry about the opposition too much. We need to see the whole picture.

- How do we defend as the shot clock winds down?

- How do we defend their best player?

Areas in Which We Must Improve

Coach Williams was worried about this team. In the last four years we have been very good on defense. We lost good defensive players. People coming back were good scorers, but weren't as good defensively. Another thing about Coach Williams, "let it be written, let it be done." We will talk about it, but once he writes it down, he comes back to it constantly.

- Toughness defensively in going for loose balls.

- Take pride in stopping their man.

- Seeing the big picture—what are they trying to do.

- Chase the rebound.

- Challenge every shot.

Defensive Stations 1997-1998

- Zigzag

- Guarding ball middle

- Guarding ball sideline

- Deny wings and low post

- Close-out—from support position and two passes away

- Challenge outside shot (1 hand) and inside shot (2 hands)

- Vision

- Retreat in the direction of pass

- Defending lateral screens
- Forming double on baseline drive
- Beat man to top of key
- Box out
- Defending rear-screen
- Defending screen at point of ball
  - show and recover
  - double
  - slide through
- Shading screens

4/4 Defensive Group Work
regular shell movement
transition from one pass away to two
Combination

This list was made at the beginning of the season and each assistant coach was assigned to certain drills he would teach for the season. The group work is team-oriented work. Here are some of our practices. I want you to see that we actually did these drills throughout the entire season. This is the first practice, 10/18/97.

Emphasis of the Day—Concentration and Effort

Thought for the Day—It's amazing how much can be accomplished when no one cares who gets the credit.

Stations:
A - Stretching   B - Jump Rope

C - Shooting Form   D - Individual Work
(Perimeter—Beginning Dribble & Offensive Moves)
(Post—Favorite Moves—Swivel vs. Mgr.)

TIME	SUBJECT
4:00	On-court—stretching
4:20	Shooting form
4:28	Individual work
4:42	Discussion
4:44	Fast-break drills #1 & #3
4:50	Defensive stance—three min. step—slide
4:54	Defensive stations 1—Zigzag 2—Box-Outs 3—Close-Outs
5:04	Introduce secondary break—5-on-0
5:11	Free throws and water
5:15	Group work Shooting Group A Defensive (Shell—Transition)
5:21	Rotate
5:27	Rotate
5:33	Shoot and water break

(Partner Shooting)

TIME	SUBJECT
5:39	Defensive Stations three minutes 1—Beat your man to top of key 2—Deny 3—Challenge outside shot
5:49	5-on-5 Box-Outs—Half-Court—10 points
5:55	Secondary Break "Through"—5-on-0
6:02	Secondary Break Game— Live
6:12	Freelance—4 possessions
6:20	Keep Away—50 passes
6:30	Conditioning

If the players don't know what the thought for the day and the emphasis of the day is, the team will run.

On-court stretching—We thought we had the worst weight program in the country three years ago. We played Virginia and they pushed us all over the floor. We looked around and we put in the Chicago Bulls' program. We spend 20 minutes, but don't do any static stretching where we just lie on the floor. Everything is movement; for example, with medicine balls.

During individual work, we are working on starting the dribble without walking, not moving the pivot foot, etc., with our perimeter people. The post people are at the other end working on their moves.

Then, after discussion, we go into the defensive drills I showed you.

We have our players broken into groups, A, B and C. When we do group work, Coach Williams teaches the group work. One group is on offense, the other on defense and the third is at the other end of the floor shooting. He has six minutes for each group and they rotate. You will see that on every practice. We will teach team defense at this station. The second practice, we will cover six more stations. The point is that you should make a plan of what you think your players can do for the year and then have enough guts to be committed to it. Don't be changing all the time.

Note—Coach Holladay also had practice plans for the 3rd, 4th, 25th, 35th, 52nd and 75th days. These were shown to illustrate the same drills were being used even into the month of March.

Defensive stations are three minutes in length and there are three of them. These are run by the assistant coaches. The players rotate and so they

have nine minutes of high-intensity defensive work. They get a lot of reps. Early in the year we do a lot of defensive stations. These stations vary from year to year as the game changes, but we stay with the stations for the year. In the defensive individual work, this is where they obviously get their individual improvement, and in group work, this is where they get the team improvement. We don't do these because we are angry. We aren't punishing them. We want to improve all year long. That's four different sets of players.

Question: You have a short time for these drills. Do you do much instruction during that time?

Answer: No, very little talking. He does not like for us to talk. We get into it immediately. Usually there is a water break after the station work. Most of you don't have the luxury of having assistant coaches. We recruit 10 players every year and three walk-ons. He takes one walk-on from the student body and he represents the 7,000 students. We have about 14 players at the most. They know what groups they are in. Let's go over some of these stations for individual improvement.

(Diagram 1)   We do zigzag a little differently. We use the entire half-court. We want to turn the ball twice by half-court.

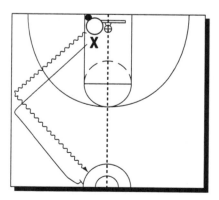

Diagram 1

(Diagram 2)   Guarding the ball in the middle. We have to adjust from year to year. We want containment. We just tell him to stay between his man and the basket. We aren't playing left hand, trying to turn him. We don't want him to get by us and turn in. The hardest thing to do is to cover the ball when it is being dribbled at us.

Diagram 2

(Diagram 3)   Guarding the ball sideline. I don't know of too many teams that do it this way. We try to get the ball on the sideline and once it's there, we play parallel to the sideline. Most teams are more at an angle (see right side of diagram). Our goal is to keep the ball out of the middle. We want to get the ball to be dribbled to the corner of the backboard, and we will trap it in the baseline area.

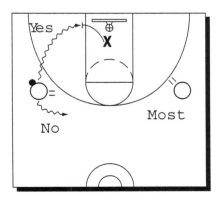

Diagram 3

(Diagram 4)   We tape the court. When the ball goes into this area, we want to keep it there.

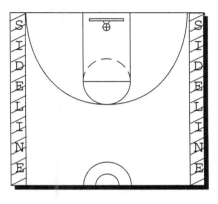

Diagram 4

(Diagram 5)   Deny wing and low post. We do not put our body in the lane. We just put a hand in the lane. Reason, our number one goal is to steal the ball. We almost invite the pass. Secondly, it is almost impossible to go backdoor on us. Our rule is that if the man goes backdoor, stay closed until that man splits your body. Then you can snap your head and look over the other shoulder. By taking two quick steps from this defensive wing position, the backdoor pass must be made in the lane.

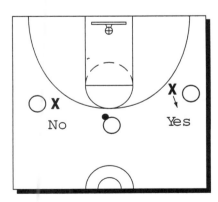

Diagram 5

(Diagram 6)   We front the low post. We play with our back against the front of the low post.

Diagram 6

(Diagram 7)　　Close-out. This comes from a support position, two passes away. Coach has the ball in the middle and passes to one of the wings. X runs full speed until he gets a yard and a half away, then he breaks down into a defense stance. The key is that he must play sideline once he gets there. His feet must be parallel to the sideline when he gets there. He comes out to prevent the shot and expects the dribble.

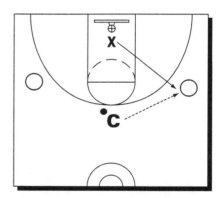

Diagram 7

(Diagram 8)　　Challenge the outside shot. We challenge the outside shot with one hand, and the inside shot with two hands. If I were coaching high school again, I would work on this a lot. I always thought they would foul the outside shooter and their man would run around them and get the rebound. All those little negatives. I didn't give my

kids enough credit. We work a lot on challenging the outside shot. We want our player to go up with the shooter and try and bother the shot. Make them shoot over the hand. We let the offensive player have one dribble, but not for the first several weeks. You can take a shooter, let him shoot 25 shots and he will make all of them. You can then stand in front of him with your hands up, and he will make half of them. It's a little contradictory to the close-out, but he will attack the guy on his shot. We leave the floor on his shot. If your man catches the ball inside, we put both hands up and make you shoot over them.

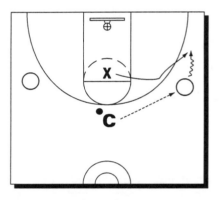

Diagram 8

(Diagram 9)　　Vision. This covers everything. Coach has the ball and the offensive man is in the corner.

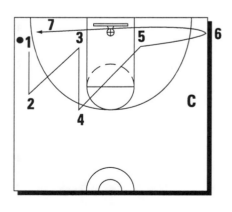

Diagram 9

- The defensive man starts in the middle of the lane.

- The offensive man comes up.

- Then down to the block.

- The defensive man is adjusting his position while this is happening. Then, the offensive man comes to the top of the key.

- The defense is denying at that point. The offensive man breaks to the low post and is fronted by the defense.

- The defensive man snaps his head after several steps if he is beaten. The offensive man breaks out to the corner and is denied. The offensive man then goes backdoor, and defensive man opens up and snaps his head after two steps.

- The offensive man clears to the corner, but the defensive man stays in the lane in help position. You have covered everything: weak-side defense, ball-you-man, deny the top of the key, retreat in the direction of the pass, and front the low post. In three minutes, you can do this drill about eight times.

(Diagram 10)   Retreat in the direction of the pass. The ball is in the middle of the floor with a manager on each wing. Pass to the wing, or manager, retreat in the direction of the pass and make the man cut behind. The cutter may stop and come back out for the ball. We would be in help position if the managers would drive.

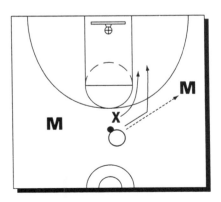

Diagram 10

(Diagram 11)   Teams take advantage of you for playing good defense. You will get screened and then the skip-pass is made.

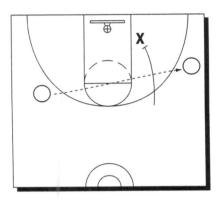

Diagram 11

(Diagram 12)   Lateral-screen. We do it differently than most. We are in a front position and help position. Coach has the ball. The man being screened is responsible for the low side.

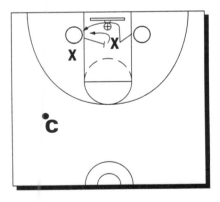

Diagram 12

(Diagram 13)   If the cutter came high, the man defending the screener must help until he gets there. We do not switch. Try not to let the screener get into your body. We keep him off with a forearm.

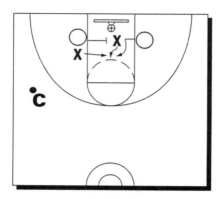

Diagram 13

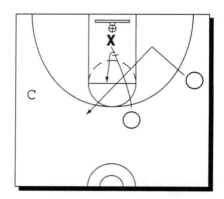

Diagram 15

(Diagram 14)   Double on baseline drive. This is an automatic trap. We want the trap outside the lane. We want an "L" trap with the legs together. We trace the ball, take it away. We must have an aggressive trap or the man will spin out and make the easy pass. We keep the trap moving. We try to get right up on the man, put our chest on him. The other three men are two interceptors and a flier. In effect, they zone the area.

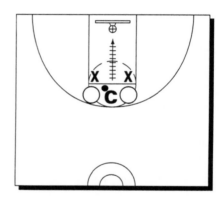

Diagram 16

(Diagram 17)   Same drill to the side.

(Diagram 18)   Specialty work for the post defenders. You can have a player flash into the lane to get the pass from the coach.

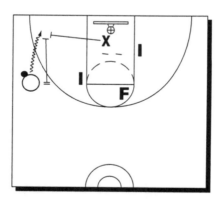

Diagram 14

(Diagram 15)   Beat the man to the top of the key. This is another deny drill. We can run this several ways. Coach has the ball. We may add a second offensive player to screen.

(Diagram 16)   Box out. We don't have any special way to box out. We never want you to lose sight of the ball.

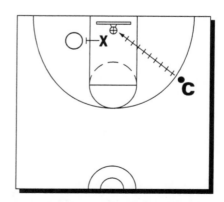

Diagram 17

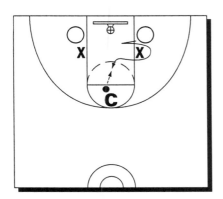

Diagram 18

(Diagram 19)   Rear-screen. The ball is passed from the wing to the coach. The post sets a rear-screen for the wing. This is just one way it can be set up. The low man is responsible to help until X1 gets there. Many teams try to screen on the ball with their best shooter and roll him out for the shot.

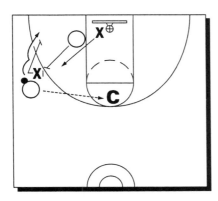

Diagram 19

(Diagram 20)   The best way is to just stay with the cutter, wherever he goes. If you do that, you must be working hard on containing the dribbler because you have taken away the help so he doesn't jump to the ball.

(Diagram 21)   Screen at the point of the ball. There are three ways to do it. You may play it one way the first round of the conference and then play it differently the second time. Up until four years ago, it was an automatic for us when someone

screened on the ball. We were going to have an automatic trap. If 5 screened and 3 dribbled off, X5 and X3 doubled him. But it turned out that 5 was their good shooter, and they would roll him away and have their best shooter shooting wide open. Now we give them different looks in addition to the double-team.

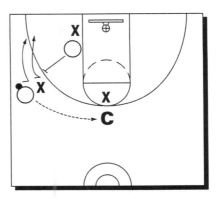

Diagram 20

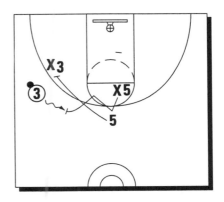

Diagram 21

(Diagram 22)   Show and recover. Some call this hedging. 5 screens for 1. X5 hedges a little. We really want X1 to go over the top and not be separated from the dribbler.

(Diagram 23)   The third way is sliding through. This is the easiest way. If the man is not in scoring position, we slide through, but if he is in scoring position, we go over the top.

Diagram 22

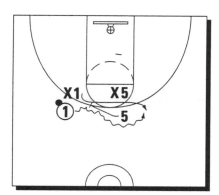

Diagram 23

(Diagram 24)   Shadow the screen. Some people call it "follow in his footsteps." Coach has the ball. We try to stay with the player getting screened by staying right behind him. The man can go either way.

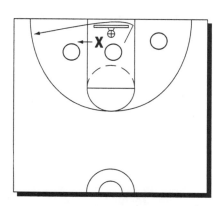

Diagram 24

(Diagram 25)   As he comes off the screen, we stay right behind him so that they can't get to our body.

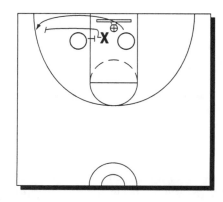

Diagram 25

(Diagram 26)   If X3 goes over the top, 3 will fade to the corner and be wide open.

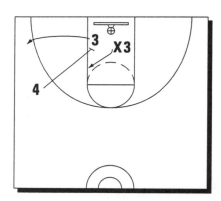

Diagram 26

Question: When do you instruct your players?

Answer: As the drill is being run. We are constantly talking to them and correcting them. We aren't going to have them stand there. We keep reminding them what to do.

Point Zone Defense

Our zone defense is a little different. We use a zone about 10% of the time. We use it for foul trouble and just for the fact that some teams don't play well against a zone. We play a point zone. Coach Dean Smith developed this, but we have some different rules. The term "point zone" comes from the fact that one of our players points to the ball. Once this is established, that means that player has the ball.

(Diagram 1)   We start with X1 and X2 on the three-point line. We start in a 2-1-2.

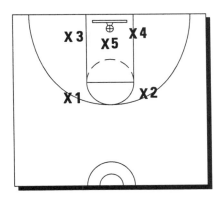

Diagram 1

(Diagram 2)   X1 and X4 are buddies, X2 and X3 are buddies. They always work together.

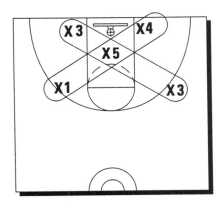

Diagram 2

(Diagram 3)   X5 is independent of everyone else. X5 always stays between the ball and the basket and this is hard to teach. When you are X5, all you do is to stay on this line. He doesn't cover anyone, even if there is a post standing beside him. He plays facing the ball with arms spread and hands up as high as his head.

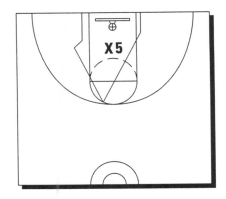

Diagram 3

(Diagram 4)   This defense is an airplane. If X1 points the ball, X1 and X4 are buddies. Anytime X1 points the ball, X4 will be under the goal. X5 will be in line with the basket. You will always get this look, like an airplane. X2 will slide down about three steps, and X3 will also slide down. X3 will always take the first pass to the left of the ball; X2 will always take the first pass to the right. This is a match-up zone. It is strong inside.

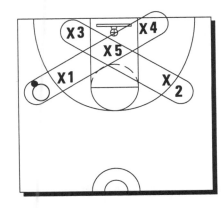

Diagram 4

(Diagram 5)   If the ball is passed to the wing, X3 is playing the ball man-to-man. X1 drops to cover the high post. Anytime the ball goes below the free-throw line, X4 crosses the lane and X2 is on the back-side. X3 is pointing the ball, and X2 is his buddy and, in general, should be under the basket, but X4 is already there. X5 is again on line between ball and basket.

the ball man-to-man. X3 moves back, X1 moves over, X5 is in line with the ball and the basket, X2 is on the weak side. Most people want to make the skip-pass; and that is why X1 is moving so far across the lane. X2 is not under the basket because he can't rebound there. He stays outside the lane. We don't think they can lob over X5 as we have pressure on the ball.

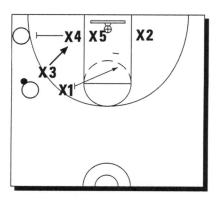

Diagram 7

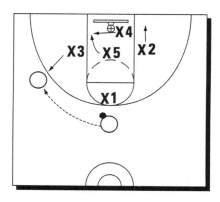

Diagram 5

(Diagram 6)   You have three players in a line, X4, X5, and X1, all with their arms extended. X1 isn't covering anyone either, but he is looking for a flash to the high post.

(Diagram 8)   There are a couple of exceptions. If X3 has the ball in the corner, and anytime the ball is below the free-throw line, X4 is across the lane. X5 is in line with the ball and the basket, so X4 stays on the weak side. In theory, X4 should come across, but X5 is already there.

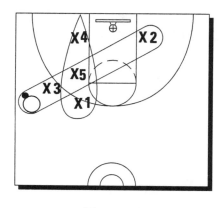

Diagram 6

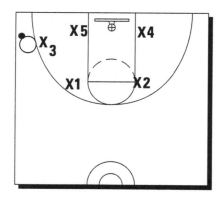

Diagram 8

(Diagram 7)   If X3 is pointing on the wing and the ball is passed to the corner, X4 comes out and takes

(Diagram 9)   We teach this working with 4-on-5. We don't have a 5 in there.

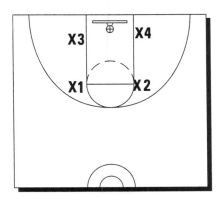

Diagram 9

cover the shooters. That's the only time. We still have X3 and X4 near the basket.

(Diagram 10)   You can also use this to play a box and 1. X1 plays man-to-man. We can work on this 4-on-5 without X1. The rules are exactly the same, but we play it a little tighter.

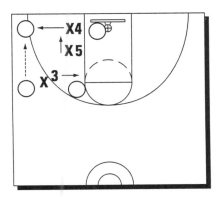

Diagram 11

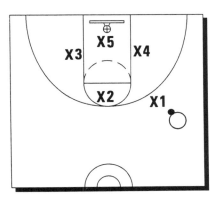

Diagram 10

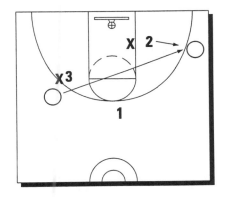

Diagram 12

(Diagram 11)   Early in the year, we go 3 vs. 4. X5 is in line with the ball and the basket. The ball goes to corner, X4 comes out, X5 slides down in line with the ball and the basket and X3 drops back to cover the high post.

(Diagram 12)   On the skip-pass and X3 is pointing the ball, then X2 is under the basket. X2 must come out to cover as X1 is covering one pass away.

(Diagram 13)   Another exception is when the opponent brings their center to the top of the key; then we must bring X5 out to cover. X1 and X2 can

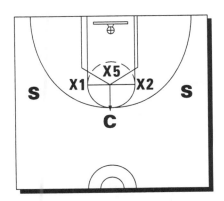

Diagram 13

(Diagram 14)   If the opponent comes down the court and lines up this way, we will stay in the 2-1-2 alignment. X1 has the ball, X2 has the first pass to the left, X3 has the first pass to the right.

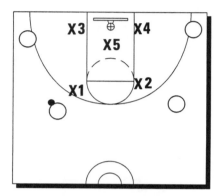

Diagram 14

(Diagram 15)   If they slide around, then X3 has the ball on the wing and X4 comes across the lane with X5 staying between the ball and the basket. If the ball goes inside, this is an automatic double-down. X1 is at the high-post area, X2 on the back side.

Diagram 15

(Diagram 16)   If X2 is on the ball, and 2 drives to the baseline, X2 guards the ball as it is being dribbled, and he has the ball until he gives it up to somebody else. X4 could call "point," and then X4 has the ball. But for us, it is an automatic trap with X2 and X4 on the baseline.

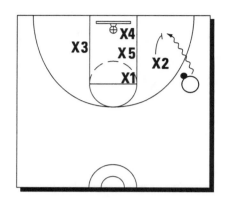

Diagram 16

(Diagram 17)   Why are they throwing it into the post man? If they are doing this so that they get a three-point shot, then X2 will go halfway until the post man commits himself by starting a move. Then X2 will go all the way to help. We are more concerned about the pass back out because we have both X4 and X5 at the defensive post position.

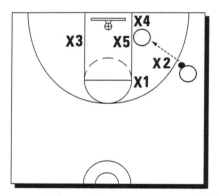

Diagram 17

(Diagram 18)   We also automatic when the ball is short-passed into the corner from below the free-throw line. X1 and X3 will double-team in the corner. We used to have another automatic double and that was on a screen on the ball, but we have gotten away from that because players were rolling back for the shot.

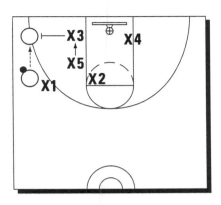

Diagram 18

Question: What about block-out responsibilities?

(Diagram 19)   *Answer:* We talk a lot with X1 and X2. If X4 is on the ball, we want X2 outside the lane on the weak side. We want X1 to drop down into the lane and box out. If X1 and X2 don't find somebody, they come out of the game. Usually X3, X4, and X5 have their hands full. All five players rebound, then we fast break.

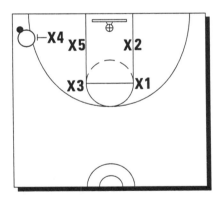

Diagram 19

(Diagram 20)   We double-team on any short pass below the free-throw line to the corner, even on an out-of-bounds play.

(Diagram 21)   We can also double-team the first pass below the free-throw line. This is a special call from the bench.

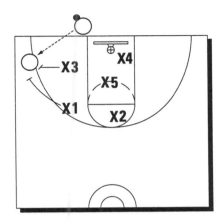

Diagram 20

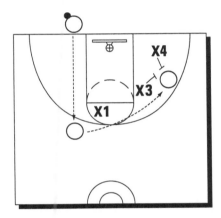

Diagram 21

(Diagram 22)   Sometimes we double the ball as it comes across half-court if we want to get the ball out of this guard's hands.

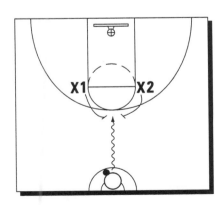

Diagram 22

(Diagram 23)   Drill. 3-on-4. X5 stays in line between the ball and the basket. If the ball is passed to the corner, X4 comes out and covers, X3 backs up, and X5 slides down to remain between the ball and the basket.

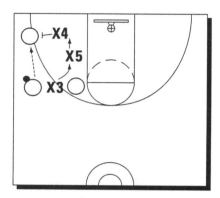

Diagram 23

(Diagram 24)   When you teach the zone with only four players, you can play a point and one without teaching anything knew. 1 will face guard.

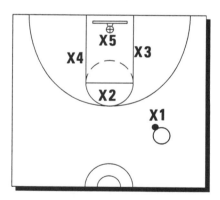

Diagram 24

Game Management

Your situation in high school is different. You may have a women's game before yours, or a JV game. But, I think that these ideas will be helpful. We stay consistent. We make it the same atmosphere for the team, home or away. We are the only team in the Big Twelve that has a winning record on the road in the '90s. In the last three years, we are 28 and 4 on the road. We always eat a pregame meal exactly four hours before we play. We feed them what they want to eat. If you give them something they don't want, they will get what they want somewhere else. We eat well: steak, chicken or fish, etc. We don't worry about the physical part as much as the mental part. We always arrive one hour fifteen minutes before the game, home or away. In high school when there is a preliminary game, you can have a time when your team will be dressed and seated before every game. Coach takes about six minutes to talk to them before the game. We go out when there are 29 minutes on the clock, and come in with 11 minutes on the clock. This is an 18-minute warm-up. That never changes, whether or not there is TV coverage. We have a shoot-around before on game days.

Scouting is divided between three assistants. Whoever is responsible for that team, we will have the roster on the board in the dressing room with their names, heights, weights, grades, and we list them in order. When we come in at 11 minutes, we let the players go in and the coaches stay out for four minutes. We go in with seven minutes on the clock, and Coach Williams will write the starters' names next to the people whom they are guarding. He then puts three points of emphasis on the board. These are major points for him. If he writes something down, we want to do it. The last thing is, he will put the jump ball lineup on the board and will designate one player to play the tap. We think we will get the tap, but we always designate one person to play their tap.

JOE HOLLADAY

Assistants' responsibilities during games: One assistant keeps track of playing time. We don't have anybody on scholarship who doesn't get at least 10 minutes a game. He also has the combinations that were in the game. Another assistant keeps track of fouls, time-outs and ball possessions. Even though it is usually on the clock, we keep those. This year another assistant kept track of what defense we were in when the other team had the ball.

Time-outs: Coach calls time-outs very seldom; he likes to save them. We also have TV time-outs, too many of them. Home and away, we have three managers who put five chairs on the floor and get away from the crowd. Coach Williams is in the middle, with the assistant coaches on each side. The players who aren't playing are responsible for being in a position to see and hear. The managers get behind and block out everybody else, including the TV cameras. There is no huddle among the coaches. He starts talking immediately. After he is finished, he looks at the assistants and if anyone has something to say, say it. There is never a case where I don't have a chance to say something. Over a six-year period, I've learned not to say anything unless I had something to say. But don't grab a player after the huddle breaks.

Substitutions: We have what we call the "tired" signal. A fist above the head means that a player is tired and he wants to come out of the game. But, he must not give that signal while coming back on defense. We had two players this year who averaged about 30 minutes a game. The only time they came out of a game is when they wanted to come out. When the signal is given, the backup on the bench can get ready to go in. Whenever someone comes out of the game, Coach Williams does not say anything to him, even if he is ready to kill him. The assistants will tell the player what he is doing wrong, praise him, etc. Coach Williams will have already spoken to the assistant. If a player came out by giving the tired signal, he puts himself back into the game whenever he is ready. Sometimes that's

tough to do, but we let it happen. That's the philosophy. Play as hard as you can play and take yourself out when you get tired. But if Coach Williams takes him out, then you sit until he puts you back in.

Foul Problems: If a player has two fouls, he will stay in until two minutes to go before half. If he has three fouls, he sits for the rest of the first half. If he picks up the fourth foul, he will sit until there are five or six minutes remaining in the game. He will have his best players in the game at the end of the game.

Halftime: We have a 15-minute halftime. Everyone sprints off the floor at the half, both coaches and players. Coaches stay away from the players for five minutes. We go into the locker room with 10 minutes on the clock. When we talk among ourselves, he asks for an offensive emphasis and a defensive emphasis to talk about. He asks for our opinions. The very first thing he will give the team is "points per possession." Every time we have had the ball, what did we get out of it? If we had the ball 40 times and have 50 points, we are 1.2 points per possession. The only way you can get more possessions than your opponent is to get offensive rebounds. That's the only way. He will then look at each assistant coach, and we will have a chance to speak.

Game Philosophy: Do you foul, or not foul? Suppose you have a three-point lead and the other team has the ball. We don't foul unless it is under seven seconds. If it is more than seven seconds, they are going to shoot the two free throws and have enough time to foul us back. That gives them another possession. One thing that I learned from Coach is when to get after the officials. I learned never to fight a battle unless I know that I am right. Coach Williams has had one technical foul in the last three years. Coach does not yell at the team at the half. He is very matter-of-fact. He picks his places very carefully. He has a business like approach. We are spoiled in that we have very good players. We lost 55 points per game off of our team this year.

We have been in the Top Ten for the past 72 weeks, four straight years. But, at the present time we are not ranked in the top 25, so this will be a little different. The expectations will not be as high. Practices are very businesslike. He picks his places where he might get after them a little. The only time that we just run is if someone doesn't know the emphasis of the day or the thought of the day. He feels we can get something else out of practice rather than by just running.

Question: What about scouting reports? Do you give them to the players the day before and are they typed up?

Answer: Each assistant is assigned to various teams and are responsible for watching three games for each team. I give one report to Coach Williams and another to the players. Each player gets one page, which will have the roster, their statistics, three favorite plays and their favorite inbounds play. We give it to them the day before, after practice. We never practice on the opponent's home court. Again, it's consistency. We did have a game on a neutral court, so we practiced in Madison Square Garden. In a tournament in Hawaii, yes, we had to. But, in the regular season, we practice at home.

After the game. The coaches go into the locker room with the players immediately. Coach Williams has never criticized a player to the press. We are out of there in a few minutes.

Filmwork: We do very little. The person who is in charge of scouting that team will put together about a six-minute tape which includes their favorite players. We will show it the night before the game and at the pregame meal the next day. Our players are student athletes. He takes two or three hours a day out of their lives, and that's it. He encourages them to be a student and be a part of the college, not just the basketball program. We have had only one player leave early for the pros. We don't take a lot of their time, but while they are there, it is very intense.

Weight lifting: We lift twice a week during the season. We do exactly what the Chicago Bulls do. We lift 30 minutes before practice. We don't do bench presses, etc. We do something entirely different. In the off-season, we have them for two hours a week. They lift for about 45 minutes and then play on their own.

Post Development

The first thing we do every day is form shooting for about 10 minutes. Our incoming freshmen tell us what their favorite move is. Whatever it is, we are not going to take that away from him. Pass the post player the ball and he performs his favorite move. You are giving your players a little freedom. Then he must develop a counter move. If his favorite move is a turnaround jump shot to the middle, he must develop a counter move to take him the opposite way. To start practice, we do the favorite move and the counter move. We do this for about a minute on each one. Then, you must have at least one move to take you to the basket. We teach the "ball fake, drop-step." Post is on the block. Post fakes, makes a two-handed dribble low between his legs and comes up with a power move to the goal. The outside leg drop-steps toward the basket. On the fake to the middle, just show the ball a little and then swing it low to take it to the goal.

(Diagram 1)   The Secondary Break Jump Shot. Managers feed 5 from the free-throw line to the top of the key. 5 must break to mid-court and come back to receive the next pass.

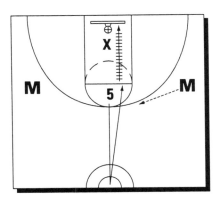

Diagram 1

(Diagram 2)   Swiveling. This is the term we use for posting up. Coach has the ball and a manager is playing defense. The offensive man must keep the manager sealed as he moves up and down the lane. We want the post to have his arms up with the upper arm horizontal and then the hands and fingers pointing up. We don't hold the defense off with our arms, we hold him off with the body. The post must continually move up and down the lane, and we try to move the defensive man back under the goal. We want the post to stay for two seconds, then move.

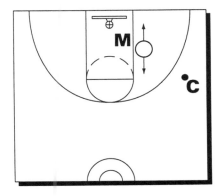

Diagram 2

(Diagram 3)   When we come down the floor on the secondary break, our big man runs the middle. 4 will start to seal off the defensive man near the top of the circle. 4 finds the man covering him and seals him high. When the pass goes to the corner, then 4 comes to the basket.

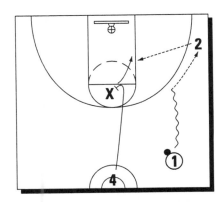

Diagram 3

(Diagram 4)   Defensively, we front if the offensive man is on the block or below. We get completely around in front with our back to him. We put one hand up, and the other hand on the man. (This hand is behind the back at belt level.) Then we lean back. How do we get that position? We can knock his arm up with our inside arm and step through. (The left arm of the defensive man knocks the right arm of the offense up.) If he is one full step off of the block, we don't front him. We 3/4 front with the offside arm extended.

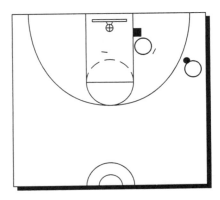

Diagram 4

(Diagram 5)   Don't go fishing and let the man get a layup. You aren't going to win every battle. Don't get caught on the high side. Try to take the backboard out of play by using your body. Put your chest on him instead of your hands. We would rather the post score over our hands than get a layup.

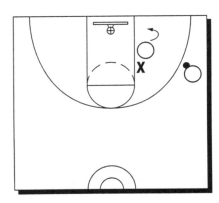

Diagram 5

(Diagram 6)   When we do defensive stations, we have two or three things that have defensive things in them. One of these things is post deny. Another is defending the lateral-screen. At Kansas, X5 is always responsible for the low side.

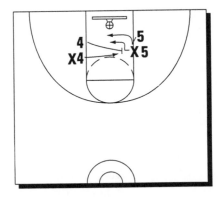

Diagram 6

(Diagram 7)   If 5 breaks up the lane, X4 holds until X5 can get there. We use flippers. If the screener gets into my body, he can screen me. But if I keep him away with my forearm, then I am in good shape.

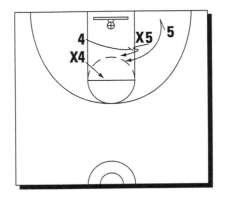

Diagram 7

(Diagram 8)   We automatically trap when the ball is dribbled on the baseline. Every time the dribbler takes a step, X5 takes a step. We want the trap outside the lane.

Diagram 8

Diagram 10

(Diagram 9)   What will the post do when his man sets a rear-screen? The ball is passed to the coach. The defensive man whose man sets the rear-screen is responsible for not allowing the easy pass. X5 cannot allow the pass to the cutter.

(Diagram 11)   Our point guard must stop the dribbler with help from the players guarding the low-post players. We would prefer the point guard take the shot instead of passing off to a post player for a layup.

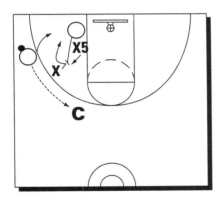

Diagram 9

Diagram 11

(Diagram 10)   When this occurs, you must be aware of the cutter fading to the corner. The man being screened usually follows his man over the screen.

The Running Game

Primary Break Rules

- Attack under control—limit those times when the ball is in jeopardy.

- Must work to box and rebound—cannot let other team have multiple opportunities.

- Be sure and quick on outlet pass. 1 must clear traffic.

- Everyone box and get the ball—then run.

- Look to pitch ahead. 2 and 3 especially must give 1 the option.

- Rebounders can also look down floor more—this may help get 2 and 3 running.

- Take the ball to basket—get fouled.

- No three-point shots on pitch ahead.

- Bounce pass is feeding pass.

- Defenses will not run back as consistently as you will with the ball—keep running and keep the pressure on. KNOW YOUR LIMITATIONS!

Secondary Break Rules

- Emphasize getting the ball inside, leave more options and have more options for post men.

- Three-point shots after penetration on skip-pass —don't look for three-point shot on pitch ahead.

- Look for drives.

- 1 should use slash to the other side a lot.

- Big men must run and let's emphasize early pass into the low post. Reward him for running.

- Don't forget kickback on hi-lo pass by posts.

- Emphasize V-cuts and spacing.

- 2 and 3 must sprint the lanes after the rebound is secured. Try to turn secondary into primary by going past people.

- Should be no hesitation on pitch ahead. Just don't put ball in jeopardy—get a shot.

- Players should understand secondary is a great rebounding offense. Get to the ball and chase rebounds.

A primary break means that there are only two defenders back. We want the shot in at least two passes. We have rebound advantage. So, we never make more than two passes. For us, we have all five men box out before we think of running. A "pitch ahead" is taking one dribble and passing ahead. We don't want a three-point shot off of a pitch ahead. Our three-pointers come off of a penetration move and pass out. The secondary break is when the defense has three or more defenders back. We do have some set plays off of our secondary break.

(Diagram 1)   Once we make the outlet pass to 1, we want him to cross the floor. We like to attack from the back side.

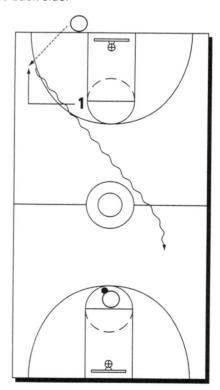

Diagram 1

(Diagram 2)   Kickback. This is a counter. If 1 passes to 5 and 3 is covered, 5 passes it back to 1. 4 stays with the ball. 2 comes up and sets a back-screen for 5. If we have a quick shot on the secondary break, we will take it. We look inside on every pass. We feel that we have a great rebounding advantage before the defense is set.

Diagram 2

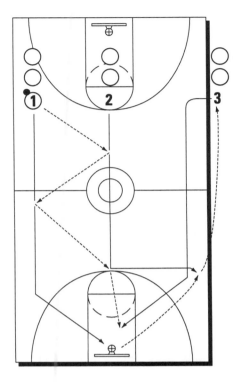

Diagram 3

(Diagram 3)   Drill #1. 1 has ball on the side. 1 makes a chest pass to 2. 2 returns a chest back to 1 and again from 1 to 2. 3 runs and times his cut, gets a bounce pass from 2 for the layup. 1 rebounds and makes an overhead outlet pass to 2 at the foul line extended. 2 then makes a baseball pass down the side of the court to the next man in 3's line. If the player in 1's position is a 4 or 5 man, he must step out of bounds after getting the ball after the layup before making the outlet pass. So, we have three chest passes, a bounce pass, an overhead pass, and a baseball pass. The person shooting the layup should hang back until he can go full speed to the basket. If the person misses the layup, he must touch the top of the field house by running the steps.

(Diagram 4)   Drill #2. 1 puts the ball on the glass and rebounds. 1 takes one dribble and passes ahead to 2 who starts near half-court. Coach stands in the way so the pass cannot be a flat pass, so we are working on our "pitch ahead." 3 and 4 are doing the same thing in the opposite direction. We teach the rebounder to pull the ball down low, almost to the floor, as he turns. Then, he takes his dribble.

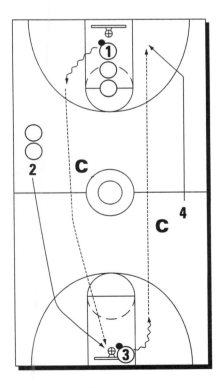

Diagram 4

(Diagram 5)   Drill #3. Coach has the ball. X1, X4, and X5 are playing defense and as the coach shoots, they block out and rebound. X2 and X3 are defensive players starting at half-court. There are two other coaches near half-court. X4 rebounds and makes the outlet pass to X1 who dribbles down the floor. X4 and X5 fill the lanes. X2 and X3 are dropping back to defend. We are working 3-on-2. The offense can only have two passes after they get to the other end. If 1 passes to 4 and he doesn't get the layup, 1 comes to the ball-side elbow for the return pass. We want him to take the shot because that puts us 2-on-1 on the boards. When the defense gets the ball, the outlet pass is made to the coach and it is 2-on-1 going the other way with 2 and 3 on offense. The former point man, 1, is on defense.

(Diagram 6)   Drill #4. This is a recognition drill. Five blues on defense and coach shoots the ball. Red team is on the side at half-court. Each red player has a number, example, from 1 to 7. Before coach shoots, the coach with the red team will call out from 1 to 5 numbers to come out on defense. Suppose it's 1 and 2. The shot goes up, outlet pass is made to 1. 1 turns and immediately must determine how many players the red team has on defense. This determines whether it is a primary or a secondary break. Blue then plays 5-on-2.

(Diagram 7)   As soon as blue scores, they come back the other way and there is another number of red players playing defense now, as determined by the coach with the red team.

(Diagram 8)   Pacers' Drill. 1 puts the ball on the glass and rebounds. 1 makes the outlet pass to 4. 4 comes to catch the ball, squares up, and starts to dribble. We often have a coach in front of 4 so he can't just turn and start to dribble without looking. 4 must pass off the dribble to 7 who times his cut to the top of the key. 10 breaks to the basket for either the lob pass or the backdoor pass.

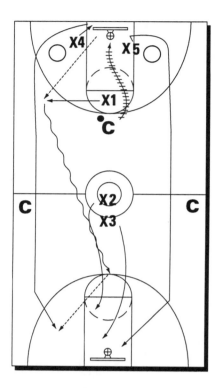

Diagram 5

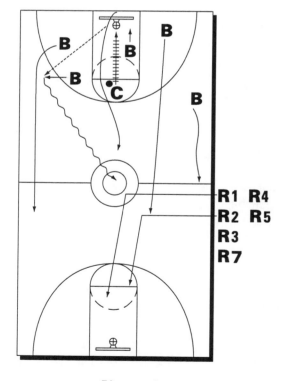

Diagram 6

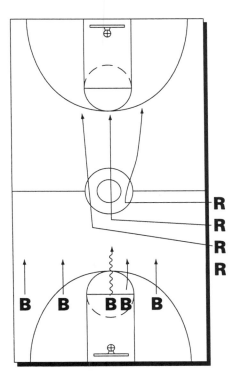

Diagram 7

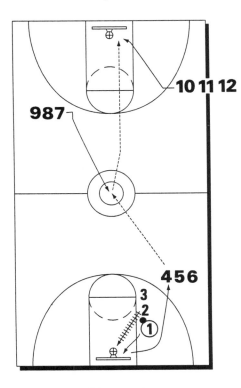

Diagram 8

(Diagram 9)   "76ers' Drill." Make 100 shots in four minutes 15 seconds. 1 makes the chest pass to 3, and 3 makes chest pass back to 1. 1 dribbles toward the top of the key and/or makes the pass to 2 for the layup. If 2 is far enough ahead, 3 can make the pass directly to 2. This is a bounce pass for the layup. 4 and 5 are on the end line, each with a ball. 2 rebounds his own shot. 1 and 3 get into position to receive passes from 4 and 5 so that all three offensive players get a shot.

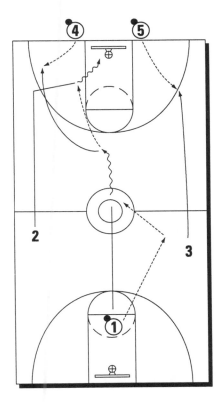

Diagram 9

(Diagram 10)   2 now has the ball, and 4 and 5 fill the lanes and the drill goes the other way. 6 and 7 are on the end line at the other end waiting to pass to 2 and 4. The drill is continuous.

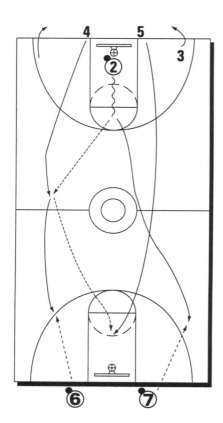

Diagram 10

(Diagram 11)   We run a 5/0 dummy secondary break drill. We want these five spots filled. 1, 2 and 3 are interchangeable, 4 and 5 are also interchangeable. The 4 position is filled by the first big man down the floor. We want the first look to always be in to 4. Suppose that 2 has the ball in the corner and 4 is overplayed at the low post. 2 should make the skip-pass to 3 or 5.

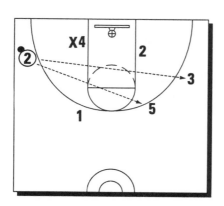

Diagram 11

(Diagram 12)   Our basic setup is that when the ball is reversed from 1 to 5 to 3, 4 follows the ball.

Diagram 12

(Diagram 13)   As the pass is being made from 5 to 3, 2 should be on the high post so he can now back-screen for 5.

Diagram 13

(Diagram 14)   3 has the ball and couldn't pass to 5. 3 passes to 2. 5 screens for 4 who always comes off on the low side.

Diagram 14

you have a decent post, you can get him the ball a lot from this secondary break. Every look is designed to get the ball low.

Diagram 15

(Diagram 15)   2 passes to 1 who looks to 4 and to 5. We don't mind a quick shot on the break. If this didn't work, we go directly into the screening game. We go from 5-on-0 to 5-on-5 for about 10 minutes. If

Philosophy

There are four things that all players, in all programs, are saying it took to be a champion.

- **Attitude**. Have a good attitude, have a listening attitude, have an attitude of togetherness and the attitude was positive. This seemed to be the gist of every story of the teams that won, the team concept. They wanted to play hard, have fun, enjoy the camaraderie and listen to what the coaches say because the coach is the boss. We all have four things in common we must be successful in to get that positive attitude.

  - Time management. How do you organize your time?

  - Competitiveness. How do we teach our kids to be competitive?

  - What do we do about discouragement? How do we handle this on a daily basis?

  - How do you solve problems? Does your personal life interfere with your professional life?

Basketball is an easy game to play, but it is hard to master.

- **Work ethic**. These players talked about how hard they worked in the preseason conditioning, worked hard in practice. They didn't care if the coach made them stay an extra half hour. Our team this year won 28 games, second in the Big Ten, and the biggest cheer I got all year was when I said, "No practice tomorrow." They hated to practice. Therefore, we didn't get from the second round in the NCAA Tournament. We didn't have the work ethic that it took to be a champion. The teams that were champions wanted to be the best. If we had wanted to

work more this year, perhaps we would have won 30 games and been in the Final Four.

- **Commitment**. These players were committed to being a champion. They worked on their own self-improvement. They loved to play. When we recruit, we want to recruit the IDEAL player.

  I — Intelligent, common sense and academic sense. My biggest problem presently is academics, making them go to class. If you are going to play for me, you are going to class and be on time.

  D — Dedicated

  E — Enthusiasm

  A — Ability, quickness and shooting

  L — Loyalty; this is most important thing of all.

- **Leadership**. We have three basic rules concerning leadership and what we expect of our players:

  - Be on time. If you are late, you run the steps of the arena 100 times.

  - Go to class every day. Why would you miss class? Because you are lazy, because you don't understand how important academics are and because you think you will pass because you are part of the basketball program. That's unbelievable.

  - Try your best. If we can do these three things, we will win the Big Ten championship. It's amazing how that works. If you are on time, it means you care about your coaches, and if you go to class every day, there is a great correlation between a student in the classroom and a student in life.

Intensity Foundation

All game habits are set by the tone of your practice intensity habits. If you don't practice hard, you aren't going to play hard in the game. We do a lot of competitive things in practice, trying to get our kids to focus under pressure. We want them to become used to it, and then they get better in the games.

We break this down into: Practice, Game, Players, and Team.

- **Practice**. What do you try to get out of your practice sessions? Aggressiveness, competitiveness, techniques and system. We have to teach more techniques today than we ever did. It used to be that the athletes played all sports. Now they don't. They used to learn to throw in baseball, get some contact in football and learn to run in track. Now we have to teach them how to run, how to throw a baseball pass, etc. We must incorporate that into our system.

- **Game**. For the game, you must have a philosophy and you must sell your team on your philosophy. This depends on your talent level. You can't fast break every year. You must establish goals. If you don't set goals for kids, they won't be motivated. Our seniors make 10 goals every year. We put them on poster board in the locker room. The players must also hang them in their rooms. If they don't see it every day, they forget them. The third thing under this part is referees. How do you handle referees? Don't think that this isn't important. You get one referee ticked off at you and he can beat you. The fourth item is management. What is your management ability? Usually, athletic directors are not former head coaches; they are corporate CEOs. Maybe you better take a class in management, how to evaluate people. If you can't, you will be left out. The AD's are interested in the bottom line. If you don't win, you are out of there.

- **Players**. It is important that you have one-on-one meetings with your players. Tell them what they are good at and what they should improve. They want to play to their weaknesses. It is our job to sell them to play to their strengths. The next

thing is honesty. If your players trust you, then you will be able to motivate them. Be positive, but be demanding. If you aren't demanding, you aren't going to win big. You must have high goals; the kids will read that.

- **Team**. There are six items and they are in no particular order. First, you must teach fundamentals. Defensive drills are boring and hard, but if you don't work on them, you won't win. Second, you must be in shape. Conditioning and weights. This is a real priority in our program. We don't want them to bulk up. We want the greyhound type. With good weight lifting, your kids don't get hurt as much and if they do get hurt, they heal quicker. Third, team morale. Do some things together other than basketball. Get your kids to coach younger teams. Then, they will understand coaching a little better. Fourth, you must have pressure defense on the ball. The greatest coaches in the history of the game have kept things very, very simple. And they always kept pressure on the ball. Fifth, you need a flexible offense. We will get to that in a minute. The sixth thing is the fast break. These six things are what our team is centered around.

Four Things to Win

I don't care where you coach, you must do these four things:

- Control your players.

- You must schedule to meet the needs of your talent level.

- Be able to adjust to the referees and the rules.

- You must have the administration behind you.

If you have these four things going for you, you'll have a good chance of having fun, keeping your job and having a good family life. Your family will not be happy if you are losing.

Competitive Drills

We think these drills help our kids play harder. I don't believe in scrimmages, but I believe in teaching. Everything we do is timed.

(Diagram 1)   Sixty-Point Game. The first team to 60 wins, but they get equal possessions. We spread the floor offensively. We do this late in the practice when they are tired. The offense tries to control the ball and score and the defense is trying to put pressure on the ball without fouling. The point guard can dribble to start the game, but this is the only time that a dribble is allowed. If he can score, he should do so. A layup is five points; a foul is four points. So, if he is fouled as he scores a layup, that's nine points. Each pass completed is one point, and a turnover is a minus two. That's the only way that you can score. You cannot set screens and cannot pass the ball back to the player who passed it to you unless it is for a layup. The same team keeps the ball until there is a turnover. After a foul, the ball is started with the dribble of the point guard again. Managers keep score. Alternate possessions on jump balls.

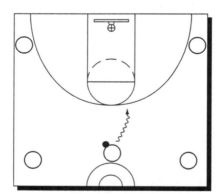

Diagram 1

One Hundred–Point Game. This is played full-court. This is played with screening and dribbling allowed. This is for offense. This may take from 15 to 20 minutes. A layup or a post move is five points. A foul is four points, a three-point shot is three points, field goals are two points. A completed pass is one point, a turnover is minus two. What we have changed is that we are going full-court, working on post moves, etc. No free throws. If you foul, the ball is taken out of bounds. We do not have equal possessions in this game.

(Diagram 2)   Rebounding, 3-on-3. Coach shoots. The defense must block out, and rotate. We rotate on this drill on the shot. The defensive man next to the coach yells, "Shot!" We want to communicate. If the defense gets the ball, they get one point. If the offense gets the ball, they get two points plus they get to run their offense 3-on-3, and when they score, they get a point. The same team stays on defense three times.

Diagram 2

(Diagram 3)   Shutout Shell Drill. The defense needs three shutouts in a row. We want the dribble forced wide. The man playing two passes away should have one foot in the lane. If the offense dribbles the ball into the lane or passes the ball in the lane, it is the same as a basket. We have about 16 drills of this type, but we don't do them every day. We select what we need. You must find ways to teach them the defensive and offensive fundamentals.

Diagram 3

(Diagram 4)   Three or four years ago, we started to extend our half-court defense a little bit. This is the way we set up in the press. It is a match-up. X4 is the trapper; X1 and X5 work together.

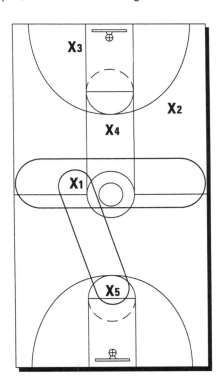

Diagram 4

(Diagram 5)   When the ball is inbounded, X3 has the ball. X4 has the option of trapping. X4 will trap two ways. X4 will trap the dribbler who is not under

control, or if the dribbler gets to half-court and picks up the ball.

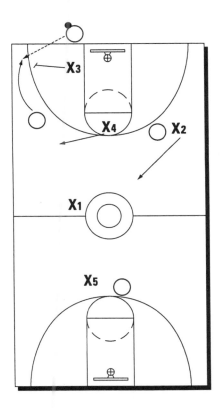

Diagram 5

(Diagram 6)   X3 has the ball in the left area, X2 on the right. X1 has the half-court area, and X5 is deep. We want them to be aggressive in this drill. Don't let them think too much.

(Diagram 7)   Seventy-Point Game. The offense can run any offense they want to bring the ball down the floor. This drill is started by a jump ball. Suppose one team scores and then the numbers line up to press. Regular scoring and we shoot free throws. This gives the press team the opportunity to set up after a made free throw. In addition to the regular scoring, a shutout is two points, a deflection is one point, a steal is one point and a trap, at the discretion of the coach, is one point.

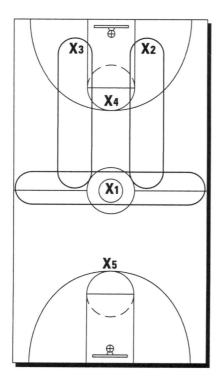

Diagram 6

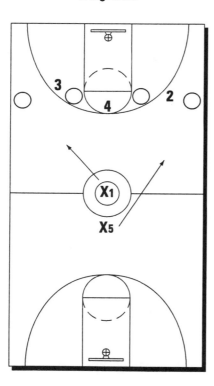

Diagram 7

(Diagram 8)   Defensive Transition Drill. There are three teams of four players each. There are three coaches on the floor. Coach shoots and the ball is rebounded by the defense. The ball is passed to the coach at the top of the circle, then to the coach at center court and then to the other circle. The third coach to touch the ball shoots. Meanwhile, the team that rebounded the first shot is fast breaking to other end. The team that started on the other end of the floor is coming out to block out and rebound. Then, the ball goes the other way.

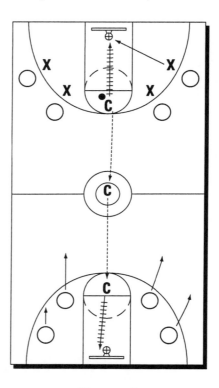

Diagram 8

(Diagram 9)   Running the fast break after a made basket. 5 takes the ball out-of-bounds and makes the outlet pass to 1. 1 starts on the dribble and passes ahead to either 2 or 3. 2 and 3 are interchangeable and the side of the floor is determined by where they were on the floor when the shot was made. 4 goes down the middle of the lane; 5 comes to the top of the circle. We want 1 to pass the ball to the first open person.

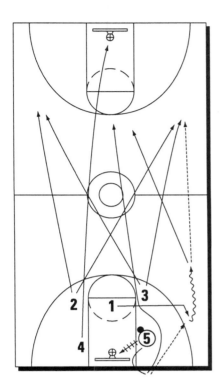

Diagram 9

(Diagram 10)   We then have good spacing.

Diagram 10

(Diagram 11)   The wings can cross underneath the basket. The right man goes low. We want the three-point shot quickly. But if we shoot it quickly, we want to get the rebound.

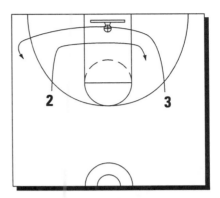

Diagram 11

(Diagram 12)   When 1 passes to 2, he cuts to the elbow on the ball side. From there he has three options. He can cut to the corner ball side. He can cut away, or he can replace himself.

Diagram 12

(Diagram 13)   If 1 goes to the corner, 2 will pass to 1 and cut through off of the screen of 4. 3 flashes to the middle and 5 cuts down the lane and then away. 5 can also screen for 2.

(Diagram 14)   If 1 goes away to the low post, 2 reverses the ball to 5. 3 down-screens for 1 and 1 pops out. 4 flashes to the post as 5 passes to 1.

Diagram 13

Diagram 14

(Diagram 15) Or, 1 can screen for 4 coming across the lane, and 5 will screen down for 1 who comes up the lane.

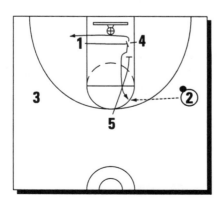

Diagram 15

(Diagram 16) If 1 replaces himself, 2 reverses the ball to 1 and cuts low across the lane. 2 and 4 set a staggered-screen for 3, and 5 screens down for 2. This is another screen-the-screener action.

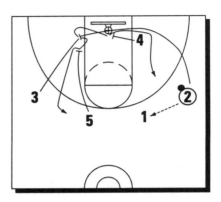

Diagram 16

(Diagram 17) Against a zone, we run the same fast break. But 1 passes to 2 and cuts to the corner ball side. 4 and 5 rotate counterclockwise on the buddy system. 3 replaces 1 at the top. We want to run the same basic break against man and zone. Run, shoot, and rebound. The game isn't that complicated, but you must practice it. If you are enthusiastic and honest, your kids will play hard for you.

Diagram 17

Selecting an Offense

I have been with programs that needed rebuilding, and the perception is, whether or not it is true, that I know how to build programs. The first thing I think you need to do to build a program is to build a consistent defense. How does that relate to offense? When we recruit, we look at them and say, "How good are they offensively? Can they score? How does that translate into them being part of what we are doing and becoming good defensive players?" I heard John Wooden (UCLA retired) say one time that you should spend two-thirds of your time on offense and one-third on your defense. I do the opposite. I spend two-thirds of my time on defense. We want them to play just the way they would play if you put them in the gym and told them to go play. How do you do that, and yet keep control? You give them a few rules, a few things they must do within that concept. You must tell them what is a good shot. The biggest problem young players have is that they all think they can shoot the 3, they all think they can dunk and they all think they are good enough to drive it to the basket and make every shot.

We tell our players that for the first week they can shoot any shot they want. But after that, I decide what a good shot is. I sit down with them individually and tell them what they can shoot. The next thing is we tell them about the things that go along with a good offense. You must have good spacing, 12 to 15 feet apart. They can understand that. We emphasize ball reversal. Ball reversal, spacing and dribble penetration are the three most important things you can do on offense, both man-to-man and zone. Then, we talk about how we screen. Most players don't like to put body-on-body to screen. It's not that they are afraid, they just don't like the body contact. This is the way we screen. Then, we tell something that is a little bit radical. We tell them we want them to take the first available good shot. Who decides what is a good shot? You do. For your best player, it may be the first open shot he gets. For your post

player, it may be within eight feet. You decide that. They must play within the parameters of what we do.

The next thing is very important to us. No matter what we are going to do on the offensive end of the floor, we teach a pattern. We teach some offensive continuity early in practice. We do that to give them the idea of discipline. We want them to be able to see where you are supposed to be and when you are supposed to be there. Everything is going to depend on the players being in the proper positions at the right time. It teaches them discipline. They must play with a sense of purpose. My assistants say that we teach the patterns, but we never run them during the season. But if everything else breaks down, we have something to fall back on. We don't go back to it much.

The next thing we do is teach them to play freelance. You might call it "motion." We give them the concepts and tell them to play within the concepts. We have already given them spacing, ball reversal, dribble penetration and screening body to body. You do all of these things in motion. Then we teach them how to receive the ball.

(Diagram 1)   We teach them the two-plane cut. The player must move in two directions. Change of pace, change of direction. They have a hard time understanding that. We want them to keep their spacing, and we want to be able to reverse the ball as easily as possible.

(Diagram 2)   We use the lane line as our spacing line. No matter where the players go, these are the spots we want them to return to. These are the spots that are most important in order to get the ball reversed, to have the proper angle to feed the post in order to have some room to get dribble penetration. If we make the guard-to-guard pass and cut, the wing man must keep the spacing by filling the vacant position at the top.

Diagram 1

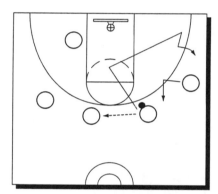

Diagram 2

(Diagram 3)　　　Why use ball reversal? To make the defense shift. If the ball is on the wing, the defense will usually play like this.

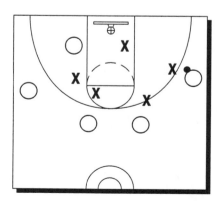

Diagram 3

(Diagram 4)　　　When you reverse the ball, this guard must move from guarding or from deny into the lane. If you are patient enough to reverse the ball several times, you cause the player to jump from denial to help to denial to help. We say that ball reversal occurs when the guard-to-guard pass is made. We don't have to make the next pass to the wing to have ball reversal. All we have to do is take the ball from one side of the basket line to the other. Make the defense move. The last thing we add are plays that feature our best players. We get our best player most of the shots. We try to put him in the position so he can take most of the shots. Then we try to find where his favorite place to shoot is. That sounds like a little thing, but it isn't.

Diagram 4

(Diagram 5)　　　Here is a play that everybody runs. I think they run it because Rick Pitino runs it. 5 steps out and screens on the ball. 1 comes off 5's screen toward the wing. 2 is a good shooter and screens across for 4. 3 and 5 then set a staggered-screen for 2 who comes to the top of the circle. 1 can pass to 4 or to 2. If you can't score on the block with 4, the play isn't very effective. Some players are more effective on one block than the other one. It will make a difference whether he is right- or left-handed. We got a great shot with this play 70% of the time. Teams can't guard box-to-box screens very well. As a last resort, many teams will switch them.

Diagram 5

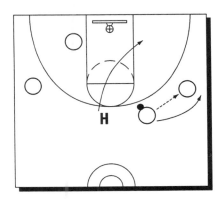

Diagram 6

I'm trying to build an offensive concept for the way we play. The next thing we have to do is to find a way to get easy baskets. How will you get the uncontested shot, the quick shot one-on-one or from transition? That is very important to every team. When we teach defense, we tell our team we are going to make the other team play us 5/5 on the half-court. Once we get set on the half-court, it is harder for them to run their stuff. So, as an offensive coach, I must teach our players how to get easy baskets, how to score either before they get set or how to score easily after they get set. Obviously, the easiest way is to run the fast break. If you watch Princeton or Arkansas play, they all run the fast break. You must run the fast break when it presents itself in order to have a chance of winning games. The second thing is that we need to find a way to get easy baskets off of our defense. We really get after people whether we are playing half-court or full-court. We must get them to give up the ball or to take bad shots so that we can get some easy baskets. The third thing are the quick hitters. We run a lot of quick hitters. We run our break into our freelance offense and then, if we don't get a shot, we run a quick hitter. We want to get a quick shot, a good shot, with the player we dictate in the position that we want.

(Diagram 6)   "Hawk." We ran this for Hersey Hawkins when I was at Bradley. The guard makes the pass to the wing. Hawk (H) runs a cut.

(Diagram 7)   2 hands the ball back to 1 who dribbles toward the top of the circle. 2 then down-screens for H, while on the other side 5 and 4 set a staggered-screen for H. We have the ball in the middle of the floor. There is no help-side defense when the ball is in the middle.

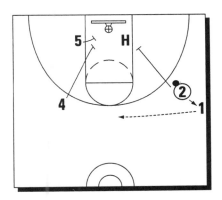

Diagram 7

(Diagram 8)   We tell H, "Go where you don't want to be. If you really want to break out on the right side, start toward the screen on the left side." H must read the screen, curl or fade depending on the defense. You have your best player shooting the shot that he wants to shoot. If H comes off of 2's screen, then 2 goes opposite and uses the screens on the opposite side.

(Diagram 9)   H could come off the staggered-screen for the three.

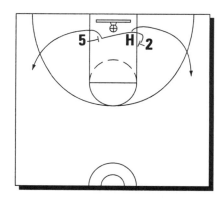

Diagram 8

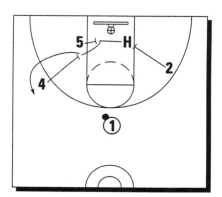

Diagram 9

(Diagram 10)   If H uses the staggered-screen, 5 turns and sets a back-screen for 4 who comes across the lane using the screen of 5 and then of 2. After 5 screens for 4, 5 ducks into the lane. 1 can pass to H, 5, or 4.

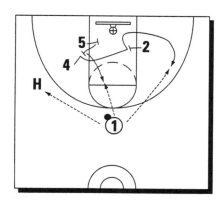

Diagram 10

(Diagram 11)   We don't send H to the corner off of 5 because of the bad passing angle.

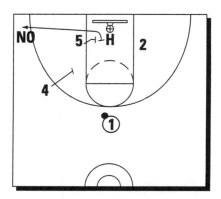

Diagram 11

(Diagram 12)   H can curl around the screen set by 4.

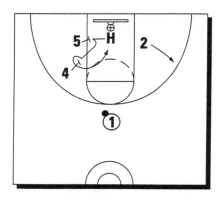

Diagram 12

(Diagram 13)   Sometimes we will run this for 4. He must curl into a post-up position. 3 steps out for a three-point shot.

When you build your offense, it's like building your defense. You must have progression. We go from patterns to freelance to incorporating plays to understanding what we are doing and to getting better. During this progression, you must really be mindful of who you are going to play. When we put together our defense, we run shell drills, and these drills are predicated on what the opponent is going to do. By the same token, we do that on the offensive end. How can we take advantage of what our opponent is going to do defensively? You must take into account what other teams are going to give you. Find something you can do better than your opponents and go with it. Lastly, we do this when things aren't going well. We have a "long play." I'm convinced that teams don't want to play defense for long periods of time. We try to make our long plays look alike. We do this against man and zone.

pulls to the corner. 2 comes off the screen down to the post. Whoever is open in the post gets the ball early.

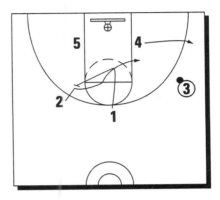

Diagram 15

(Diagram 16)   If 2 isn't open, 5 breaks to the top of the circle off of 2 as 2 cuts by and gets the pass from 3. As soon as 5 catches the ball, 1 makes a cut. Here's the rule. If you get to the three-point line and you are denied, we want you to take one more step out, and backdoor cut.

Diagram 13

(Diagram 14)   "Pull." We start in a stack. 1 passes to 3.

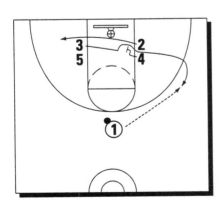

Diagram 14

(Diagram 15)   3 has the ball; 4 and 5 are in the posts. 1 cuts to screen for 2. 4 posts up and then

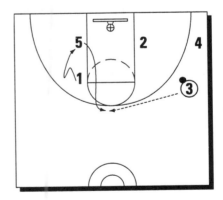

Diagram 16

(Diagram 17)   If 1 wasn't denied, he gets the pass from 5. 2 back-screens for 4, and 5 down-screens for 2. 1 can pass to 4 or to 2.

Diagram 17

(Diagram 18)   If 1 is denied, 1 makes the back-cut to the basket.

Diagram 18

(Diagram 19)   Sometimes we hold the screen by 2 for 4, pass to 1 and he can go one-on-one with no weak-side defensive help.

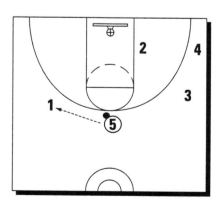

Diagram 19

(Diagram 20)   "Coppin." Starts the same way with 2 and 3 crossing to the wings. Rule, 1 passes to the wing and screens away to the opposite block. If 1 passes to 2, then he down-screens for 4 who comes high.

Diagram 20

(Diagram 21)   2 reverses the ball to 4, and 3 down-screens for 1 who gets the pass from 4.

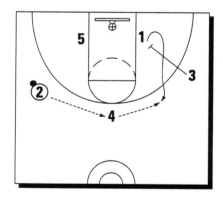

Diagram 21

(Diagram 22)   3 screens across the lane for 5, a block-to-block screen, and 4 then down-screens for 3 who comes high. 1 can pass immediately to 3 before he sets the screen for 5, or 1 can pass to 5, or to 3 who comes back to the ball. Our long plays are almost a pattern, and you can run them over and over.

Diagram 22

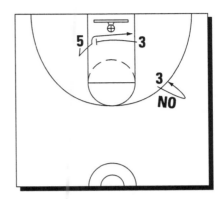

Diagram 23

Question: How do you teach the timing?

Answer: If you teach a two-plane cut, it will slow down your offense and help your timing.

Question: Will you define a two-plane cut?

(Diagram 23)   *Answer:* A two-plane cut is a cut in two directions. If 3 is coming to screen for 5, we want 5 to walk his man in the other direction first, then off the screen. If you just cut out and back on the same line, that is not a two-plane cut. You should run your offense very slow. Watch the pros. They run it slowly. They try to execute what they do. They take their time and they execute. You must tell the player receiving the screen, "Don't go off the screen until the man who is going to throw you the ball has caught it."

(Diagram 24)   On the screen, 3 comes to screen. 4 cannot pass to 5, so he reverses the ball to 2. 5 must time his cut, he must wait until the ball is passed. We want the ball delivered to 5 when he is on the way to the post, not after he gets there.

Diagram 24

Defense

Defense wins championships. That's an old phrase, but I'm sold on it. You can play a lot of different kinds: half-court soft, half-court in the passing lanes, full-court pressure, full-court passive. It depends on you. I believe you can teach players to do something the wrong way and they will be successful at it if they believe what you told them was the right way. Think about that. They will make it happen, anyway you teach it, but you must convince them that it is right. I say that to make the point that you need to have confidence in what you are teaching. I believe in the way we play defense. We can defend anyone on our level. If our team plays within themselves and doesn't try to overdo, we can do it.

(Diagram 1)   Let's put up a 3-out, 2-in offense. The ball is at the top of the circle. We want both defensive men one pass away to be on the line, up the line. In the post, on the line, up the line. In the high post, we deny on the ball side, and he is the one man who can hug his man. He can't front because of the lob. We put a big premium on ball pressure. We want the man guarding the ball to get right up on him. Don't worry so much about getting beat as you worry about him making the pass or making a sharp cut to the basket.

(Diagram 2)   When the ball is on the wing, we don't want reversals. We front the low post. We want the weakside player to get on the basket line. We want him below the ball on the basket line and if you are the lowest man on that line, your responsibility is the lob pass. We play the ball head up, but parallel to the sideline. You can't get beat middle. There is no help from the defensive man on the top because he is denying reversal by hugging his man.

Diagram 2

(Diagram 3)   We want you to drive the ball sideline to end line. You must prevent the straight line to the basket cut. Drive it to the end line and square the ball up.

Diagram 1

Diagram 3

(Diagram 4)   If we can get the ball near the end line, we are going to play 4 vs. 2. We will eliminate three players, and not let them throw the ball back out. The man at the top of the circle will deny reversal and when the ball gets to the baseline, the man guarding the low post will come out to help with the other players rotating down.

it straight up, make him go to the side. If the ball is on the wing, play your man parallel to the sideline, drive him sideline–baseline. We want them to go to the baseline. Even though it looks good to the offense when he is going there, we will have so much help it isn't good. In the post, we front as often as we can.

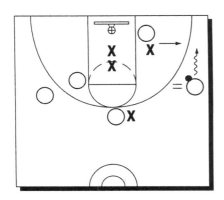

Diagram 4

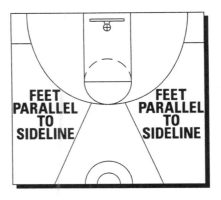

Diagram 6

(Diagram 5)   The man fronting the post gives early help and recovers. The deepest man in the lane plays the bottom side of the post, and the man from the top of the circle is responsible for the top of the post.

If the ball is driven toward the baseline, we want everyone to the level of the ball. Make them throw the ball back out. We would prefer shooting a jump shot while we are rushing at him than have a man driving into the middle and taking a shot. One weakness, if you play against a good player who can drive it and shoot it, when you drive him to the baseline and get beat a little bit, some can drive and before your post can come out to help, he can jump and shoot it.

Diagram 5

(Diagram 6)   We mark off the court. In the corner areas, we play straight up. When the ball is in the middle at the top of the circle, we want you to play

(Diagram 7)   Drills. I'm real big on 2-on-2 drills. I don't like combination drills because you lose the emphasis when you combine the drill. If you combine two drills, you now have two points of emphasis. Deny guard-forward entry. The defense puts great pressure on the ball. The forward starts low and the other defensive man is on the line, up the line. Teaching point! How far up the line can the man go? He can get as far away as he can, depending on the speed of his recovery. Remember, we have great pressure on the ball and the pass will not be a bullet pass. It is hard to get your players to move up the line. They think if their man scores, it is their fault. We try to convince them that if the other team makes a basket, we all lose. We want them to have enough confidence to get up the line, but we must have great pressure on the ball. F makes a two-plane cut, catches the ball outside the three-point line. As F comes up the line, the defensive man comes up higher and then denies to the three-point line. After the three-point line, we don't mind if he catches it, we just want you to square up on him.

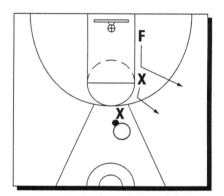

Diagram 7

(Diagram 8)   Add to that same drill. After the pass, the defensive guard must deny the give-and-go cut. He jumps to the ball and gets into the passing lane. We want him physical, jump to the ball, deny, and make the man cut behind. Then you can deny to the low box.

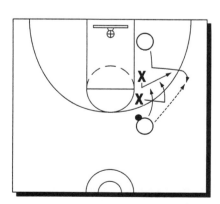

Diagram 8

(Diagram 9)   Deny all the way to the low post, where he fronts.

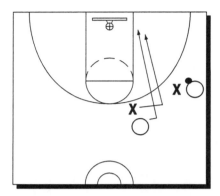

Diagram 9

(Diagram 10)   You can make this a continuity drill if you have the wing man dribble to the top of the circle. The players have exchanged positions, and you can run the drill again.

Diagram 10

(Diagram 11)   Screen down. Coach has the ball with the defensive man on the line and up the line. The defensive man lets the ball go from the coach to the wing. Coach rolls the ball to the wing to emphasize the line of the ball. As the ball goes to the wing, we front the post. The wing passes back to the coach and defensive players get on the line of the ball again. Initially, we tell the man setting the screen for the post not to really screen, but to run to the box.

Diagram 11

(Diagram 12)   On the screen down, we want both players to open up and exchange. Both players are on the line, up the line. After the players get used to that, we allow the offensive man to really screen. But, the screen must be made high because you are off the post, we say, to take the path of least resistance getting around the screen. We think it usually is under the screen because there is so much room. If you go over the screen, he may fade to the corner and you will have a hard time recovering.

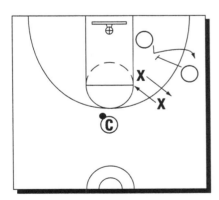

Diagram 12

(Diagram 13)   Box to box. We have definite rules. If you get screened box to box, you must go over the top. We don't care where your man goes. When coach has the ball, both are on the line, up the line. Coach passes to the manager. Front the low post on the side of the ball, get in the help side on the away block.

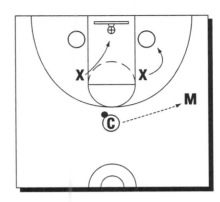

Diagram 13

(Diagram 14)   Screen comes. The man defending the screener turns so his back is to the baseline. We want him to absorb the screen. Most offensive men will go underneath. The defensive man must see the ball, but has his arm up and absorbs the man coming across. The man being screened comes over the top, and when he gets there, he must verbally say, "I got him." Once that happens, the other man releases.

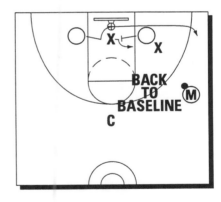

Diagram 14

(Diagram 15)   Good teams will eventually start to roll back on you. The man that sets the screen comes high. We tell our man to stay and absorb. The other defensive man must get into the passing lane and deny.

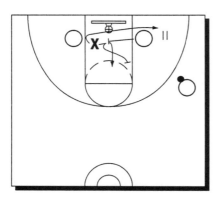

Diagram 15

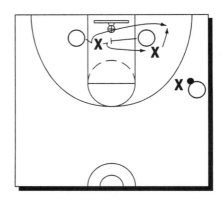

Diagram 17

(Diagram 16)   Back-screen/cross-screen. Combine two drills near the end of the season. Coach has the ball. Both defensive players are on the line, up the line. The post makes the back-screen. The lower man calls out "screen," and opens up to the ball. I must see the ball. I must take away the lob pass.

(Diagram 18)   If the cutter didn't go low, the defensive man must check him and drive him higher. Get your arm into him and drive him up the lane.

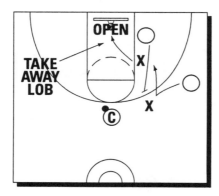

Diagram 16

You may get a jump shot, but you aren't going to get the lob. We tell the top defensive player to "skinny up and get through." We want him to slide through and deny.

(Diagram 17)   When the ball is passed to the wing, screen across. The defensive man goes over the top and the other man absorbs the cutter. Keep intense pressure on the ball.

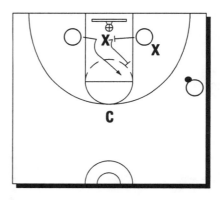

Diagram 18

(Diagram 19)   Help and recover. The man on the line up the line must help when the coach starts to penetrate. The coach will back out on the dribble, and the defensive man must recover.

(Diagram 20)   Next, the coach will dribble at the defensive man and then pass to the wing. Stop the dribble and recover back to the wing.

(Diagram 21)   The wing will be made to dribble to the baseline under ball pressure. The man fronting the low post will help and recover, and the defender at the top of the circle will help on the post defense.

Diagram 19

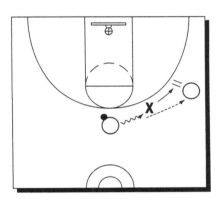

Diagram 20

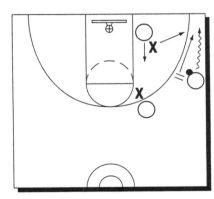

Diagram 21

(Diagram 22)   When the pass is made into the post, the defensive man must come from the top of the key and get a piece of that pass. Each of these segments is run three times.

Diagram 22

(Diagram 23)   Rotation drill, ball on the wing. Deny at the top, two men who are two passes away are on the basket line. The bottom man is responsible for the lob. Front the low post and put pressure on the ball.

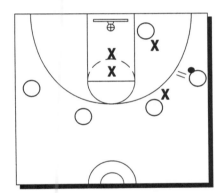

Diagram 23

(Diagram 24)   Eight-man recovery drill. 4/4. The ball at the top, wing defensive man is on the line, up the line. The other perimeter defensive man is denying ball reversal by hugging his man. The defensive man two passes away has sagged into the lane. The ball is passed to the wing and taken on the dribble toward the baseline. The defensive player on the line and up the line must recover and get to the dribbler. The dribbler must be stopped outside the lane. The defensive player on the top drops down the lane. The man in the lane comes across to help on the dribbler, and the guard at the top drops deep into the lane.

Diagram 24

interchange. The most important thing is to stop the ball. When the ball is thrown back out, the man who stopped the ball must follow the pass and stop the shot.

(Diagram 25)   If the ball is passed back out and the perimeter players can shoot it, they shoot it. When the ball comes back out, they must rush their man under control; run, slide, slide, with the hand up. Eventually, the two men on the weak side will

Diagram 25

Approaches to Playing against Zones

I thought I would talk about approaches to playing against zones, whether it be half-court or full-court. I'm going to preface what I talk about with a story from several years ago. We are getting ready to play Notre Dame. Notre Dame had a very good team and they pressed a lot, and they used different presses. We had seen them play several times. They played hard. They picked up man-to-man, used a match-up press and then they would set up in a standard 2-2-1. They were doing four or five things. We were practicing several days before the game. I have a very smart kid named Quinn Buckner playing for us, and he happened to have rotated out. We are trying to recognize the presses. Bob Donewald, one of my assistants, was setting up the Notre Dame game plan. We are getting our players to recognize it. If they are in this, we are in that; if they do that, we are in this.

Buckner is standing beside me, he says, "Coach, can you recognize the difference in those presses?" He had a very good point. I'd give anything for a kid like that. To have a kid who thinks, and who asks you good questions that make you think as a coach, that kid is an invaluable player. He wasn't trying to be a smart aleck. I stopped practice. I set up what we would do, no matter what they did. It came down to handling the ball, cutting to get open and screening when it was possible to screen without trying to recognize what type of press. We went up to Notre Dame and played very well. We had one turnover in that game against the press. It wasn't anything that I did, it was the question that Buckner asked. I've always felt that if we can simplify whatever we are doing, it will certainly be to our advantage.

Pete Newell has a great comment. He feels that we overcoach and under-teach. I agree with that. We spend a lot of energy and practice time in coaching, rather than teaching. Instead of having something different for each press, what we really had to do was to cut hard enough to get open, catch the ball and not throw it away once we had it.

There are three things that are really important in playing against any type zone. The first of these three things is the dribble. I think when playing against the zone, the dribble is probably the least used asset that people have in zone attack. Many years ago there were two standard thoughts. You move people against man-to-man, and you move the ball against the zone. Pass the ball. That concept has been tinkered with less than any standard traditional concept in basketball. The dribble is really underused against zones.

Let me mention passing for a second. The cross-court pass is not a pass the zone is really set to cover. The zone is really set to cover the one person away pass. It is set to cover the penetrating pass. Several years ago, I was trying to pick a word to use when attacking a zone defense. The word I came up with was "Distort." The thing you are trying to do is to distort the zone. You are trying to distort the movement of the zone. You are trying to distort the configuration of the zone. You are trying to keep the zone from sliding with the ball. Every zone has slides. All of that is geared to the position of the ball. There are three or four different ways to distort the zone. The very first one is with the dribble. There are three ways you can distort the zone with the dribble.

(Diagram 1)   The first one is to just dribble the ball off the top of the zone. Just taking the ball from the top of the zone to the side creates some problems for the zone. The three-point shot has really hurt zone offenses. Too many teams and players mainly shoot threes against the zone. Whether this is a point zone or a two-man front, it doesn't make any difference. Who's going to cover the dribbler and how far? That's a question that the zone must answer. We can take the ball all the way off the top, and bring A down with him. Take him as far as he will go.

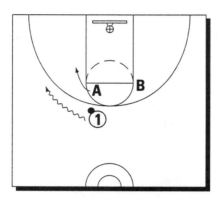

Diagram 1

(Diagram 2)   If it is a one-man front zone, often the player on top will go to the edge of the lane or maybe one step further. We teach our dribbler to come back in on him and hold him in that position. We break all of this down into simple drills that you can visualize. We will play one man on top; we will play 2 vs. 3, 3 vs. 2, etc. The first use of the dribble is to take the ball off the top. Another thing you gain is that you don't have to have someone on the wing because you dribble the ball to that position. Now you can use one player with the dribble instead of two players with the pass. We can utilize that man in a better position, in another location, or against the zone. So, we use the dribble to take the ball off the top.

(Diagram 3)   We use the dribble to take the ball out of the corner. The ball has been thrown into the corner. Whatever the zone is, someone has come out to guard the man with the ball. How far will he go with him? What is created by bringing the ball out of the corner and passing the ball back to someone filling the baseline? We call this "circle." I'm taking the ball out of the corner, and someone is coming in behind me.

When we are playing against a man-to-man team, I am thinking that way. In your man-to-man defense, you can determine who your players are going to guard. This is really important in your preparation. Let's say that you like to switch. Now, I can

determine a little bit who they are going to guard. If you don't like to switch, then I can determine what your biggest problems are in your man-to-man defense. That may involve little screening big, or big screening little. When you like to switch, you start your best defensive player on my best offensive player, then I can maneuver your poorest defensive player to guard our best offensive player. But, you start out determining who your people are going to guard. If you throw the switch into it, I have a little to say about who they are going to guard.

Diagram 2

Diagram 3

Regardless of the switch or not, against man-to-man, I can determine where your people are going to play. You have a little quick player who is going to play my guard. He is tough on the perimeter, but I'm going to play him in the post. I'm going to make him play post defense. If you have a big strong player that we can't play inside, I'm going to take him to the top of the key. When we are playing against man-to-man, I can determine where your players are going to play. You can determine who, but I can determine where. If you determine who, and I allow you to determine where, then I've given you an advantage and then I have none. But, if I put them where I want them, that could be to my advantage. That's one of the reasons we have always used the kind of offensive movement we have against man defense.

(Diagram 4)   Now, this changes against a zone. You set up a zone. You determine where your players are going to play in the zone. Most teams are right-handed so they are going to do most of their shooting from the right side of the court. You position your biggest man on the baseline for the offside rebounding. You have determined where this big kid is going to play, but I'm going to determine who he is going to play against. It's not going to be against our biggest player. I'm going to put a quick kid in here somewhere. When he comes out to guard, he must stop a driver, not a player like himself. If I have a 6'5" kid and he is no better than yours, I'll play him in the high-post area, but if I have a really quick 6'2" kid, I'm going to play him against your big kid. I can determine who your player has to guard, and I can do that throughout the zone and that becomes my advantage. If I allow your big player to be matched up with our big player, then you have the advantage. When we prepare for you, we try to create advantages for us and disadvantages for you in terms of the match-ups that exist.

(Diagram 5)   The next thing you can do with the dribble against the zone is penetrate the gaps of the zone. Take the ball into the gap. Basically, there are five gaps against a zone. A gap means the space that exists between two players or a player and the baseline. These five gaps don't always exist against every zone. If you visualize a 2-3 zone, you would really have those gaps. If you look at a 3-2 zone, you would have four gaps and then still drive the

baseline. So, the gaps will vary depending upon the configuration of the zone. A pass is guarded by movement of the zone. The dribble must be guarded almost entirely with the double-team. If I can get a step on someone and start to dribble, someone must help. Dribble penetration brings about a 2-on-1 situation that leaves us with a 2/1 situation somewhere else in our favor.

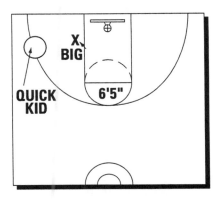

Diagram 4

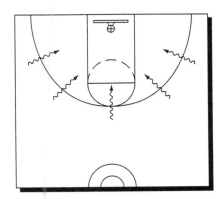

Diagram 5

(Diagram 6)   We spend much time preparing against a zone, working three people against four. This is almost a trapezoid. We are working to penetrate, bring two people to the ball, pass one way or the other and look to drive the gap all the way to the basket. We want them to penetrate hard enough so they can take the ball all the way to the basket.

Diagram 6

(Diagram 7)   To vary that, we will play 4 against 5 and do the same thing. We try to bring two players to the ball and make the penetration until we get the shot. We start out by having one man penetrate against two, then two against three and then we move on to what I just showed you. With one against two, we really aren't looking to get the shot. We want the penetration and then make a pass out to a manager.

Diagram 7

(Diagram 8)   Two against three, we are looking to penetrate and make the pass to each other. When we go three against four or four against five, we are looking to get the shot. The dribble is so important in creating opportunities to score that you can use it against any zone. This past year we have had too

much catch and pass. We have not had enough dribble penetration. You aren't going to penetrate every single time you get the ball. We try to have some rules for offensive play that overlap and cover both zone and man defense. One of them is this. Any time you get the ball on the perimeter, you face the basket and hold for a count of two, just to see what's going on. I think that opportunities to get the ball inside against any defense are missed more often because the kid catches and passes, than for any other reason. When he catches and passes, the player with the ball does not take the time to look inside to see if anybody is open. Kids don't see inside very well. They get it; they get rid of it. If I face the basket, I've got to see if somebody is open inside. There are two exceptions to that. If, as I catch the ball, I have a shot, I must recognize that and go into my shot move. If, as soon as I catch the ball, I've already seen that somebody is open, then I pass it immediately. If I have neither the shot nor an open person, I face the basket for a count of two, to see what is going to happen. So, we can dribble off the top or we can dribble out of the corner, taking the ball as far as the defensive player will go with us.

Diagram 8

The second thing we can do is penetrate the gaps, bringing two defenders to the ball. The more often we do that, the more often we are going to set up a shot situation.

(Diagram 9)   Let me show you an example. The ball has been taken off the top against a 2-3 zone. It has been taken to the left side. The ball is brought back, and B has had to move to his right, and now the ball is brought back. The ball is driven hard into the gap. B moves to cover, but the man on the baseline must also come up to cover. This penetration move might free us up for a very good shot in the corner. The second thing you get from that is the big slow player in the middle of the zone, out of necessity, coming out to cover the baseline, and having to cover a good driver. But dribble penetration has set that move up.

Diagram 9

(Diagram 10)   The third use of the dribble is "freeze dribble." This is an example. 1 takes the ball off the top and A is defending. This is against a 2-3 zone. 1 quickly reverses the ball. B's movement is the standard movement in the 2-3 zone, dropping back into the middle. 2 steps out and receives the ball from 1. 2 now has B almost directly in front of him. 2 freezes B by going right at him. 2 does not wait for A to reposition himself. 2 does not wait for B to come out. 2 immediately goes at B. One of the things I have found wrong with kids attacking the zone is that they put the ball over their head. By the time he gets it up and starts looking, the zone has adjusted and there is no distortion in the zone. If 2 is successful in getting into B, there is a good hole on the wing. If C comes up to help, there is a hole on the baseline. Here we have used all three forms of the dribble. We

have taken it to one side, brought it back and frozen the defense, then we have the penetration from the wing or baseline for the shot. This same idea can be used against any zone you are going to play. I think the dribble is the most important thing to use against a zone.

Diagram 10

Let's talk about passing against a zone. The most important thing is the pass fake. If I am on top and make a pass fake, the zone moves. The zone is keyed to move on the pass. Jim Crews, who has been coaching at Evansville, is as good as we have ever had with the pass fake. I asked Jim, "Why are you such a good pass faker?" He said, "Coach, I'm too slow to dribble." That's a darn good answer. Everytime we get a good pass fake, something good happens because the zone moves. The zone doesn't wait to see if the ball is going to be passed. The zone moves on the anticipated direction of the pass. The pass fake is the first thing you consider when passing against a zone. The second thing is putting the ball right where your player can catch it and step into his shot. Don't throw it at his feet. Let's throw the ball where the kid can catch it and shoot it.

The last thing is that when we throw the ball inside, let's use the bounce pass. Henry Iba and I used to argue for hours. He hated the bounce pass. But I don't like the ball being thrown in the air into the post. My reasoning is that the defensive post man is much more likely to get a piece of the ball thrown high rather than low. I want the ball to be delivered where the post man can catch it at his knees. When that happens, that puts the ball underneath the inside defense. That's too low for most inside people to get. Secondly, when I get the ball at knee level, I am ready to play. When I get the ball high, I must change my position to get ready. I must bring the ball down. But if I get it at the knees, I can fake, I can drive, I can turn, I can shoot. I am ready to play in that position. I mentioned before that there can be a lot gained by throwing the ball cross-court, particularly against a zone that really moves toward the ball. When I throw a cross-court pass against a zone, I want the ball thrown over the top to either a very good shooter or a very good driver. The shooter will have room to take the shot; the driver would be able to take advantage of the zone recovering to the ball by getting past the recoverer.

(Diagram 11)   The shooter. I'm on the three-point line and move to my left. I'm right-handed, so I'm also a right-footed shooter. What we want for everybody is this. As I move to my left on the perimeter against the zone, I always want to be open to the top of the key, left foot forward. If the ball is below me in the corner, I am closed to the ball. I keep my right foot back, no matter where I am on the perimeter. On my left side, I am open to the top of the key, closed to the corner. We want the kid to have his feet in a shooting position when he catches the ball. He will step into his shot with the left foot as the pivot foot. He can drive from this position; he can pass from this position. He is down and ready. He can also shoot from this position. When he catches it, he is ready to step into his shot.

(Diagram 12)   On the other side of the floor, as a right-handed shooter, I am closed to the top of the key and open to the corner. My right foot is back. I am ready to catch the ball and step into the shot. That gives me enough of an advantage to get a clear, open shot as opposed to catching the ball, turning, and stepping. That gives the defense time to get into me and I must take the shot under pressure. Footwork in shooting is always important, but the

setup of your feet is very important on the perimeter against a zone.

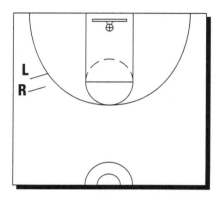

Diagram 11

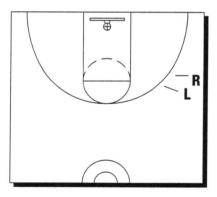

Diagram 12

(Diagram 13)   Same thing right on top of the key. I am open to the right, closed to my left. I step right into the line if I am capable of having three-point range.

The next thing with the shot is the shot fake. As I catch the ball, I turn to go into the shot motion. That does a lot of things for me. I face the basket and see if someone is open inside. Catch, look, step in, start the shot. I see the defense coming hard, shot fake. What have players in the zone been taught to do? Come out with a hand up. He has already extended himself vertically. This is a great situation for me to drive against. We tell our kids, "Look at the feet of the defensive player and drive to the side of the extended foot. Go past him." With the shot fake you get him up higher, then go past him.

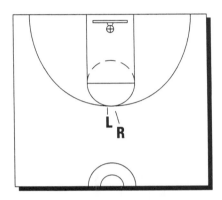

Diagram 13

Shot fake sets up dribble penetration. Dribble penetration really distorts the zone. One way that we work on this is to wait until he catches the ball and we call out either "shot" or "shot fake." He must react to the verbal command. Then we go one-on-one and we tell the defensive man to vary it. If he comes out slow, I must take the shot. If he comes out quick, then I will shot fake and drive. This takes concentration. There is nothing in this game that is more important than concentration. I think the best teams occasionally have the best players, but when they do, they also do the best job of concentrating. Really good teams who do not have the best players are teams that can really concentrate.

(Diagram 14)   Here are a couple of other thoughts against a zone. When the ball has been taken down one side or the other of a zone, 1 passes to 2. When the ball comes back, 1 must cross to the other side of the court before the ball can be returned to the same side. If 2 passes back to 1 and 1 immediately passes back to 2, that does nothing to the zone. If you are playing zone and you get a team to play catch with the ball, that's the best thing that you can have. When 1 gets the ball back, he has these

choices. He has a shot, a shot fake, he can pass, he can reverse the ball, he can dribble, but he cannot pass directly back to 2.

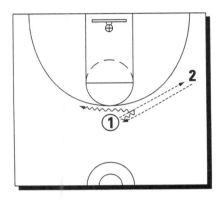

Diagram 14

(Diagram 15)   2 is a good shooter. 1 passes to 2 and he is covered immediately. The ball comes back to 1. Take the ball across the center of the court. The defense moves with the ball. 1 can now pass back to 2. The shooter has B in a bind. B must recover quickly. If he is too quick and too high, he can drive. If he is too slow, then he can shoot. Since this is a good shooter, B may stay a little man-oriented and may not move as far as he would normally.

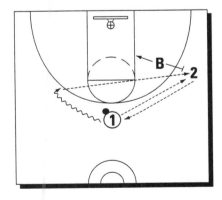

Diagram 15

(Diagram 16)   If he does that, he opens up a gap we can attack with another player. Whenever the defense makes an adjustment, we must make a counter adjustment on offense. Remember, we take the ball to the other side of the court before making the return pass to 2.

Diagram 16

(Diagram 17)   Here's something that you might want to do. We are playing against a 2-3 zone. Put in the five defensive men. You are talking to your team. "Look at the holes in that. We can rip this thing apart. Look at the gaps in here. They can't cover us if we are quick with what we do."

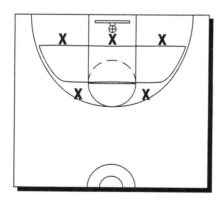

Diagram 17

(Diagram 18)   Now, if you are going to play a 2-3 zone, you show them this. "Where are they going? There is nothing that they can do against it." That's my psychology lesson for today.

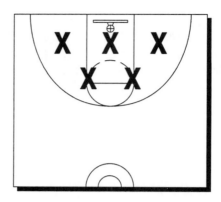

Diagram 18

(Diagram 19)   Another thing we do against a zone from an inside standpoint is this. 1 takes the ball away from the post. The zone will slide. I think you really waste an inside man against a 2-3 zone if you have him cut toward the ball. He is too easy to play. When he comes, the defense slides and cuts him off.

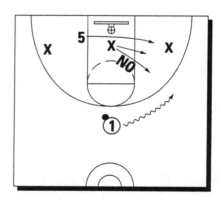

Diagram 19

(Diagram 20)   If he will have a little patience and hold his position, we can reverse the ball and hit him as he steps up. We can also pass directly from 1 to 5. Take the ball away from the post, then bring it back to him.

(Diagram 21)   Playing the back man behind the zone is very important. Playing him in front, as shown in the diagram, is a mistake. All five of our players are above the defense. If he is behind, they are stepping back and creating more space for you in the lane, or they forget about him altogether.

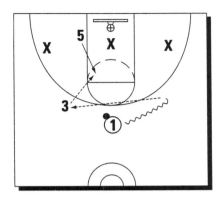

Diagram 20

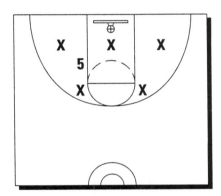

Diagram 21

your weaknesses, and play to your strengths. Let's understand what everybody else can do. If you have a choice of two players on the break, give the ball to the better shooter. If we are going to be any good, we must all understand what we can do and what we can't do. The kid who loses the ball against the press because it was thrown to him when it shouldn't have been, is not at fault. It's the kid who threw him the ball to begin with. Then, we must play our kids with their strengths and weaknesses in mind.

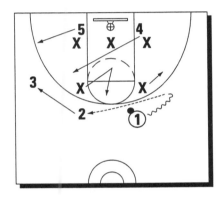

Diagram 22

(Diagram 22)   Being patient is important. The ball is dribbled off the top by 1. 1 passes back to 2 and 2 then reverses to 3. The back man must come up and 5 will step out ready to shoot the ball. If only one of our post people can shoot, we always take the ball away from the man who can shoot. The ball goes from 1-2-3-5 or 1-2-3-4. Speaking about confidence in shooting — the one person who I want to have confidence when the shot is taken is me, not the kids, because they and their mothers think that they can make any shot they take.

Shot selection for kids is amazing. We had a kid we were trying to set up as a screener. He asked when someone was going to screen for him. Real team concept. The answer, "When you learn to shoot." It is really important that we know what our kids can do and can't do. I don't have any hesitation telling kids what they can and can't do. Stay away from

Another thing that we try to do in ball reversal is reverse the ball to three people. That's when we will dribble it off the top. (See Diagram 22 again.) If we only reverse it to two people, we don't have enough options. You do the most damage against the zone reversing it to three people. Bring the zone one way, reverse the ball and make the zone recover. That's where most of the opportunities are.

(Diagram 23)   One thing we can do against a 2-3 zone is to use a stack. We stack 4 and 5 on the baseline, 2 and 3 at the elbow. Right away, the zone must make some adjustments. They may bring D in, bring C up and they have created several holes.

(Diagram 24)   Run a triple stack. What will they do? We can also screen from this. Few teams play zones against us, so I would have to believe from that, people have some problems with what we do against a zone.

Diagram 23

Diagram 24

(Diagram 25)   Three people on the perimeter and move them. We may not dribble penetrate. 1 passes to 2 and cuts through and out the ball side. 2 dribbles to the top and 1 replaces 2. You can run this to either side. This is really important against a match-up. You need to make shortcuts against a match-up, that's important.

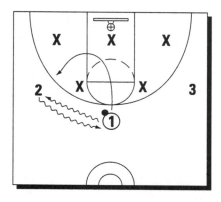

Diagram 25

(Diagram 26)   Start with a stack inside. 1 takes the ball away from the stack side. 2 steps out, and 5 comes across. 5 probably will not be open. The ball is reversed from 1 to 2, and there should be a hole near 3 for a shot.

Diagram 26

(Diagram 27)   Screening against a 3-2 zone. 1 takes the ball away from 3 and 4. The zone shifts. 4 sets the screen on the low man in the zone, and 3 is the shooter. We will also screen the bottom man in a 1-3-1 zone. I think it's hard to screen the match-up, but the bottom of the 3-2 is easy to screen. The reversal of the ball will keep the wing man honest and keep him from helping.

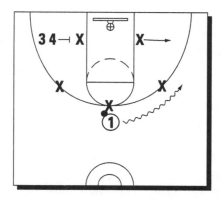

Diagram 27

General Comments

Passion—Sometimes I ask someone to give me one word to describe a coach. "Passion" should be the word. If you don't have a passion for coaching, you need to get out and do something else. Another key phrase is "paying your dues." So many kids today think there should be instant gratification. Many of the top coaches have done a lot of dirty little jobs to make their programs better. A key phrase for you is to "know who you are and what your game is." There is nothing wrong with being an assistant your whole life if you find the right person to work with. Your players need to know who they are and what their game is. That's big. If they don't, you aren't going to win any championships.

I want to ask you some questions.

- Who on your team is tough and competitive? That's a big question to ask. Every year you need to take your squad list and go down and ask that question about each one. There are so many coaches who talk about making practices competitive and game-like. Run if you lose. Do something to distinguish between winning and losing. We don't distinguish between winners and losers in today's society. We have participation trophies. Give everyone a trophy. Society is dumbing down. We have seen the morality of our country dumbing down. For your team, you can't dumb down competitiveness and being tough. Doug Collins had a great saying when he coached the Detroit Pistons. "An army of asses led by a lion will be defeated by an army of lions led by an ass." In your school you get a certain type of kid to work with. Don't complain about what the other coach has until you've been there. But you've got to get tough kids.

- Will he fight the battles if he doesn't have early success? Many people don't. We give no awards in our camps. There is nothing more useless. Here's the biggest battle you will have to fight in coaching, again from Doug Collins. "A man bent on revenge must first dig two graves." Don't get angry at every coach in your league. We have some coaches we don't like, but don't let your team know it.

- "Most people can run all day on one compliment." That's from Mark Twain. You must apply this to your treatment of your assistant coaches. How can your kids be together if your staff isn't together?

- Strive for significance rather than success. Do you want to be a Division I coach? Maybe you should think again. Maybe it's not for you. You want to have a significant life.

- Look for the teachable moment. If you spend time watching tape with a player in your office, that's a teachable moment. That's showing your player you have made an extra effort to teach. Sometimes it's better after a loss. If we win a game big, I talk about other things, about people less fortunate. You must have a love for teaching.

(Diagram 1)   Shortcuts. I think you can do this against any zone, particularly a match-up. Keep a handler between two shooters. If the handler gets outside the two shooters as he loops, we have an automatic rule that we screen the top of the zone when the ball goes away and then slip into the middle of the lane looking for the ball.

(Diagram 2)   Through Cuts. If a forward is guarding the ball, we go near the baseline.

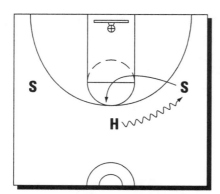

Diagram 1

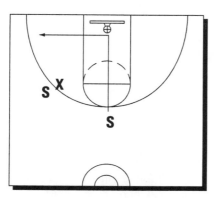

Diagram 2

(Diagram 3)   If a guard is guarding the ball, we go away. A great phrase is that in March you can't run plays, you must make plays. You need to go to the options of the plays.

Diagram 3

Put this idea down first. "Small minds talk about people—average minds talk about things—great minds talk about ideas." The biggest jerk in town knows everything about everybody. The average minds talk about money, success, etc. But great minds talk about ideas. That's the significant difference.

Post Play

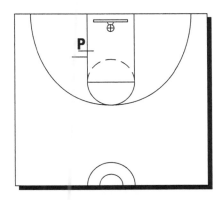

Diagram 2

Defensive Ideas

Post man on transition, take three hard strides before you look over your inside shoulder to find the ball. That's a Celtic rule. Do this in all drills.

If X4 man gets down the floor before X5, explain that it is permissible for him to guard X5's man until he gets there. It is then permissible to change back at the quickest opportunity.

(Diagram 1)   Denial stance. You do not want to be level or lower than your defensive man. If he is lower, I get into him and bury him.

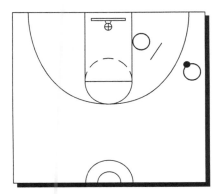

Diagram 3

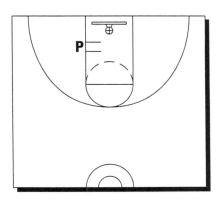

Diagram 1

(Diagram 4)   If you get sealed on the high side of the post, the dribbler can get a layup.

(Diagram 2)   If we are defending, we want to be above the post on the line and up the line.

(Diagram 3)   If the ball is on the wing, we play dead front on the low post. If you want to play behind, that's fine. You want to take away angles and block out. You don't want the player to be able to roll down the lane from a higher position. So, you never play dead front on anything except the low post. The key phrase here is "do not give up angles." Basketball is a game of spacing, angles and momentum. The defense does not get beat on the help; it gets beat on the recovery.

Diagram 4

(Diagram 5)   If we play someone who gets their help from the defensive post, we wait until he goes to help and then we send the post out for a three-point shot.

Diagram 5

(Diagram 6)   The Red Sea. A special situation. Shoot it off the front of the rim, step in, and lay it in.

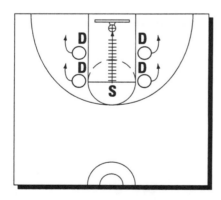

Diagram 6

(Diagram 7)   Front the post on his favorite side; play behind on his un-favorite side. If my post man is slower than your post man, why should I ask him to try to front both sides? If we have a post man who is skinny and quick, we front both sides because it would be death to play behind. Post defense is an individual thing. Don't ask a kid to do something he is not physically capable of doing.

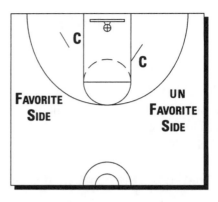

Diagram 7

On skips, if you are fronting, you need to go under so you don't give up the baseline angle on the skip-pass. The first thing on post offense is to hold your seal as long as possible without chasing the ball. So, what's the number one thing on post defense? It is to destroy the seal. Don't let them get to your body.

If you are going to play behind, start out as if you are playing on the high side and then force them out a little. Don't stand behind them right away because then they will take up the slack. Make them think they need to step out. Don't ever give up that baseline angle. If you play on the hip, I believe a good post man can score on you.

If you are caught behind, show your hands to the official. You can do a lot of things with your lower body that you can't do with your hands.

If you have a post man who is slender, take him away from the basket and have him drive to draw the foul. You won't get the foul in the post. You must step him out and drive.

Emphasize positioning without fouling. Don't ever foul from behind. Don't jump on a power move; it will be a foul. If he is shooting a jump shot, you can jump. If he is making a power move, umbrella. Don't jump when the ball is in the lane. When the ball is driven to the middle, you fake, but you do not come out. Fake up and go back. Make the player take a jump shot.

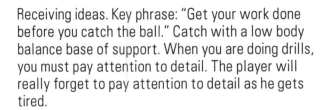

Flashes. Meet all flashes with your chest.

(Diagram 8)   Cross-screens. We don't switch unless it is an emergency. Duke switches the low cut and stays with the high cut. Indiana stays with the low cut and stays with the high cut. You must have consistency in your defense. This is what we do. Take a step toward the man, get your body on him and ride him over either way. The man guarding the screener opens up and protects the basket and then recovers in the passing lane. Tag them. Get your arm out and tag screeners. There is no excuse for being screened. You can't get screened with your arms out.

Receiving ideas. Key phrase: "Get your work done before you catch the ball." Catch with a low body balance base of support. When you are doing drills, you must pay attention to detail. The player will really forget to pay attention to detail as he gets tired.

(Diagram 9)   Catch perpendicular to the line of the pass. Catch the ball and then turn a quarter turn in the air. Turn your body in the air. On the perimeter, you "square in the air." In the post, you make about a quarter turn.

Diagram 8

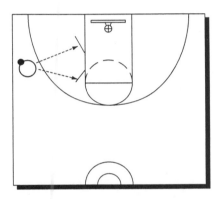

Diagram 9

When a player curls, we chase, but it is all keyed on the player guarding the screener. He is the player guarding the curl.

We trap ball-screens. We don't want the ball to get to the screen. There are different kinds of ball-screens, but we trap them all the same. If they are not out far enough to stop the ball from getting to the screen, they are not trapping well enough. Help with the body and don't reach. Recover to where the man is, not where he was.

Close-outs. Post men always close out short with high hands. You will almost always be driven by a non-post man. Hold the lane when guarding a post man who can't shoot and steps out.

Posting position. I want the post to be able to see the backs of his hands. The fingers must be vertical, head high. You catch the ball with your feet, your eyes and your hands. Your feet get you into position behind the ball, your eyes see it in, and your hands catch it.

In the post, you get open and stay open. You receive safely and you score simply. That's all post play is. When you get open and stay open, that entails holding your seal. Do not run after the ball and release your seal. If you are playing against a great shot blocker, you do not want to give him space, you want to take up space. You take everything to his body. You get your body on his body. Receive the ball safely, chin on the ball. Score simply. You don't need to dunk. Each post should have his own workout. Work with your players to develop his own workout.

Catch the ball close to the basket. Make a move to get closer to the basket. Try to play the game with two feet, two eyes and two hands shoulder-width.

On any dead ball or dribble use, the post releases pressure. If the dribbler is in trouble, I don't care where he is, the post goes to the ball and gets it.

When the post makes a turn to shoot a jump shot, he should turn with the ball on the shoulder that is away from the direction in which he is turning. Keep the ball up. Don't keep it under your chin. Have it chin high on the shoulder.

When a player works by himself, he should throw himself a pass by tossing the ball out from him with a backspin on it. Or he can throw himself a lob pass. If you have a passer for him, have him throw him bad passes. Make it difficult to catch the ball.

When your perimeter players catch, they catch with their feet in the air. They land facing the triple threat chin. The eyes look at three things in this order: the rim, the post, and the action. The action is the screening action taking place between the other three players. The action is going to take time to develop while looking at the rim and the post. Slow the ball down. Here is a great drill for perimeter play, 4/4/4. A partner is guarding him. He holds it for four seconds, dribbles it for four seconds and holds it again for four seconds. It teaches handling the ball under extreme pressure. On any back-to-the-passer drill, have the post score.

The Rodman Drill. Post is facing you. You throw the ball off the backboard, he must turn and catch. He shoots, scores, and passes the ball back to the coach. Have two players passing two balls back and forth between them. Feed the post with a tennis ball, a wiffle ball. Do one-hand passing and catching. Don't let them buddy up. Make them push each other. A good post man should be a little selfish. He should look to score first, every time.

(Diagram 10)   Passing Ideas. The darkened areas are the pro spots. There is another spot in the corner but that spot is only filled if a player makes a cut under the post, called a Laker Cut. We believe that you can't spot up four people on the perimeter. We need one player diving. We use our worst shooter to dive, but we can't call him that, so we call him our best cutter. We have three men spotting up in the pro spots. Anytime you don't know what to call something, call it "pro." After feeding the post, the passer adjusts to an open spot. The man in the corner can make a Laker Cut and the post can reverse the ball to the opposite corner. This cut is good against heavy sags or zones. We always want ball reversal into three people.

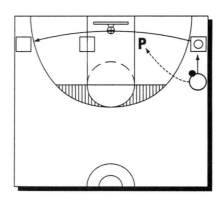

Diagram 10

We like to play zone because we want a sandwich on the post. In a match-up, they can clear you out. You've got to give a shot up somewhere. There are four reasons to play a zone: 1. The other team can't attack a zone. 2. You can't guard man-to-man. 3. To sandwich the post. 4. Can't control the guards.

On any cut off the post, try to be six feet away from the post. When your post man goes high, he looks down, he looks opposite, he looks back. There are four key words: top—down—opposite—back. That will give you the timing.

"Sweet" is the first side post feed to the post. It is not "sweet" if he has to make a move. This means a non-created shot by the post for a layup.

Try to get the ball on top. You look down, you look opposite to the weakside and then you look back to where it came from. That's just about the timing that you need for screening action.

On any duck-in pass to the low post, the bounce pass is long, low, and hard. The only way that you can throw this type of pass is if the ball is released low.

Double-team. When the post catches the ball, his first move should be to look to the middle. If the pass is thrown to my face, I know my defensive man is directly behind me. I need to know where the double-teams are coming from. I know the two pro spots will be filled and maybe a Laker Cut into the corner.

You need to have a move to the baseline when you don't have angles. There is always power if you have angles. If you don't have angles and they are playing behind you, you must have a sequence of moves and it will be different for every post man. A "go-to move" is the move everybody knows that you're going to make and they still can't stop it. You are no good as a post man if it doesn't take two people to guard you.

(Diagram 11)   Here is a great drill if you do individual workouts. When you feed the post, have the feeder trap the post. You can back-dribble out of a double-team, screen in on the weak side and throw across. Even a bad post man can do that for several dribbles.

Think about limiting the movement of the post. Find the favorite side and limit him to that side. He can go to the other side one time, let him flash one time. Then have him work his way back over. When the ball goes away from me, as a post man, I should take a step off the lane so I can receive a screen or get

the angle to screen for someone else, or I can flash toward the ball. It improves spacing, and I am in a much better position to go to the board.

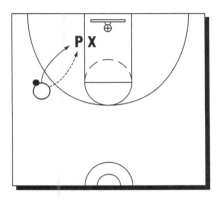

Diagram 11

When you run your secondary transition, we have an air dummy there and he must seal it. Run to the rim, and bury the defense. I don't like going to the box. Why give up all that space? A post man takes up space; the guards create space for a shot. If the ball is reversed, I don't go to the box. I find the next man in the zone and I seal him. Put your body on first.

Shooting Ideas. Always put back the miss. Shot fakes. I see shot fakes that don't look like shots to me. A shot fake is where you start your shot and stop it. We want two-inch shot fakes with no foot fakes. That's for everyone.

The quality of your shot selection is the number one thing that determines whether you win or lose. Less is more.

Never give a three-point shot to a three-point shooter. Rick Majerus has a rule about threes. You must shoot it, you must defend it and you must rebound it. You must learn how to rebound a three. If you can rebound a three and take another three, you never miss.

(Diagram 12)   Three-on-two. The guard attacks the opposite side from the best finisher. If he can penetrate past the first guard, it is now a 2-on-1 with the best finisher. If he can't penetrate past him, the other player moves behind him for the European Three. That is the hardest thing to defend in basketball. Anytime the ball is driven, go behind the driver to get the automatic three.

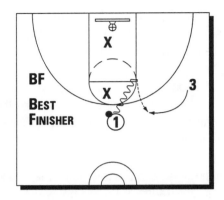

Diagram 12

Zone Offense

Two things about offense. If you had two things, and only two things, you could have a decent offense. They are good shot selection and spacing. These are the two hardest things to teach in offense. Every kid wants to shoot every shot. Shot selection is one of the first things you should get straight with your kids every year because you know your team better than anyone else. If you let the players shoot the shots they want to shoot, three years from the time you allow them to shoot those shots, you won't be there. They will get you fired. We shot 51.5% from the field and we weren't that good. We only had two players who could shoot. They literally took over 65% of our shots. You can't let people shoot who can't shoot. We chart our shooting drills from day one. After a week and a half, one player was shooting threes at a 7% clip. I sit the team down and tell each one which shots he can take and which ones he can't. This player with the 7% fought me every day. He wanted to shoot threes. In a game, he said they weren't guarding him. No kidding! He still thought he should shoot that shot.

(Diagram 1)   Spacing. Put two players in a circle and tell them to go 15' to 18' away. I'll guarantee you that one of them will only move 6'. They do not understand spacing. Great point guards understand spacing better than anybody.

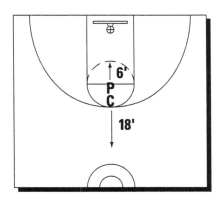

Diagram 1

Every kid plays against man-to-man all summer long. They are comfortable when they see a man defense. When they first see a zone, they want to just shoot over it. Teach them what the coverages are. If they understand the coverages, they know where to attack and they will do a better job. Every zone looks at you the whole time. The man with the ball must pull two players together so we have 4-on-3. With the shot clock, you must attack early and well. Kids don't shoot as well when they are running out of time. I think there will be a shot clock in high school in the next few years.

(Diagram 2)   On the first day, we put up the areas of coverage for the players of that zone. We want to attack where the circles intersect. There are about five to seven gray areas in each zone. If you attack the gray areas, and pull two people together, you will get much better shots than if you attack around the outside. I learned more about attacking zones by watching John Chaney (Temple) practice for two days than any offensive concepts I have ever seen. I think John Chaney is one of the great zone coaches in this country.

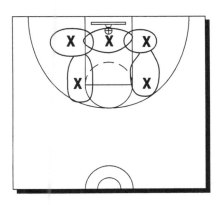

Diagram 2

(Diagram 3)   The thing they always talked about was that when they came up to guard a player, to attack the dribbler's inside shoulder and push him to the outside. This keeps him from drawing two players together and you can then overplay him one-on-one.

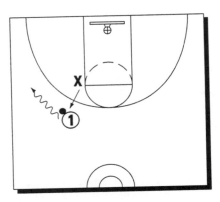

Diagram 3

(Diagram 4)   So, it makes sense that I want to attack the inside shoulder of the defender. Force two players to come together.

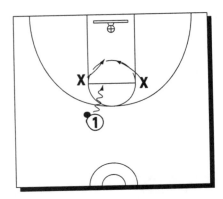

Diagram 4

(Diagram 5)   Behind the zone. We want to attack from behind the zone. Realize that 70% of your shots come from "the back of the head." When the ball is on top, this area is behind the zone, flash on top, flash to the middle.

(Diagram 6)   If the ball is on the wing, 70% of your shots are coming from this area. He should be working on penetration, skip-passes and ball reversal to get shots for the person flashing to the ball. If he passes into the corner, he will be covered.

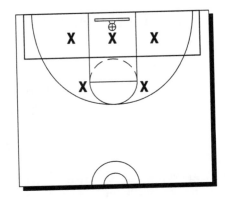

Diagram 5

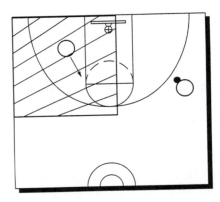

Diagram 6

(Diagram 7)   If he passes the ball into the post, the worst thing he can do is pass the ball back out to the same man. That is the easiest coverage in basketball. The man digs down, recovers back out. There is no pressure on the zone.

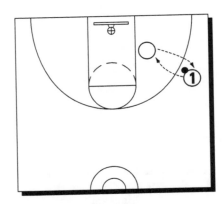

Diagram 7

(Diagram 8)   The post should look to pass the ball to this area. Every zone overreacts to every post pass.

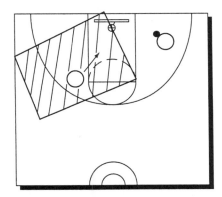

Diagram 8

(Diagram 9)   When you attack from behind, we talk about two lines. We want to attack behind both of the lines of defense. When we attack a 2-3 or a 1-2-2, we call the middle the runway. We want to get the ball into the runway as much as we can and are attacking from behind at the same time. If you attack both lines of that defense from behind, you are really putting pressure on them.

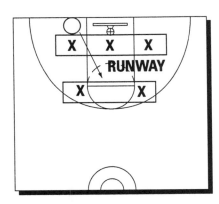

Diagram 9

(Diagram 10)   There are two types of movement. You must have side-top-side, and you have to have inside-out. We all have to coach according to our

talent. We want at least one side-top-side, and one inside touch. We want the zone to play strongside defense, topside defense and then weak-side defense. If we can get the zone to move, we can get better shots than just coming down the floor and shooting over the zone. Make the defense move and get them out of their areas of coverage.

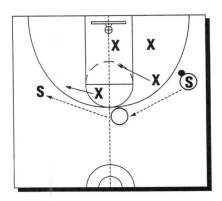

Diagram 10

(Diagram 11)   I had a good point guard and I learned something from him. He asked why I was asking him to penetrate against the two quickest players on the defense (the guards).

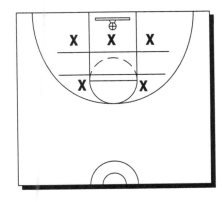

Diagram 11

(Diagram 12)   He suggested that he (1) pass the ball to the wing and make an inside cut. 2 will dribble back to the top and pass the ball back to 1 who can then penetrate against a slower person. It makes sense to find those players in the zone they are trying to hide defensively, the weak areas, and attack them with your best people.

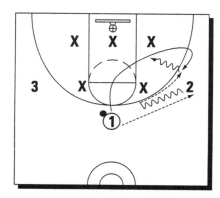

Diagram 12

(Diagram 13)   3 is the best shooter, 5 is the best post player. Always put both of them on the same side of the floor and put them on the side of the floor where the zone's weakest defender is. Always take the ball opposite these two and then bring it back. This makes the zone recover and makes it more difficult for them to guard.

Diagram 13

(Diagram 14)   Create a 3-on-2. Work 3-on-2 in practice; it will help their confidence.

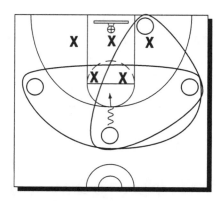

Diagram 14

(Diagram 15)   "Pop Three." We would run this with eight seconds on the shot clock. Dribble penetration from the top, pass to the wing and take a jump shot. They must know they can get a shot on that zone. When we were successful with that, the back men would start coming up to help and then we could attack from behind. We always wanted a player to come up the court to help or across the lane to help. If we could get that, he could not make a two-pass recovery.

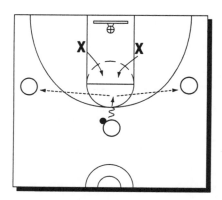

Diagram 15

(Diagram 16)   We all have rules for our players. If one is a nonshooter, you must find a way to help him help your team, but you must have a rule to keep him from doing something stupid. With our post players, we always attack Big Triangle, Small Triangle. Put your worst post player just outside the block. He can screen in on the triangle and he's not allowed to do anything else. He should get rebounds. He plays the triangle. You need a post player who can step out now and then so that you have 4-out and 1-in to get an advantage on the perimeter. If you have a good point guard and a four man who can play both inside and outside, you have a chance to have a good team.

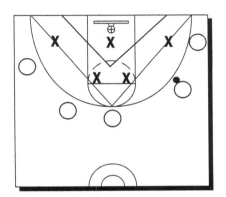

Diagram 16

(Diagram 17)   If the ball goes in to the post, his first option is to shoot. If both his feet are outside the lane, this is a 22% shot, for players I have coached for nine years. If both his feet are inside the lane, it is a 55% shot. If you throw it in and one man of the zone is behind, and two players are helping him, that is a bad shot.

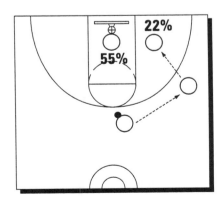

Diagram 17

(Diagram 18)   Reverse the ball, then you've got the 55% shot. When the ball is reversed, everybody looks at the ball.

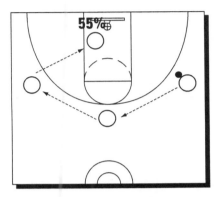

Diagram 18

(Diagram 19)   With the ball in the post, pass over the top to the weak-side wing and then flash for the return pass.

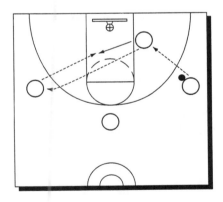

Diagram 19

(Diagram 20)   The weak-side post always thinks he is put upon. We think he is the most important player opposite the ball that we have. We want him to flash middle and pass back from where he came.

(Diagram 21)   Screen in and float to score.

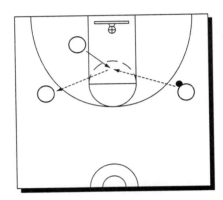

Diagram 20

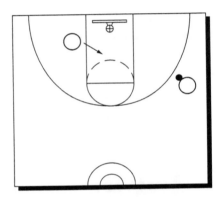

Diagram 21

(Diagram 22)   Hit the baseline, block out and
rebound from the baseline out. If he does one of
these three things, he is occupying people and
making things happen. Everyone should spend a lot
of time with offensive rebounding against a zone.
Get behind the zone and then push out to rebound.

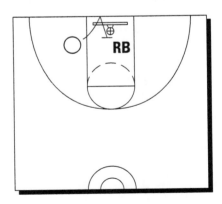

Diagram 22

(Diagram 23)   Perimeter players. We want at
least one skip-pass per possession. It moves the ball
quicker and changes every recovery the zone has.

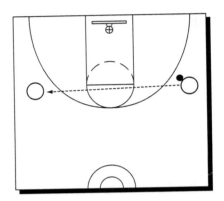

Diagram 23

(Diagram 24)   If I dribble-penetrate and kick to
here, the two defensive men have a one-pass
recovery. Good zones will get there.

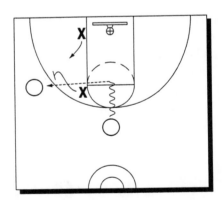

Diagram 24

(Diagram 25)   If I make the skip-pass now, there is
a two-pass recovery with time to penetrate, get an
open shot and time after the skip-pass to have our
people flash.

(Diagram 26)   Years ago, everyone taught the
quick reversal. Moving the ball around the outside of
the zone is not going to help your zone offense. Any

good zone wants you to pass the ball around the outside. The only time we quick-reverse is if we know the guards will play like this. Then, the second pass causes them problems.

Diagram 27

Diagram 25

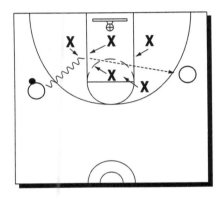

Diagram 28

(Diagram 29)   This is also true when the perimeter shooter comes in behind the penetrator. This man must sprint to that spot.

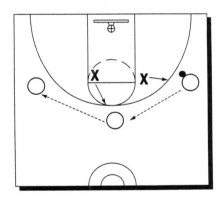

Diagram 26

(Diagram 27)   It really helps the penetration if you will make the pass fake before the penetration.

(Diagram 28)   We want to get at least two dribbles with the penetration. If you can get that and then the pass, you will get a shot. You must spend a lot of time with your perimeter players to be shot ready. They must catch the ball in the ready position.

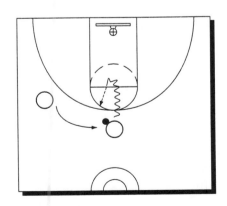

Diagram 29

(Diagram 30)   Flare out. 1 dribbles the ball to the wing, and our best shooter goes through to the corner. 3 slides to the lane lines extended, 4 comes high, 5 screens in.

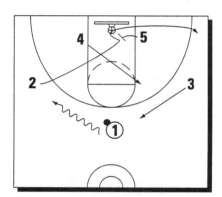

Diagram 30

(Diagram 31)   If you come down the floor and set up an overload like this, it is no good. The defense will see this and match up to it. If you take the ball away and bring it back, it is harder for the defense to react.

Diagram 31

(Diagram 32)   1 now has the ball on the wing. We have overloaded the right side. We have taken the ball away from the overload, and now we will bring it back. As we begin to reverse the ball, we put pressure on these two players.

Diagram 32

(Diagram 33)   As the ball is reversed, 1 passes back to 3 who is in the chute (lane lines extended.) 3 passes to 4. If 4 can shoot, the pressure is on the deep man to come up. 4 can pass to 2 in the corner. 5 posts up on the block. On any ball reversal, post behind that ball reversal. 5 doesn't look for the ball until he has found the body of the defensive man. Attack the defense and then look for the ball.

Diagram 33

(Diagram 34)   As soon as 4 makes the pass, he goes to the short corner opposite. If the ball is reversed again, 4 is open.

(Diagram 35)   "Corner Call." 4 and 5 are on the blocks. This is predicated on overloading one area of the zone and bringing the ball back to it. 1 passes to 3. The post man on that side steps out. 3 passes to

4 and dives hard to the block. 2 will loop in behind to set a stack with 5.

Diagram 34

Diagram 35

Diagram 36

Diagram 37

(Diagram 36)   4 has the ball, 3 is on the block. On the pass back to 1, 4 screens in for 3, and 5 screens the deep man in the lane. 2 and 3 go to the corners. They have three players guarding our four men. I am convinced that you should throw the ball in from the top against zones rather than the wing.

(Diagram 37)   Screen on the ball vs. zone. 1 makes the pass to 3. This shifts the zone. 3 passes back to 1. 4 comes up and screens the guard, and 1 dribbles off of the screen.

(Diagram 38)   1 can turn the corner and get a shot or he can pass to 2 on the wing. 4 steps out high. The back man on the zone has to make the decision of whom to guard. 5 does a low duck. Everyone is watching the ball. 1 can reverse the ball to 4 and to 3, who has faded into the corner. 4 then goes to the low block.

(Diagram 39)   If 3 doesn't have the shot, the ball is reversed to 1 and then to 4 with 5 screening in the lane. Screening is really hard to guard.

(Diagram 40)   Double High. 1 brings it off the top. 5 screens the guard, 4 screens the other guard. As 1 comes off the first screen, 5 dives to the block diagonally. After 4 screens, he pops out. 1 passes to 3. 3 can hit 5, or reverse to 4 to 2 in the corner.

Diagram 38

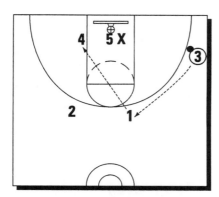

Diagram 39

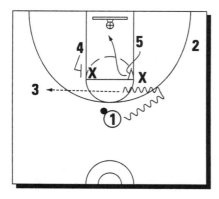

Diagram 40

(Diagram 41)   This is my favorite. 2 is the best shooter. 1 takes the ball to the side away from 2. 2 breaks to the corner and gets a pass from 1.

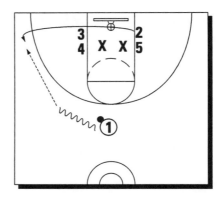

Diagram 41

(Diagram 42)   As soon as 2 comes off of the double-screen of 3 and 4, they screen-in the two players in the lane. 2 is being guarded by the third deep player in the zone. Now, 5 comes off the screens of 3 and 4 and gets the pass from 2.

Diagram 42

(Diagram 43)   When the defense starts to play the play, 5 breaks high, 4 sets the screen and then turns and seals for the pass from 2.

(Diagram 44)   Out of bounds vs. a zone. Start with a double-stack. 1 pops out and gets the pass from 2. 3 and 4 screen in. 2 ducks in the lane and then goes to the corner for the pass from 1. 5 is in offside rebounding position.

Diagram 43

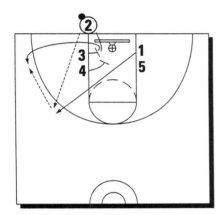

Diagram 44

(Diagram 45)   Versus a match-up. We have a simple rule against a match-up. The match-up zone plays the next pass before it's thrown. If 3 has the ball, the guard is already up playing 1. Match-up zones can be stretched so there is more open area than a regular zone. They all have man responsibility.

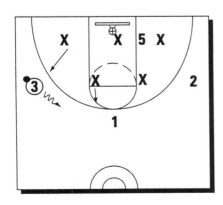

Diagram 45

(Diagram 46)   We want the ball to be dribbled up from the wing and thrown back to the baseline. We make the deep man in the zone take 3.

Diagram 46

(Diagram 47)   If the ball is on top, take it down and 4 will break out for the reversal pass to 3.

Diagram 47

(Diagram 48)   No shot, 4 goes to the short corner; 5 works the short triangle. You should work on every type of zone. Don't be surprised by a 1-3-1 trapping zone. If you are a bad team, you will see a lot of zones.

Question: How about the secondary break against zones?

Answer: We have one we run.

Diagram 48

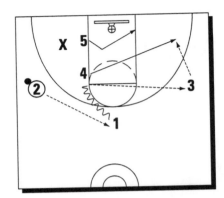

Diagram 50

(Diagram 49)   The ball is on the wing, and the ball is reversed to 1-4-2. 5 follows the ball and 4 goes to the high post.

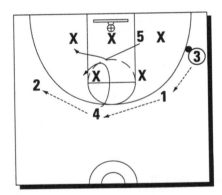

Diagram 49

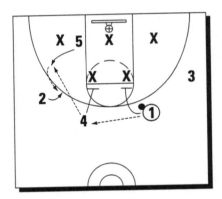

Diagram 51

(Diagram 50)   As the ball is reversed back to 1, he drives into the lane to hold the defense, then passes to 3. 4 goes to the short corner, 5 flashes into the lane and then goes to the block.

(Diagram 51)   Special. 1 has the ball. 1 passes to 4 to 5. 4 and 1 double-screen the top two men in the zone, and 2 comes off the double-screen for the pass from 5 for the three-point shot.

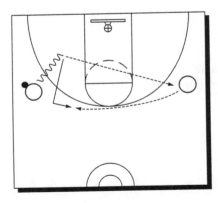

Diagram 52

(Diagram 52)   When you make a skip-pass, tell the passer to be ready to shoot because the ball is coming back after the receiver penetrates.

(Diagram 53)   When the ball goes into the post and the post passes out to the weak side, the post should flash following his pass.

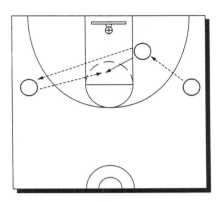

Diagram 53

Man Defense

You must find one defense and make that your trademark, one that the kids really believe in. The first thing you must do defensively is don't give up easy baskets. We put a real premium on not giving up an easy basket in transition.

(Diagram 54)   Last-second shot for a three-point play. 2 is in the corner, 3, 4, and 5 screen the bottom players on the zone. Then, 3 and 4 break high. 2 runs the baseline and gets the pass from 1.

(Diagram 1)   We use the middle of the floor, the "chute" area. When the shot goes up, our two guards go directly back. They do not rebound offensively under any circumstances. If you designate who rebounds and who doesn't, you have a better chance of being a good offensive rebounding team and a better defensive transition team.

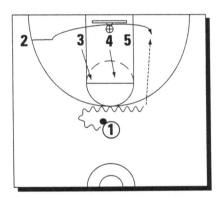

Diagram 54

Here are a few general comments:

When you penetrate, use your strong hand.

Offensively, go make contact with the defense.

Start all your offensive drills on the far side of the center circle.

Our challenge as coaches is to make the players believe.

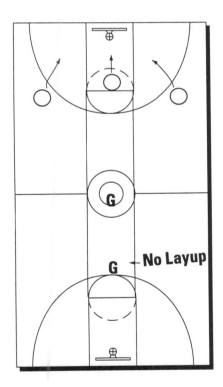

Diagram 1

We send our two guards back every time, one to the center circle, the other behind him. They give ground enough to slow the ball, and the back man is responsible for not giving a layup. If he has to go to the rim, then he has to go to the rim. Our other three players' only job is to go rebound. Our three front liners, unless we are in "three back," go to the board every single time. There are no questions asked. The three players on the board become very important in transition defense. We never contest the rebound. We want to run down the middle of the floor, and don't "buddy run" with your man. Never mind your man. Where is the ball?

(Diagram 2)   We want our players to run to the lane and cover out. Stop the ball, get it off the middle of the floor and keep it off. If the ball is dribbled to the side, we want to keep it there. If your man is trailing, we want to double-team the ball.

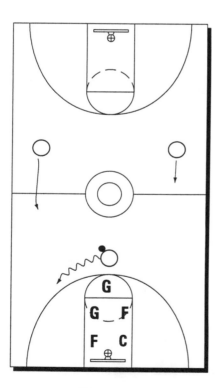

Diagram 2

(Diagram 3)   One of the hard things to do in transition is, when the shot is taken and our players are back, here comes the trailer down the lane and

dunks the rebound. You must really spend some time on transition rebounding. You must get your body on him.

Diagram 3

(Diagram 4)   In half-court, our main concern is this area around the basket. Most things happen in this area. If your team can control that area and really rebound the ball defensively, you have a chance to be in most games. We check the ball and deny penetrating passes. We never deny non-penetrating passes. If you aren't doing either of these two things, you are on the help line. The fourth place you can be is on the bench if you aren't in any of those three.

(Diagram 5)   We spend a lot of time teaching stance, but not in terms of where the feet are. If we aren't driving the ball to the side, we play them straight up, don't let them go by. If we can stop the penetration, now they must shoot over us. If we are off the ball, we want to be on the help line with our back parallel to the baseline, but the head is turned.

The arms are out. See the ball first, see the man second, see the ball third. We want to have an advantage guarding the ball, one man on the ball and four men helping.

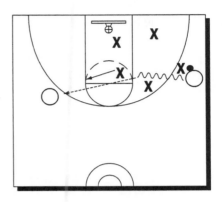

Diagram 6

(Diagram 7)   Don't come up the floor to help. The only time you come up the floor is to draw a charge. You give up the layup.

(Diagram 8)   We spend a lot of time with close-outs. Make it realistic. Make it like a game situation.

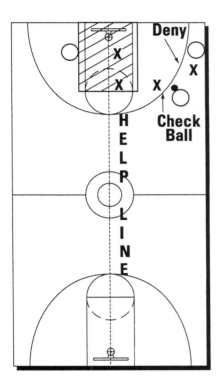

Diagram 4

Diagram 7

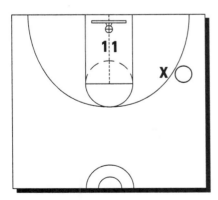

Diagram 5

(Diagram 6)   We don't want to allow the penetration and pass. The man who has to close out must come from too far.

Diagram 8

(Diagram 9)   The ball is passed into the post. The defensive guard drops down to help on the post. The ball is passed back out to the other perimeter player and the guard must close out on the player with the ball.

Diagram 9

(Diagram 10)   Skip-pass over the top. Recover, take away the dribble-drive. If he is a shooter, make him dribble. If he is a dribbler, make him shoot. There are not many players who can do both. If you close out on the shooter, sprint and go by him. We are not into blocking him out, we are into changing his shot. Get to them before the ball is eye high. At the worst, make him move it a little. We run at the ball.

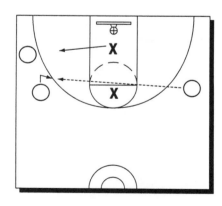

Diagram 10

(Diagram 11)   We talk about pursuing the ball. The man closing out must turn around and get back in the play. Recover and get back to rebound.

Diagram 11

(Diagram 12)   Same thing with penetration. Get back and recover. Pursue.

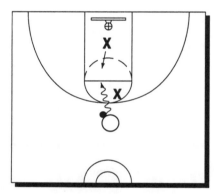

Diagram 12

(Diagram 13)   If you can scramble well, you have a chance of being a good defensive team. No matter if you play man, zone, or press, your team guards in a scramble at least 7 out of 10 times. Somebody is getting by one of your players. We have simple rules. If a player gets beaten, the closest player runs to the ball and we cover everybody else behind on the pass. The other players are headed toward the lane.

(Diagram 14)   If the pass is made, we are scrambling to recover and pick up a man. The closest player picks up the ball. You must learn how to play in broken situations and you must practice it. I've always said, "How could we let him get an open shot?" This stresses team defense. On defense, you must have unselfish players. They want to hug their man; they don't want to give up their man to stop the ball.

to the other end. The two guards go back. This really gives the offense an advantage.

Diagram 13

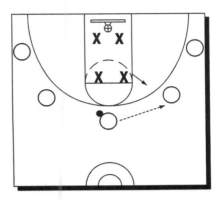

Diagram 15

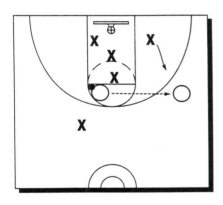

Diagram 14

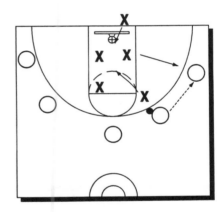

Diagram 16

(Diagram 15)　Drills. Five-on-four scramble. Our rules are these: closest player covers the ball; the other players are in the lane unless you are covering the next pass. Sprint to the lane. We play until we score; losers run.

(Diagram 16)　5/4 to 5/5. It's hard to get people to talk. When the fifth man comes in he must yell 5-on-5, match-up, scramble and cover the ball.

When we do this full-court we put our big player at mid-court. As soon as the shot goes up, he takes off

(Diagram 17)　Switch and Change. Bring the ball over half-court to start the drill. When I say "switch," the offense drops the ball. The players on defense grab the ball and attack the same basket. The key is the offensive players cannot guard the player that was guarding them.

(Diagram 18)　Ball-side Screen. Screen on the same side as the ball. The defender wants to shortcut over the top. We play footsteps and chase. The man guarding the cutter chases. The man guarding the screener plays on top of the screen, bumps the curl or switches if he curls to score. We never go over the top to allow the man to go to the corner for the open shot.

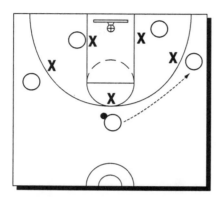

Diagram 17

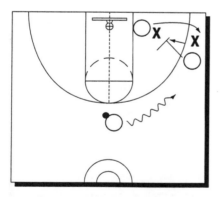

Diagram 18

Diagram 19

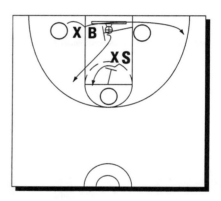

Diagram 20

(Diagram 19)   Flare Screens. On the flare screen, we play it just like the ball-side screen. As he goes off the flare, we chase the flare over the top. The player guarding the screener holds the middle of the lane, ball side.

(Diagram 20)   Triangle action. Small to big or big to small. Small screens across, then a down-screen. We want the big player going under on any cross-screen. Small player comes high and we chase the footsteps.

(Diagram 21)   Ball-screen. We put lines on the floor. The outer circle is the scoring range line. The help line is in the middle of the floor. The other line is the motion line. We also have the chute area. We play ball-screen based on scoring range. If the ball-screen is outside of the scoring range, we go behind. If it is in scoring range, we play it one of three ways.

(Diagram 22)   If he is a nonshooter, we are off and go under to take it away.

(Diagram 23)   If he is a shooter, we play a "half double." We double-team two dribbles. We show a double-team and sprint back.

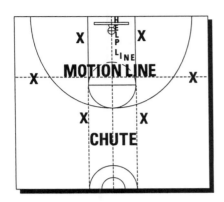

Diagram 21

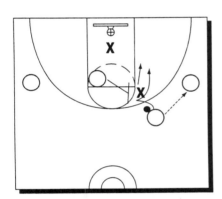

Diagram 22

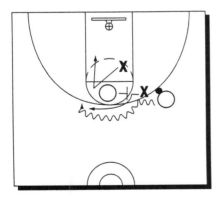

Diagram 23

(Diagram 24)   If we double-team, we chase until they pass the ball. The others are protecting the lane first, jump shot second.

Diagram 24

(Diagram 25)   Flashes. We do it 5-on-5. On any ball reversal, we want the weak-side man cutting and the other two players filling. We want 2 to cut, and then immediately after 3 passes to 4, we want 3 cutting right behind him with 1 filling at the top.

Diagram 25

We run a 4-on-4 shell drill with some aspect of screening, etc. Anytime there is a perimeter ball-screen, we switch it.

(Diagram 26)   We saw this often. Dribble over, screen across, double-down. Eight teams in our league run this.

(Diagram 27)   Purdue runs this. Ball on perimeter. 5 screens for 2, then 3 screens for 2. 1 passes to 2. They run this very well. We will work on three or four of these plays every day.

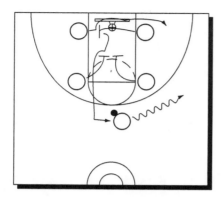

Diagram 26

Diagram 27

Diagram 28

(Diagram 28)   Rebounding. When the shot goes up, block out on the ball-side perimeter. The one you must spend time with is the man guarding the player two passes away. You can't charge at him. Both are moving. I don't run at him anymore. He goes to the lane line extended; wait for him, and use a hard arm bar. Our point guard does not block out. He just rebounds. His man is going back. Our point guard should be the second best defensive rebounder.

We have three defensive situations we practice every day: fouling a three; switching all screens up six points or more when they need three; when they need to score a basket, we drive the ball to the side and have our big man front the post. We don't normally front. If you let it go to the post, they will get something.

We play defensively straight up, toe to toe, shoulder to shoulder. We don't drive him baseline or to the middle. We say do not let your man get in the 15-foot area.

(Diagram 29)   I'm a big believer in always doing things the same way so there are no surprises. On ball-side screens, we are at the level of the screen, just off the shoulder. The man being screened always follows footsteps. I don't want my man to have an option. X2 chases him every time. X1 bumps the cutter as he curls. If he continues to score, we switch it regardless of size.

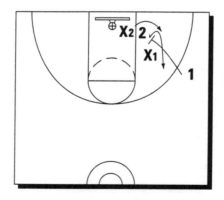

Diagram 29

Out of a double-team, pursue the ball to the rim. Don't run at the ball, go to the rim.

If you have to give up something, give up the jump shot.

(Diagram 30)   Close-outs two passes away—go to the lane line and let the offensive man come to you.

Diagram 30

Practice

Don't think you have to make practice fun and have different drills every day. Basically, we follow the same practice plan every day. When we condense our practices from three to two hours, we just shorten the length of the drills, but we do the same thing. We post the practice plan two hours before practice. I have the assistants in the locker room one hour before practice. If any of our players want to talk about any of the drills, now is the time. There is a benefit having your assistants spending time with the players; they are somewhat of a buffer between the players and the head coach. Sometimes stretching becomes a joke. They lie down and just talk about their social life. Now I have our trainer lead the drills and it is good. Stretching is important. We go from a light stretch into 15-20 minutes of skill work. Then, we stretch again. We didn't have one pulled muscle last year.

We lift and run year round. We lift four times a week off-season and run twice a week for 45 minutes. If your muscles are in great shape, you don't get hurt. When we start practice, we get on the end line and run the length of the court six times, in 31 seconds. We call that the Deep Six. If you don't get it in 31 seconds, we go again. If they know we are going to start practice that way, they are focused to do it. Then we come together and have one of the players say something to start practice. We then go into team ballhandling for 10 to 15 minutes. We pass and catch with two hands. Nobody works on passing and catching on their own. We do:

- 2/0 full-court air pass, call name of receiver on the way down.

- 2/0 full-court bounce pass, on the way back.

- 3/0 full-court air pass, down.

- 3/0 full-court, bounce pass on the way back.

(Diagram 1)   Two-pass Drill. 1 passes to 2, 2 passes to 3. The ball should not hit the floor, but we allow the dribble to keep from traveling. That's one of the most used passes in the game, but we never practice it. We use it as a diagonal vs. pressure, a lead pass on the fast break. The player in the middle must catch the ball as it goes through the net. If they have a turnover or a miss, they start over. If they can't make the pass and catch with no defense, how are they going to do it in the game?

(Diagram 2)   We then do some sort of spacing drill.

(a) We dribble to the side and pass back to a partner.

(b) We also do it with three people.

(c) This is 2-on-1 trap. Coach passes to partner, two defensive men trap him, hard pressure. The first time he has one dribble to get out, the second time he has two dribbles. Pass back to the coach.

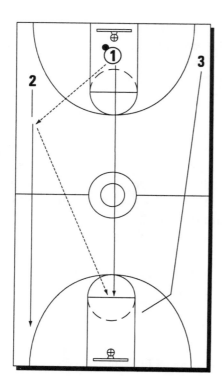

Diagram 1

(d) Three-man passing. The defensive man is in the middle for 30 seconds. Change positions. The man with the most deflections wins, the others do pushups.

We do some sort of 1-on-1 full-court every day. I am really big on team defense after the break. You must be able to check the ball at some level sometime in the game. Defense is a team game, but you must be a good individual in the group if you are going to help.

(Diagram 3)   1-on-1 Half-Court. The player starts moving and the coach passes him the ball. The defensive player must stop the dribble and push it toward the sideline. We cover all our screening situations every day.

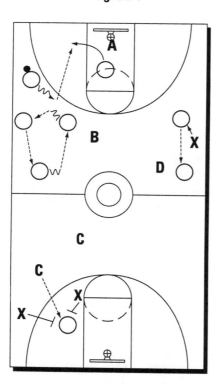

Diagram 2

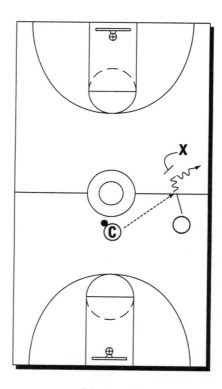

Diagram 3

We will play some 5-on-5 early in practice for about 20 minutes. We break it into segments of about seven minutes each: vs. pressure, vs. half-court traps, vs. whatever. We will pick three. If you always wait until late in practice, they might be too tired to be effective. We spend 15 minutes a day with the dummy fast break. The more I do it, the more I think we need to dummy, press break, special plays, etc.

Then, we work on screening, 4/4 shell, and 5/5 shell. We do three transition defensive drills. Don't change your philosophy from day to day. Don't press one day and walk the ball up the next. My team knows what we want to accomplish. We then go 5/5 vs. man and 5/5 vs. zone. If you don't practice against a zone every day, someday you will get killed. We do three possessions against a 3-2, a 2-3, a 1-3-1 and against a half-court trap. We run close-out drills at the end of practice. If you can check the ball from the help position, you can be a good defensive team.

The hardest thing for us to do is to get our team to talk. They talk better if they are better players. I got this from a walk-on. I asked him why he never talked. He said that he was having all he could do to keep his head above water without helping someone else. Better players will talk more. We shoot a one-and-one between every drill, or we will break for two minutes and shoot free throws. We shoot 100/day outside of practice and record them. We can't make them make free throws, but we can give them the opportunity to get better. As coaches, after training table, we sit down and watch the video of the practice. We work at night on the next day's practice. You need input from your assistants about the practice, and also from your players.

I sit down with my players and make sure they understand the terminology we use. Talk with them outside of practice. It makes the practices more effective. We then do some last-minute situations. I believe in practicing long and hard, except the day before a game when we have a light practice. On the day of a game, we practice for an hour, very hard, at 7 o'clock in the morning.

Building a Program

Here are some things you ought to think about. Picking a job. There are about fifteen schools where the coach will be in the Final Four on a regular basis. That's the bottom line. People leave jobs for money, location, family, or conflict. Those are the reasons you leave a job at any level.

When choosing a job, know what the expectation level is. The jobs where you must start from scratch aren't always the worst jobs. Go where you know you can get the job done.

When you get there (in college), fire everybody; the trainer, the academic advisor, the managers, especially the coaches. I took over a program that won five, five, and six games. No one there could have known what it took to win. When you take over a single-digit win program, you are taking over a mess.

Anybody who needs a campus visit to decide on the job, you don't want. You cannot get involved in an interviewing process and get turned down and have to go back with your tail between your legs. I didn't need a campus visit to Northwestern before I took the job. If you do tell somebody that you are going to take the job, then take the job. You must have some sort of reputation that says you are trustworthy. If you are taking a job, take it, and stay. That's all there is to it.

Meet with the players the first day you are there and explain how you are going to be as a coach. First of all, you usually don't get a good job. You get jobs with poor players in them, who were allowed to do whatever they wanted. That's why you got the job. Meet with the players and have a short meeting; give them their weight lifting schedules, etc.

When you have the meeting with the players, establish the fact that you are going to respect them if they will work hard. You are basing your respect on the fact that they are going to work hard in the classroom, represent the program well and work hard in everything you ask. If they will do that, they will have a chance to be part of the program. When you make the meeting short, make sure they know you are going to have individual meetings. Every time I have taken over a program, the players were slumped down in their chairs, with hats on. First thing I tell them is to sit up straight, take your hats off, look me in the eye or get out. That's one of the few rules that I have. If I am talking to a player, he is going to look me in the eye. Mutual respect is the big thing to establish when you first get a job.

Be realistic about your program, but be urgent. We talk to our players about having a sense of urgency. You must have a sense of urgency to win. Whether they win or not is a different thing.

Have few, but good rules. The only rules I have are: be on time, play hard, play together and learn to hate losing. You can make them hate losing. I know how to make them miserable when they lose. I am lousy to live with two or three days after a loss. They will hate losing and hate you. But if they give their best and we lose, that's all right. Chances are, they aren't used to winning.

You must have some program priorities. Ours is simple. Defense, rebounding, good shots, no turnovers. Every locker has that sign in it. Every time we send them something in the summertime, those four things are at the top of the paper. We think it is important to establish what you believe in so they will believe in it. You must be player oriented. We list three things: our players, prospects, recruits. Do everything for the players. Do everything first class and spend time with them off the court. I never go more than two days without talking to our players. If I am out of town for five days, I call them twice in that period. They know

better than anyone whether you care about them or not, and they will tell other players.

If you take over a double-digit win program, your hardest year will probably be your second year. If you take over a single-digit win program, your third year will be your hardest. Even if you have two recruiting classes in, you will not be very good your third year. It happens. Downplay any type of optimism until you are sure. If you know you're going to be good, don't go around saying that you aren't. Then you lose credibility. Be sure you tell your players in advance anything that you are going to tell the media. You must spend time conditioning their minds to understand that you believe in them.

Parents. I never take a call from a parent or have a meeting with a parent about basketball. I send them a letter at the beginning of every year saying just that. You can call me about your child's welfare, academics, but the second you mention basketball, the conversation is over. Stay away from boosters. As much as they may want to help you, the same group might be against you down the road. Never take anything from a booster. There is a price that comes with any of that and don't think for a second that it's not going to happen to you, because it is.

Hiring the staff, particularly in college, is critical. You must have the same type of chemistry that you have as the team that you will recruit. You must have good people. I have three classifications for people: good people, bad people, really good people. You must have good people around you. We are going to work together 15 to 18 hours a day.

Recruiting players. Don't duplicate players; don't duplicate staff members. We have a blend of players who get along really well and you have to have a blend. We have one player who is the most level-headed, laid-back, good kid I ever met. I need someone like that around me. We have another kid who is an aggressive go-getter. You can't have two of them. I know who I need around me.

Scheduling. For us, with a bad program, you must schedule some wins. In March, all they want to know is, did you win or lose?

You must make sure your players do well academically. The first time you aren't winning, academics are the first thing they are going to throw at you. Then it will be verbal abuse, and difference in philosophy, they don't care, and style of play. If you are winning and playing slow, then it's great. If you lose, you're too slow. If you are winning and playing fast, great. If you lose, then you are playing out of control. So plan your job. Have a long-term plan.

When rebuilding, do not let them know they are getting to you. You are going to have some bad times. That just comes with the territory. Do not go away from what you believe in and are doing.

Motion Offense

Diagram 2

If you are a control freak, you won't like it. Once you give them the rules, and the game starts, you are not going to know everything that is going to happen. Since your players change from year to year, you must decide where you want to get your shots from and who you want to shoot them. Your rules won't change much, but you must make your players understand how, through the rules, you are going to have the right players shooting the ball in the areas that you want.

(Diagram 1)   We want to get shots from these spots. It seems as if when we want a three-point shot, we shoot from these three spots. If we are playing against a zone, we get them from the corners. In both our motion and our set plays, we will probably get our shots from these spots.

Diagram 3

(Diagram 4)   We call this area "the Box," and this is where we want to get the ball. If you can get the ball in this area, all defenses break down.

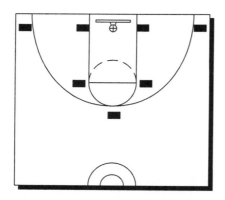

Diagram 1

(Diagram 2)   The best shot is still the layup, and we go backdoor. 1 should never stay in the middle. We want him to one side or the other. 5 comes high, and 3 goes backdoor and gets the pass from 1 for the layup.

(Diagram 3)   To relieve the pressure, we will use an early post exchange and then the low post coming high.

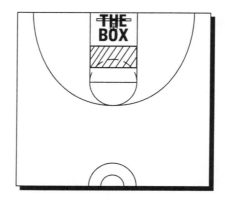

Diagram 4

When we come down to set up, we want the point guard to come down the middle and then to go to one side or the other. We want the wings at the free-throw line extended with their backs to the sideline one step outside of the three-point line. We want our wings to be able to see the point guard, the middle of the floor and the low post. The offense starts with the baseline players. We want the post men with their backs to the baseline, just above the squares with 15- to 18-foot spacing.

(Diagram 5)   How are you going to guard the low post? If you play defense on the side of our posts, we like to make a point-to-post entry.

Diagram 5

(Diagram 6)   If the defense plays up the line, we can't run the low post high or flash. 2 must read and set the down-screen or else the post will come up and set the back-screen for 2.

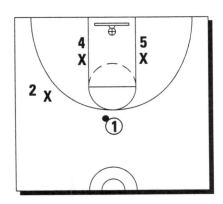

Diagram 6

What you do on ball reversal is the most critical part of your offense. Timing, spacing, and to understand if you are a screener or being screened, are critical. It is important that you have a man who can screen block-to-block on ball reversal, then flash and catch it in the lane. On ball reversal, the opposite wing reads his post man. If the post flashes and the wing V-cuts, it clogs up the area.

Basic Rules of Motion

- First entry—the point guard chooses a side—the ball-side wing down-picks, and at the same time the weakside post back-picks the weakside wing.

- On all picks, the screener must call the name of the player he is screening for.

- On all down-picks, the cutter must read the defense, circle, flare, or cut to the elbow while the weakside post is back-picking the weakside wing.

- After the initial down-pick and back-pick, there will be a post exchange.

- On every pass in the offense, the passer will receive a back-pick. The cutter should read circle or flare.

- On ball reversal, there will be a back-pick on both sides. Weakside post has the option to back-pick or flash post, so weakside wing must read.

- If you feed the post, the passer will be back-picked by the new point. The passer-cutter will read circle or flare, and the screener will flare to the ball-side corner outside the three-point line. The opposite wing will relocate outside the three-point line and look for a pass from the post.

- If the post makes a pass back out, he will receive a back-pick from the opposite post and should look to circle or pin his man.

General Rules

- Cutters on back-picks will cut ball side. The cutter will become the new post man and look to post exchange.

- Improve the passing angle to the baseline only if you're going to feed the post.

- On post exchange, the ball-side post initiates movement, and the cutter must read the defense and cut high or low. On all switches, the cutter must go high, and the screener must roll back low to the ball.

- If there is a switch on the post exchange and we have a high-low post on one side and the ball is reversed, the high post back-picks the passer and the low post back-picks the opposite wing or button hooks and picks his man.

- The screener must call the cutter's name.

(Diagram 7)   Strongside Drive. First, 1 makes a six-inch jab step and reads. If the defense reacts, then take a long step and drive to the basket. You can get to the basket in one dribble.

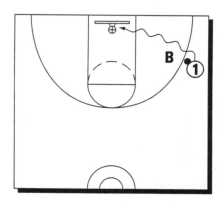

Diagram 7

(Diagram 8)   Now with the jab step, long step, and drive over the top.

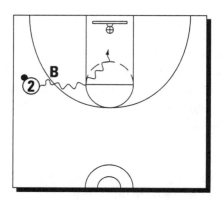

Diagram 8

(Diagram 9)   Jab step, long step, crossover, two dribbles.

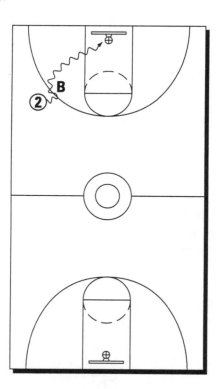

Diagram 9

(Diagram 10)   Jab step, long step, crossover, dribble to the baseline, the dummy defender cuts him off, make one spin dribble and shoot the layup.

(Diagram 11)   Jab step, long step, one dribble to the elbow, reverse pivot and shot.

Then jab step, recover, and shoot. Early in the season, we do this every day. The defender plays easy. Later, the defender will go all out.

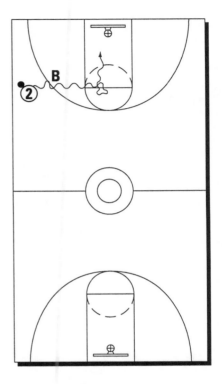

Diagram 11

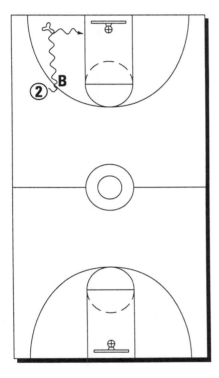

Diagram 10

(Diagram 12)   The weakside wing must first read where the point guard is going. We never give the point guard the option to pass and screen away. We did it for years, and we never got the shot off of that, so we stopped that option. We tell the wing to stay for a second, then come to the top of the key, and if they overplay this wing, cut down the lane to the box.

(Diagram 13)   Wildcat Drill. F must make a cut toward the basket, plant his foot and show his hands. Then, he makes a hard cut into the lane, catches and goes straight up with the shot.

Diagram 12

(Diagram 14)   Next, same drill except instead of getting the pass in the lane, he goes to the elbow, and back-cuts to the basket for the short jump shot.

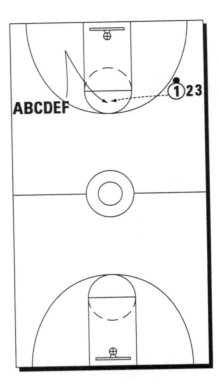

Diagram 13

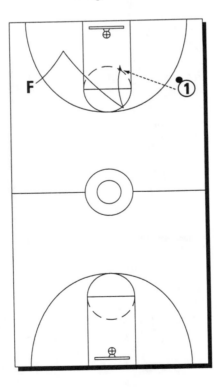

Diagram 14

(Diagram 15)   Is a layup guarded by a 6'8" player as good as a shot taken from the bottom of this circle unguarded? Can your players take the ball on the dribble, go hard to one step below the free-throw line, stop, go up, and shoot it soft? If you can, you will get a lot of wide-open shots.

Diagram 15

(Diagram 16)   Perimeter-Post Drill. 3 has the ball. If he were to pass it into 5, 3's man would probably double-down and help with the post. We want 3 to take one step and cut to the box. He gets the return pass and shoots it.

Diagram 16

(Diagram 17)   If his man turns toward the middle, 3 would cut to the baseline for the return pass.

Diagram 17

(Diagram 18)   3 dribbles to the baseline. 5 backs across the lane and draws his defensive man with him. If he doesn't go with him, 3 passes to 5.

Diagram 18

(Diagram 19)   Also, 5 can reverse pivot, and back up the line. 3 makes the hook pass to 5.

Diagram 19

(Diagram 20)   If 3 dribbles into the lane, 5 fades into the short corner.

Diagram 20

(Diagram 21)   Screening. There is no screen if there is no contact. 2 down-screens for 4. The timing is crucial. 1 goes away and comes back to receive the pass from 2. 4 steps out, cuts towards the basket and then comes off of the screen. 4 can also go to the short corner.

(Diagram 22)   You must now read circle or flare. If your man follows, circle.

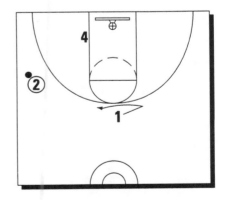

Diagram 21

(Diagram 23)   If your man goes over the top, flare. Teach the screener that the screener will probably be the one who is open.

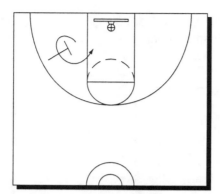

Diagram 22

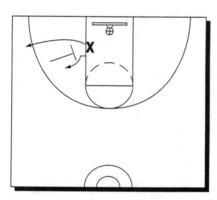

Diagram 23

(Diagram 24)   2 has the ball; 4 screens away for 5. This is a poor screening angle.

Diagram 24

(Diagram 25)   Have 4 come higher to get a better angle and screen 5 at somewhat of an angle. 5 comes off the screen, and 4 steps out and either back-picks for 1, flashing to the middle of the lane or to the elbow.

Diagram 25

(Diagram 26)   Shooting Drill for Three-Point Shot. 1 passes to 2 and cuts to the corner. 2 makes a skip-pass to 1. 1 does a reverse pivot and catches the ball with his right foot back. He steps into his shot when the ball is in the air.

Diagram 26

If the Mind Can Perceive It—
The Body Can Achieve It

My topic is a little different, but all coaches need to understand this. Before you can start coaching, you must teach first. If you don't teach, you can't coach. Kids must understand the things you are trying to get them to do. I want my kids to understand what they are doing and why they are doing it because it gives them a better concept of what they are trying to do.

If we are playing defense and we are going to trap, let's assume that the paint is Fort Knox and that's the gold we want to protect. So, we want to force the ball away from Fort Knox. The bottom line is that you are trying to get to the paint because that's where you score. So, you must perceive what is going on before you can get your body to adjust to it.

Basketball is a game of reaction; you react to a situation. It's repetitive. You do things over and over until they become part of their learning process. You don't have time to think on the court. You do your thinking in practice. You need an automatic response.

React! I don't want them to think. I want them to get out there and play. If you take time to think, the game is passing you by.

In practices, we make our drills short. I don't want any drill to last over three minutes. We do the same thing every day. We work on the offense, but we break it down into phases. When we go to team play, that's when we put it all together. That's what we mean when we say, "If the mind can perceive it, the body can achieve it." Don't ask the body to do something it doesn't understand. The other part is that we want to make it as simple as possible.

Good coaching is determined by how the kids execute on the floor. Give your plays simple names. One coach named his plays after cars. Another named his after colors. You don't want your players thinking about X's and O's. All you want them to do is know how they are going to execute, what they are going to do and how they are going to do it. So you simplify it. We want them to be comfortable.

Kids can't play if they are stressed. I've coached at all levels, from elementary to college, both public schools and private. I've never told a kid that we must win this game. I never talk about winning. I talk about competing. I talk about maxing out, doing the best you can do. That's all you can ask. You don't need to put any pressure on them. That will hurt the team effort. Players must believe in their coaches. They must believe in what they are doing. Some coaches can't adjust to their personnel, they want the personnel to adjust to them. That's crazy.

Coaching is determined by getting the players to execute. I walked into practice one day and asked, "How many of you know your teammates? How many of you know their abilities, their weaknesses and their strengths on the court? I know everybody's strengths and weaknesses, and you should too." We just sat down and began to talk. I asked various players to say what some of the strengths and weaknesses were of some of the players. They were reluctant to say. But, we went through the whole team doing that.

I told them that when we get into a game situation, they needed to know who to go to, who has the hot hand. You need to know who can handle what type of pass. You need to know the people who are playing with you. That is important in bringing the team together. Some coaches coach players, but never coach teams. They never put it together as a team. If you can't motivate, it is tough to coach. You must get the kids in the right frame of mind to play, and the next thing is to be ready to motivate.

(Diagram 1)   We run a little 2-1-2 offense. If 1 passes to 2, 4 goes to the short corner on the baseline. 1 and 2 exchange. 4 looks inside to 5.

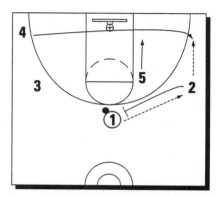

Diagram 1

(Diagram 2)   If 4 can't hit 5, 4 reverses the ball to 1 to 2 to 3, and 5 comes high and sets an up-screen for 2. 2 curls. 5 slides down the lane.

Diagram 2

(Diagram 3)   We run a series from that play. Whatever number we call first indicates the person who is going to set the screen. If we call twenty something, that means that 2 is the screener. The second number is the player that we are screening for. So, "24" means that 2 will screen for 4. 1 passes to 2 to 4 in the corner. 2 then sets a ball-screen for 4. 5 sets an up-screen for 3, and 3 comes into the middle.

Diagram 3

(Diagram 4)   "54" means that 5 will set the screen for 4.

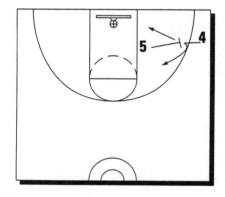

Diagram 4

(Diagram 5)   "31," 3 screens for 1. 1 looks for a give-and-go. This offense can be used against a zone or a man.

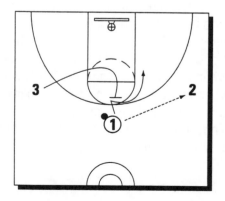

Diagram 5

(Diagram 6)   You can also run this offense from the left side. 1 to 3 to 4. 5 cuts across to the ball side, and 3 goes away.

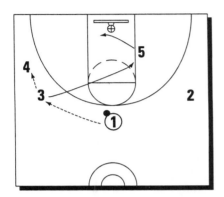

Diagram 6

(Diagram 7)   If 4 has the ball in the corner, then 5 cuts down the lane to the low post on the ball side. If 5 doesn't get the pass, she up-screens.

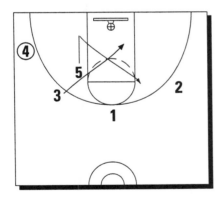

Diagram 7

(Diagram 8)   The player who will be open the most is 3.

Another part of basketball is conditioning. We want to prevent knee problems. When boys run track, the first thing they pull is a hamstring because the quads overpower the hamstrings. With girls, just because of the bowness in their hips, the emphasis is put on the lateral muscles, not the medial muscles. We have an exercise that strengthens the knees. We use the buddy system. One girl sits on the floor and the other girl stands over her. The first exercise is started with the legs closed and the sitting girl exerts pressure against the legs of the standing girl. The sitting girl tries to open her legs. The standing girl has her legs at the ankles of the girl who is sitting. Then do the opposite. Open the legs of the sitting girl and try to close them.

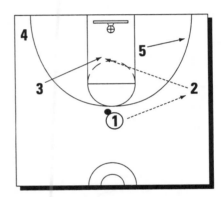

Diagram 8

We need to stabilize the knee. We do five reps of 10 seconds each. We also have a series of 21 exercises that stretch the body from the neck to the feet. We run for 10 minutes before we stretch. We do not stretch a muscle that is not warm. We spend three or four seconds on each one. You must be ready to play, mentally and physically. Be focused. I want your undivided attention from 15 minutes before the game to 10 minutes after. That's all I ask.

(Diagram 9)   Drill, Post Shuffle. The ball is reversed from 1 to 2 to 3. The post shuffles around the lane, following the ball. 3 will pass to the post for the shot.

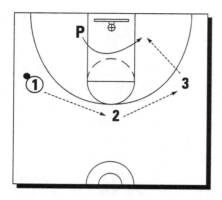

Diagram 9

(Diagram 10)   A variation has only two perimeter players. The post comes high and then slides down for the pass and layup.

Diagram 10

I tell my players they are in a theater and they are in a performance. What is your character? Basketball. If you make a mistake, I tell them they weren't in character. Stay in character. The difference between a good player and a great player is a player who is able to create his own shots. When you can do that, it shows that you have some confidence in your ability to handle the ball.

Girls are a different breed to coach. Their temperament is different. You have to be very patient. You have to know who you can yell at and who you can't. Some you must pat on the back. But you must know they believe in you, that you have won them over, that they have confidence in your ability to coach and that you are giving them something meaningful. Kids want to hear something from the coaches that they can use. Parents want their kids ready to go to the next level. You must get the mind set for what you want the body to do. Remember, if the mind can perceive it, the body can achieve it.

(Diagram 11)   Drill for the fast break off of the free throw. We put five people on the lane. 5 rebounds and outlets to 1. 2 breaks into the middle for the pass from 1. 3 and 4 fill the lanes; 5 trails on the side opposite of the outlet pass. 1 is on the side of the outlet pass. If 3 or 4 do not get the ball, they cut to the basket. The one on the right side goes low. Both go through the lane, do a V-cut and come back and replace themselves.

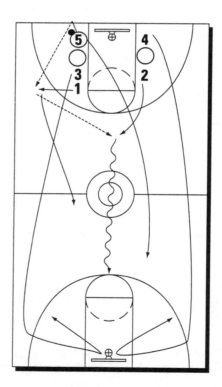

Diagram 11

(Diagram 12)   If the ball is rebounded on the other side and 4 rebounds, 2 breaks out for the outlet pass, 1 cuts across the middle and gets the pass from 2, and 3 and 5 fill the outside lanes with 4 trailing on the side opposite that of the outlet pass and 2 trailing on the side of the outlet pass. The trailers run down to the post position. You must teach rebounding. Three things. First, assume that every shot is a miss. Second, get your hands above your head. Third, move to the flight of the ball and jump as high as you can. If there is another-colored jersey between you and the basket, you are in the wrong position. If you are on defense, there is no reason a player with the ball should beat you down the floor when you don't have a ball.

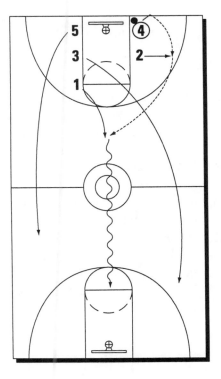

Diagram 12

Set Plays

Every good play must have a good counter. At the college level, for the long-term use and effect, the counter needs to have a counter. The end of a game is the time to run such a play. I want to start with things we do out of our secondary break.

(Diagram 1)   This is the way that we end our secondary break. 4 and 5 are interchangeable; 2 and 3 are interchangeable. 1 passes ahead to 2. The ball is reversed back around to 3. 5 follows the ball. As the ball is reversed to 3, 2 comes in and sets a rear screen for 4. 4 can get a lob pass. You can get the lob pass and get the layup.

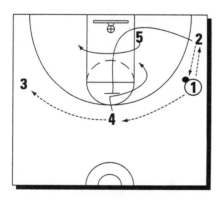

Diagram 1

(Diagram 2)   After 2 sets the screen, he steps out to receive the ball. 4 screens across for 5, and 5 always goes to the baseline side. We then have the ball in the middle of the floor, 4 and 5 working together inside. This is the fundamental part.

The defensive basketball world today is used to set plays. Defenses are used to set offenses. Fewer of us are running a set offense every time down the floor because the defenses take away the predictable. That's why more people are running motion and freelance offenses. We want to attack

in a set way on the run. How many teams have defenses coming back in transition and recognize what is going on quickly enough to stop a set play in transition? I want to show you some things we run in transition. These plays come off of our fundamental secondary break. Now come the options.

Diagram 2

(Diagram 3)   Start in the same positions. 1 passes to 4 but 4 cannot pass to 3, so the ball is reversed back to 1. In the regular secondary break, 2 comes in to get into position to come high to set the rear-screen (see Diagram 1).

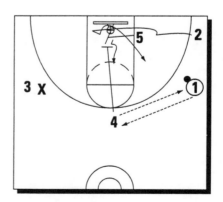

Diagram 3

Since the ball wasn't reversed, 2 continues across and screens for 5. 4 then down-screens for 2. This puts a burden on X5, the man guarding 5.

(Diagram 4)   4 sets a ball-screen for 1 who dribbles off of 4's screen. 5 is following the ball; 3 is fading or spotting up. 2 sees the ball-screen occur, and he then back-screens for 4. 4 goes to the basket for the lob. 1 can pass to 3, 5, or 4.

Diagram 4

(Diagram 5)   If 1 can't use those options, 2 steps out for the reversal. 2 then can look to 4 for a hi-lo pass.

Diagram 5

(Diagram 6)   You can also use this for a three-point shot. After 4 sets the ball-screen, he spaces up. 1 passes to 4 for the shot.

(Diagram 7)   As 1 passes the ball to 4 for the apparent reversal, 3 V-cuts to the basket. He has the

entire side of the floor open. 5 and 1 set a double-screen for 2 who gets the pass from 4. 5 is on the outside, 1 on the inside of that double-screen.

Diagram 6

Diagram 7

(Diagram 8)   This is the counter. 2 goes at the double-screen, but cuts to the basket. 5 then screens in for 1 who curls out to get the pass from 4.

(Diagram 9)   The ball is reversed from 1 to 4 and then to 3. 5 follows the ball and then follows the ball back. As 4 passes to 3, he follows the pass and sets a ball-screen. 3 dribbles off the screen of 4 as 1 comes across and sets a screen for 4 who goes for the lob. 3 has the jump shot option, has 5 coming across the lane, and has 4 on the lob, or if nothing happens, he passes back to 1 and 1 can pass back into 4.

Diagram 8

Diagram 9

(Diagram 10)   1 reverses to 4 as 2 goes through. 3 down-screens for 5. 4 passes to 2.

Diagram 10

(Diagram 11)   2 has the ball. 5 comes off of the screen of 3 as 4 down-screens for 3 who comes high. 2 can pass to 5 or 3.

Diagram 11

(Diagram 12)   This is the counter to Diagram 10. This is used if you have a wing player who is a good post player. 1 dribbles toward the corner. 5 comes high as 2 posts up. 1 looks to 2. 4 slides over and then sets a diagonal down-screen for 2. 3 fades to the corner. 1 can hit 2. Or 1 - 5 - 4. Or 1 - 5 - 2. If 2 gets the ball, but doesn't have a shot, we want him to swing it through and take it to the basket going to his left. The only defensive man on that side of the floor is X3.

Diagram 12

(Diagram 13)   Out of our regular secondary break, we can change it so that as the ball is reversed and 5 follows the ball, 4 will down-screen for 2 who pops out for the jump shot.

(Diagram 14)   If we can't reverse the ball to 3, 3 will V-cut and go backdoor as 5 and 2 come high.

This clears out the entire side of the floor. If we don't get this, we go right into our motion offense.

Diagram 15

Diagram 13

Diagram 14

Diagram 16

Diagram 17

(Diagram 15)   If you have a good-shooting post player, 5 sets a back-screen for 1 who cuts to the basket. 4 down-screens for 5 who pops out for the shot. The ball goes from 1 - 4 - 3 - 5. This play keeps the defense honest.

(Diagram 16)   Another way is for 1 to pass to 2 and cut through. 3 and 4 will replace and 1 replaces on the opposite wing.

(Diagram 17)   The ball is reversed from 2 - 4 - 3 - 1. 5 sets a back-screen for 4 who cuts to the basket. 5 then pops out for the shot. 1 can pass to 4 or 5.

(Diagram 18)   This is the counter. The ball cannot be reversed to 1. 1 V-cuts and goes backdoor. 5 sets a back-screen for 4. 4 cuts to the basket, and then uses the staggered-screen of 1. 3 has 1 on the backdoor, or after several dribbles, he can pass to 4 on the low post.

and then to 3. 2 is the shooter. 5 back-screens for 1, and 4 down-screens for 5. 3 passes to 1 on 5-2.

Diagram 18

(Diagram 19)   If 1 cannot make the pass to 4 because he is overplayed, 3 will loop in and set a back-screen for 4 who cuts to the basket. 3 then steps out and gets the pass from 1.

Diagram 19

(Diagram 20)   3 takes it on the dribble as 5 and 1 set a staggered-screen for 2. 1 looks to 4 and then to 2.

(Diagram 21)   If we get to a point where we want to get into something a little more structured, we run what we call a "four man flex" out of the secondary. It is the same alignment; 1 passes to 4

Diagram 20

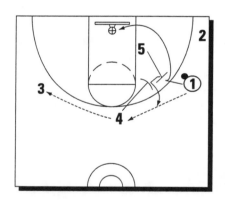

Diagram 21

(Diagram 22)   3 reverses the ball to 5 to 4. 1 sets a back-screen for 3 and 5 down-screens for 1 who pops out. This is a four-man flex with one man stationary in the corner, 2, who is a good shooter. The faster you cut, the better it works. We go from this into motion.

(Diagram 23)   Out-of-Bounds Plays. We score so much on our out-of-bounds plays that sometimes we take the ball to the baseline and call time-out so we can run one. 1 is the inbounder. 3 curls back for court balance. 4 and 5 set staggered-screens for 2. We say that it is staggered, but 5 really doesn't care about 2. 1 passes to 2 and goes away.

Diagram 22

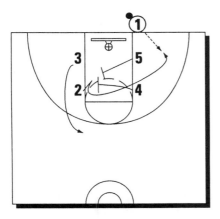

Diagram 23

(Diagram 24)   2 has the ball. 4 takes one step away from 2 and then comes back off of 5's screen. 5 will roll to the basket so it is a fake staggered-screen.

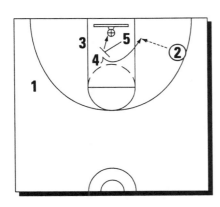

Diagram 24

(Diagram 25)   2 is the best shooter. 3 cuts to the ball-side corner. 4 comes off of 3's back. 5 comes into the lane and sets a screen.   2 takes his man under the net and comes off of the screen of 4. 2 will be open in this area. This is a congestion play. This is a much better play against a team that plays off the ball and plays under the basket to stop the layups.

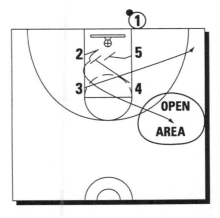

Diagram 25

(Diagram 26)   4 sets a cross-screen for 3 who gets the pass from 1. 5 comes on a diagonal away from the ball, but reverses and sets a back-screen for 1. 1 gets the pass from 3.

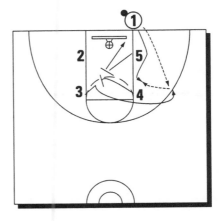

Diagram 26

(Diagram 27)   As a counter, 4 could down-screen for 2, and he could come high and shoot the jump shot.

Diagram 27

(Diagram 28)   1 dribbles across the lane as 4 comes down toward 2. X4 thinks it is a screen and gets off to help. 2 takes one step up, and then cuts behind 5's screen. 4 rolls across the lane to get the bounce pass from 1.

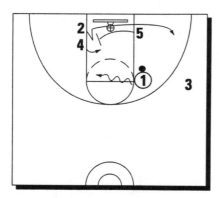

Diagram 28

Late-Game Situations

We have a great late-game philosophy. Do you have one? Do you work on it every day? How successful you are in late-game situations is going to directly depend on how much time you spend doing it. Do you practice it every day, every other day, every week? We practice a late-game situation four out of six days. We end practice with some type of late-game situation almost every day. What would you do if you had two seconds to play, the other team was at the foul line and they were behind by two points and they only had one shot, so you knew that they had to miss the free throw? What would you do? Obviously you would put all five of your players in there to box out. How about committing a lane violation? Find out what they are going to do. If he messes up and he makes it, you have the ball out of bounds. If he misses, then you know what they are going to do. Do you think about the different kinds of situations? You want your kids to experience success. I want them to get used to winning. My kids have already come into the huddle with little time left in the game and said, "We do this every day."

(Diagram 1)   Here is a last-second play to go the length of the floor. 4 is very athletic; 1 is a good shooter. 2 must have a good arm. 4 cuts to a certain spot. 2 throws to that spot. When the ball goes in the air, don't stare at the ball. As the ball goes by, X1 will follow the flight of the ball. As soon as X1's head turns, 1 takes off. 4 catches the ball and flips the ball to 1. 1 has the shot.

You need to have a time-out cutoff. If the other team ties the game or puts us behind, 10 seconds is our cutoff. If 10 seconds or less are on the clock, we will call time-out. If it is over 10, we get it and go. We already know what we want to do.

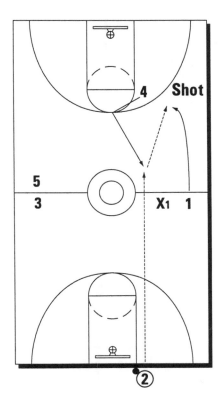

Diagram 1

(Diagram 2)   Down 3, you are at the line for one shot. In general, we have had success in tapping the ball to a certain area rather than trying to rebound it. If 5 goes hard to the board, he could have a foul called on him. But, if 5 steps back and screens the next man, 3 could come in and tap the ball to the side where 2 has moved to on the shot. 2 could then get the shot.

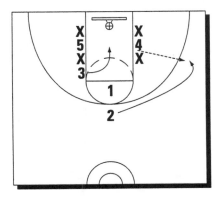

Diagram 2

(Diagram 3)   If you are down 2, then 5 can screen and 3 steps into the lane. 4 also screens the man above him and 2 goes outside and around for the rebound.

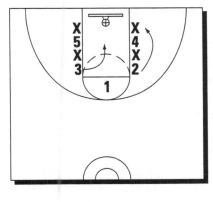

Diagram 3

Question: If you are down 4 or 5 points, when do you go for two and when do you go for three?

Answer: If we are more than one possession down, then we will go for two. If we are down six, then we will go for three.

Question: Late in the game and you are up three, do you foul and put them on the line?

Answer: It depends on how late. We will foul if there are under 10 seconds left. Do you want to have a chance to win the game with your defense or do you want to have a chance to win it with your offense?

Quick Hitters into Motion Offense

I really believe in the motion offense, but I also believe in different variables of it. I believe in running transition into motion, but I also believe in quick hitter sets in the motion. When we put in the motion offense in October, it is usually ugly. The coach must have patience. If you run a set offense, it will look good in a few days because your team will pick it up right away. But, so will your opponents. Motion is hard to scout, and the players like to play it because it gives them a lot of freedom. But it is structured. Basically, you must have players who are interchangeable parts. You can run this without a true center. When we start, we break things down. We go from 2-on-2 to 3-on-3 to 4-on-4 to 5-on-5. That's the best way to implement your motion offense because you have to give your players a feel for reading each other, how to use screens and you must have good spacing.

(Diagram 1)   We do 4-on-0, with a coach. This is a spacing drill. We will do different variations of screening. They must make 10 passes before looking to shoot. The middle is not clogged, and they get a good feel about reversing the ball. We want at least one reversal before taking a shot. Make your rules in practice. Never stand still.

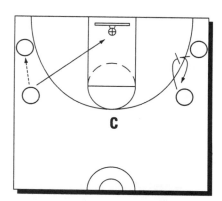

Diagram 1

(Diagram 2)   If we need a reversal pass, it is automatic. We will flash someone from a low area to the top of the circle. We also screen the passer.

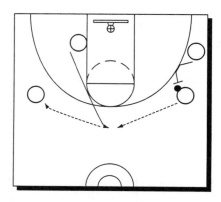

Diagram 2

(Diagram 3)   We also go 3-on-3 with a coach. This teaches your players to read the screens, and we always screen the passer.

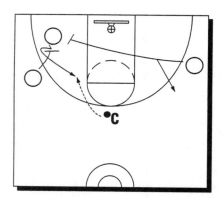

Diagram 3

(Diagram 4)   Motion reverse. Sometimes I put the guards down low.

(Diagram 5)   We don't have any specific positions. 3 can make the pass and cut through, and 5 can flash to the top for ball reversal. It is constant movement and the floor is balanced. You never want more than three players on the same side of the floor.

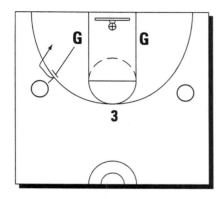

Diagram 4

Diagram 6

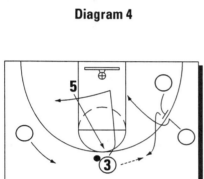

Diagram 5

Diagram 7

(Diagram 6)   In a motion offense you must be able to read the defense. Coach has the ball. If 1 down-screens for 4, 4 must read the defense. If the defense follows him, he curls. If the defense goes over the top, he fades to the corner. If his man gets picked, he pops out high. The screener (2) knows that if they switch, he comes back to the ball. Make these drills competitive. Keep score.

(Diagram 7)   We will re-screen. We start with 5 and 4 high, and 1 and 2 low. 3 can play high if he is a decent ballhandler. If you don't put 3 there in practice, he won't do it in the game. 2 and 1 back-screen for 4 and 5. Then 2 and 1 will re-screen down again for 4 and 5. This is good against pressure.

(Diagram 8)   We do 4-on-4 with a coach. The coach can be used as a reversal man. We work on all of our screens. Along with the other screens, we have a flat screen where the man in the post sets a screen for the wing. If we score, we set up the press and the other team tries to beat it. They can now use the coach against the press.

(Diagram 9)   If they don't get the shot, they can use the coach for reversal.

(Diagram 10)   Sometimes the coach will hold the ball as a signal for the man to go backdoor. That gets them in the habit of moving. Anytime a man leaves an area, another man must fill it.

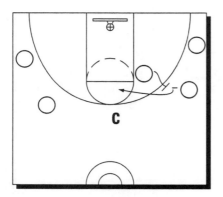

Diagram 8

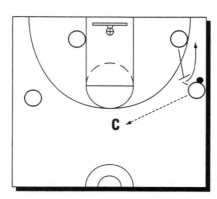

Diagram 9

Diagram 10

to the spot or the lane. We designate one player to take it out-of-bounds. We spread the floor by sending two men to the corners, one man down the middle and he comes ball side. We have variations off of this. 1 has the ball and reverses the ball to 4 to 2. 5 flashes to the ball side, and 3 back-screens for 4 who comes off the screen for the lob pass.

Diagram 11

(Diagram 12)   If that doesn't happen, 2 reverses to 3. If 5 is fronted, we will pass from 3 to 5 for a hi-lo.

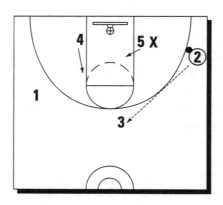

Diagram 12

(Diagram 13)   If not, 3 reverses to 1. 5 back-screens for 2 and screens for 3. 4 can post up.

(Diagram 11)   We run a transition set into motion. We fill spots. This is similar to a numbered break, but we don't number the players. We tell them to go

Diagram 13

(Diagram 14)   We can do this. 1 to 4 to 3. 2 back-screens for 4 who looks for the lob. 5 flashes and posts up.

Diagram 14

(Diagram 15)   If the ball is reversed from 3 to 2 to 1, 5 will screen for 3. 3 will set a back-screen for 2 and steps out. 2 cuts to the basket.

(Diagram 16)   If 1 reverses to 3, 4 will back-screen for 1. From this we go into our motion.

(Diagram 17)   Transition Loop. Same situation, 1 to 4 to 3. 2 back-screens for 4 and 4 cuts. 5 flashes ball side.

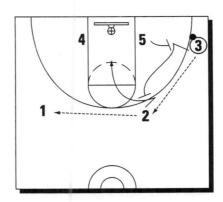

Diagram 15

Diagram 16

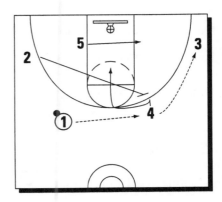

Diagram 17

(Diagram 18)   As the ball reverses, 4 screens across for 5 and ducks up the lane.

Diagram 18

inside. 1 passes to the wing and cuts away. The forward screens laterally for the wing who breaks to the short corner.

(Diagram 19)   Through. 1 dribbles and pushes 2 through on the baseline. 4 slides down. 3 pops out to the head of the circle and the ball is reversed. 4 sets the down-screen for 2 as he comes through.

Diagram 20

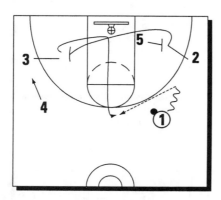

Diagram 19

Diagram 21

(Diagram 20)   2 must read the screen, often he can curl. 5 will post in the middle of the lane.

(Diagram 21)   Stagger. Same spots and the ball is reversed from 1 to 4 to 3. 1 and 4 set a staggered-screen for 2 who gets the pass from 3. 5 can post.

(Diagram 22)   Quick Hitters from Motion. They are not designed to score on the first or second pass. What they are designed to do is to give different looks to get us into the movement of motion. We start in a 1-4, point, two wings and two forwards

Diagram 22

(Diagram 23)   The ball is reversed, the forward screens down for 1 and the wing screens down for the man on the baseline.

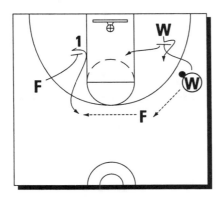

Diagram 23

(Diagram 24)   Curl Series. Start with a 1-4. Wings cut to the baseline, inside men screen down. This is good against pressure. We want to enter the ball from the foul lane down. From that, we can go into the motion.

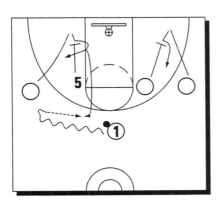

Diagram 24

(Diagram 25)   An automatic motion rule is that when the ball goes opposite, you don't screen across. We want to isolate down low and have a man at the top for reversal. So 5 down-screens for 3 who can curl or widen out. 4 goes to the top of the circle.

Diagram 25

(Diagram 26)   Zipper. 2 curls up around 5's screen and then 4's.

Diagram 26

(Diagram 27)   The ball is reversed from 1 to 2. 3 comes higher and then goes backdoor if he is overplayed.

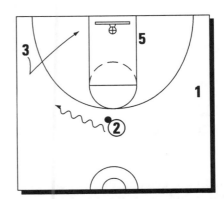

Diagram 27

(Diagram 28)   If not, 2 dribbles at 3, and 3 gets the handoff and dribbles to the top of the circle. 4 screens on the ball. 5 ducks in. 3 just came off of a staggered-screen by 2 and 4. Don't let 1 creep up. Keep him down for the three-point shot in the corner.

Diagram 30

Diagram 28

(Diagram 29)   Gold Series. 3 dribbles to the side. 4 and 5 double-screen down for 1. 2 fills the spot vacated by 1.

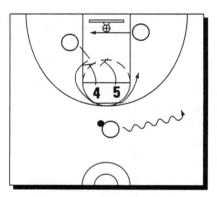

Diagram 31

(Diagram 32)   If the first cutter comes higher, then look for the hi-lo pass to the other cutter coming off of the double.

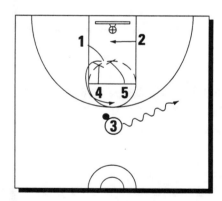

Diagram 29

(Diagram 30)   3 passes to 1. 4 and 5 continue down and set a double-screen for 2 coming off the weak side.

(Diagram 31)   Look for the first cutter curling around the double-screen set by 4 and 5.

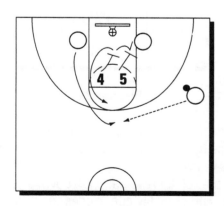

Diagram 32

(Diagram 33)   We can run this as a sideline out-of-bounds play. We ran this if the ball was below the foul line.

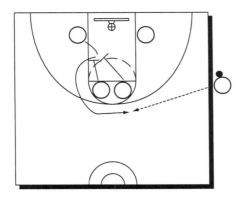

Diagram 33

(Diagram 34)   Another sideline play. Immediately, 2 comes off the screen and goes to the deep corner. 4 and 1 hold for a count. 4 screens away as 2 comes off the screen of 5. 3 passes to 2, and 2 can make the lob pass to 5 if he is fronted.

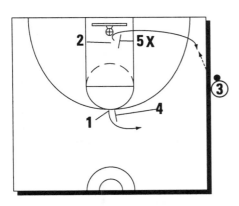

Diagram 34

(Diagram 35)   Sideline Play. 2 screens down for 1 and then comes off the double-screen set by 4 and 5 in the lane. The ball goes from 3 to 1 to 2.

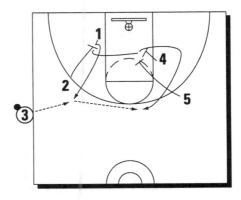

Diagram 35

(Diagram 36)   If you have a point guard who can score, run the Flat series. 1 passes to 2 and cuts off the screen of 5 to the basket. 1 can post up.

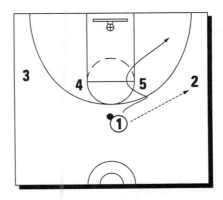

Diagram 36

(Diagram 37)   I want more than one option. The ball is reversed from 2 to 5 to 4. 1 will set a back-screen for 2. Then 5 down-screens for 1, screen the screener.

(Diagram 38)   1 comes off for the three-point shot.

(Diagram 39)   If 1 can't shoot it, he looks to 5 posting up. 2 comes off the staggered-screen of 3 and 4. 1 can pass to 2.

Diagram 37

Diagram 38

Diagram 39

(Diagram 40)   Isolate and Misdirection. Start the ball on one side and reverse to get the isolation on the weak side. You must move the defense first,

take away help. We call out the number of the man who we want to isolate, let's say #41. 4 screens down for 2. 1 passes to 2 and cuts to the corner.

Diagram 40

(Diagram 41)   5 back-screens for #41 and 2 dribbles to the top of the circle.

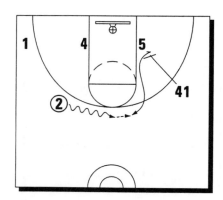

Diagram 41

(Diagram 42)   2 passes to 5 as 4 flashes high. 2 should dribble across high.

(Diagram 43)   5 skip-passes to 1 in the corner and 41 flashes to the ball and is isolated on the box.

(Diagram 44)   Four-Out Stagger. We don't run all of these plays every year. 4 and 5 start high, 3 is in the corner, 2 at the short post. 1 dribbles off of 4's screen. 2 back-screens for 3 coming out of the corner. 3 posts up. 5 and 4 set a staggered-screen for 3 coming high. After 3 clears, 2 pops out to the three-point line. 1 can pass to 3 or to 2.

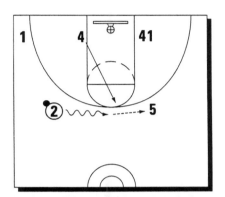

Diagram 42

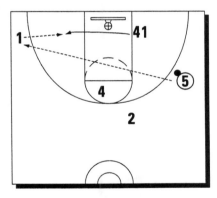

Diagram 43

Diagram 44

(Diagram 45)   Power. 1 dribbles off of the screen of 3. 2 screens across for 5.

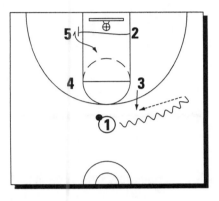

Diagram 45

(Diagram 46)   1 passes to 3. 4 down-screens for 2, a screen-the-screener action. 2 either pops out or curls and gets the pass from 3.

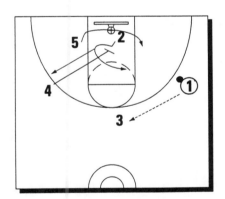

Diagram 46

(Diagram 47)   Scissors Series. We spread the court possibly with three guards. 2 passes to 4 who hits 3 in the high post. 1 and 2 run a scissor action by 3. 4 then screens down for 1, and 5 screens down for 2. This spreads the floor.

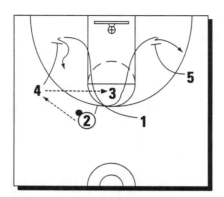

Diagram 47

(Diagram 48)   Backdoor Drill. Coach is under the basket. When you are being pressured, you must be able to change direction. You must practice the backdoor more, going away from the ball. Even though there is no defense in this drill, the wing must V-cut, square and pop before he receives the pass. The passer cuts to the basket at the coach. The other wing must cut high and then go backdoor to the opposite corner of the first cutter. The ball is dribbled to the top and the drill continues.

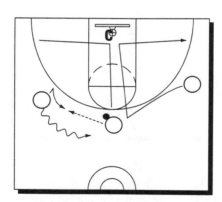

Diagram 48

(Diagram 49)   Baseball. This is 4-on-4 half-court with no dribbling. You get one point for a pass. You can't shoot a jump shot, you can only take one bounce for a layup. You get three points for a layup. The defense comes up on you to stop the passing and this makes you move without the ball and go backdoor. Give the defense a point for a deflection,

five points for a charge. We don't want our players to look at the ball on offense. We want them looking at their defender because that is the person you must beat.

Diagram 49

(Diagram 50)   Backdoor Special. 1 passes to 2 on the wing, and 4 screens away for 5. 1 and 3 exchange.

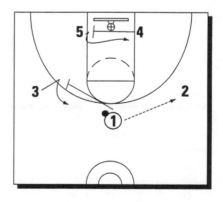

Diagram 50

(Diagram 51)   2 reverses to 3 and screens down in the corner for 5. 4 steps up the lane, and 1 goes backdoor.

(Diagram 52)   Start with a stack; 2 is the shooter. 2 screens across for 3, 4 and 5 set a staggered-screen for 2.

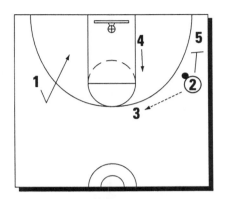

Diagram 51

Diagram 52

(Diagram 53)   Run this for a three-pointer late in the game. 1 passes to 2 who looks to 5. Even if we need a 3, we may drive it into the post. The defense will sag. 1 and 4 set a staggered screen for 3 who comes to the top of the circle for the three-point shot off of the pass from 2.

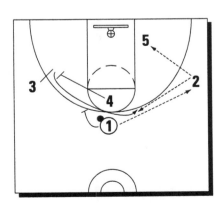

Diagram 53

(Diagram 54)   Another version is to put 4 on top and make a dribble handoff from 1 to 2. 2 continues on the dribble and uses the side-screen from 4. 2 can shoot it or make the pass to 3 in the corner.

Diagram 54

(Diagram 55)   Hi-lo. We like to swing through and then down-screen. 1 passes to 2 and goes opposite.

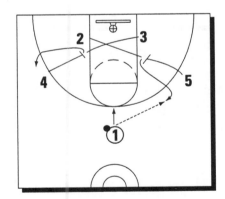

Diagram 55

(Diagram 56)   2 passes back to 3, and 4 and 5 set back-screens for 2 and 3. 3 passes to 1.

(Diagram 57)   I like the 1-4 with the screens from the elbows to the wings. Players aren't used to defending this.

Diagram 56

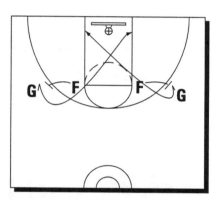

Diagram 57

(Diagram 58)   After 5 flashes to the top, 2 and 4 must do something. They just can't stand still. They must move without the ball.

Diagram 58

(Diagram 59)   The Four-Spot Shooting Drill. Manager shoots and 5 rebounds and outlets to 1. 1 V-cuts, receives the pass from 5 and dribbles down the floor and makes the pass to 2 who is breaking to the ball. Manager hinders 1 when he starts to dribble. 2 receives the ball and turns, and another manager hinders him as he dribbles. 2 dribbles to the wing and then feeds 3 who posts up on the block with the manager behind him.

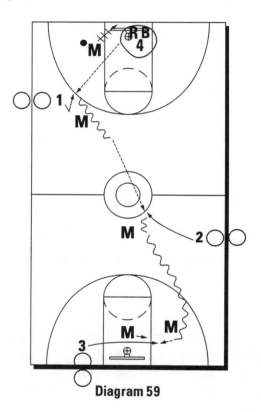

Diagram 59

(Diagram 60)   Two-Man Break. Outlet pass to 1. 1 passes back to 4 for the layup. Run the same drill for a jump shot on the wing. Then repeat except instead of 4 shooting, 4 returns the ball to 1 for the jumper at the elbow. Run this both ways, changing positions.

(Diagram 61)   4 outlets to 1, and 1 dribbles sideline and 4 is the trailer. 1 passes to the trailer for the shot. Run the drill again, this time 4 goes to the box. Run the drill again, and 4 goes to the opposite corner for the three off the skip-pass.

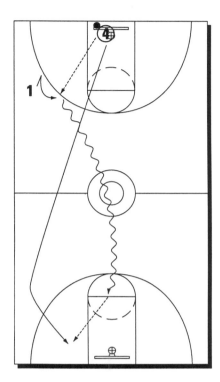

Diagram 60

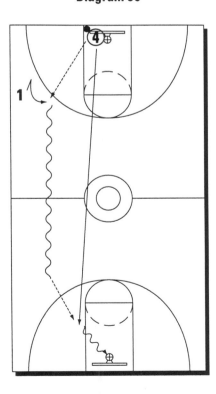

Diagram 61

(Diagram 62)   Two-Ball Shooting Drill. Have a shooter, a passer and a rebounder. Shooter shoots, rebounder passes a second ball to the passer as the shooter changes his position. The passer makes the pass to the shooter as the rebounder rebounds the first ball. The shooter goes between wing and corner. Then, you can add one dribble before the shot.

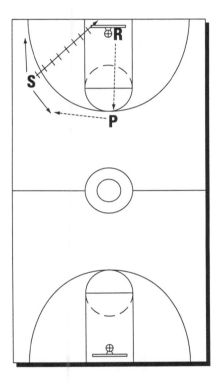

Diagram 62

(Diagram 63)   A good team drill for the end of practice. Three teams of four players each, black, red, and white. Drill starts with red team playing offense against black. When black gets the ball after a make or a miss, black takes the ball the other way with red playing defense until half-court. Then white is on defense against black in the other half-court. After a make or a miss, white takes the ball the other way against black to half-court where red takes over.

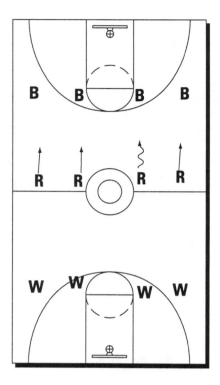

Diagram 63

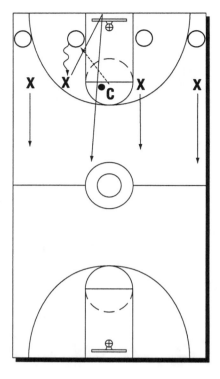

Diagram 64

(Diagram 64)   Recognition Drill. Four offensive
men on the baseline, four defensive men at the foul
line. Coach throws the ball to one of the players on
the baseline and calls out the name of one of them
on defense. That player whose name is called must
sprint and touch the end line before getting into the
play. It is 4-on-3 full-court until he catches up.

Changing Defenses

You must make certain decisions about your team regardless of the level you are coaching. I decided that if a player didn't guard his man, he didn't play. You must back up your decisions with playing time. If you are going to win, you need to get across the team defensive concept. You must get your players to believe in your defensive philosophy. Winning basketball must start with a good defensive philosophy. We play man-to-man about 90% of the time, put in a little zone and some combination defenses to help us in certain games. First, let's talk about some of the subtle changes we made in our man defense.

(Diagram 1)   When we talk about guarding in the half-court defense, we are talking about guarding this area. If your man has the ball here, you are putting pressure on the ball at the three-point line. We will sag off of the other men, depending on where the ball is.

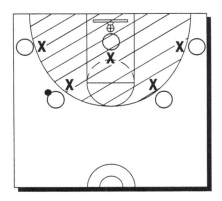

Diagram 1

(Diagram 2)   We make adjustments based on our scouting. If your man can't shoot, we don't play him. We will stay in the lane. We will dare him to shoot.

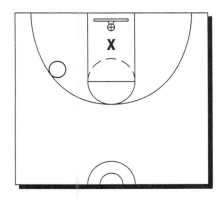

Diagram 2

(Diagram 3)   We vary our post positioning based on the weaknesses and strengths of the post players on the other team. Some coaches teach all their players to play defense on the post a certain way. You can do it if you have players who can do that. If you insist your players do things they can't do, you are hurting the team. We do the defensive post drills that everyone does. Two coaches moving the ball between them and the defensive player adjusting his position to the position of the ball. As the ball goes from high to low, go over the top. As the ball goes from low to high, the defensive man will go behind. If you have a player who does it differently, but their man doesn't score, let them alone.

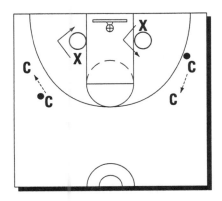

Diagram 3

(Diagram 4)   We must help on post feeds. Every time the post dribbles, we go after the ball.

Diagram 4

(Diagram 5)   Based on personnel, we extend our man-to-man full-court. Some of the teams we played had a post player take the ball out of bounds. If he passed to 1 in the corner, we would double-team 1, and everyone else would deny. We wanted the ball thrown back to the post. We would dare 5 to dribble down the floor.

Diagram 5

(Diagram 6)   We will trap up and down based on the first pass. 1 dribbles to the side and 4 screens for 2. When the pass is made to 2, we trap him. Everybody rotates. We will front the low post and bring the offside man up to the high post.

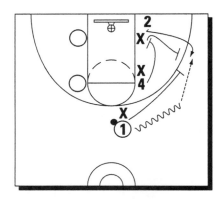

Diagram 6

(Diagram 7)   Also, we would run up at the dribbler and trap him. The other three men zoned.

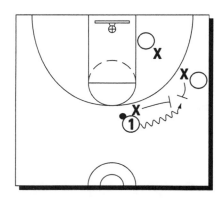

Diagram 7

(Diagram 8)   Although we played man-to-man, we would zone a little. We played a 2-3 zone, but we changed it a little and called it "blitz." If they were in a 1-3-1 and the ball was passed below the foul line, we would trap the ball. The middle man in the zone would front the low post, and the offside deep man would come up in the high-post area. The offside guard would look to run through the return pass. This was effective for us on out-of-bounds plays. We would do it for a possession or two after a time-out. We would stay in this if the other team was having trouble shooting.

Diagram 8

(Diagram 9)   A Triangle-and-Two. I am amazed how things I thought were true end up not being true. My theory was that a triangle-and-two would be good for a few possessions. But, often it is effective much longer. Once we played it for an entire half and what we did was about as simple as you can get. We put our smartest and best athlete at X1. We put our two big men on the baseline, and we chased the two guards with X2 and X3. We pressed full-court and then dropped back into this as a half-court defense.

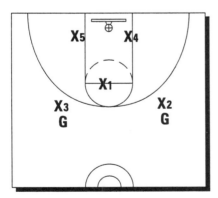

Diagram 9

(Diagram 10)   We fronted their good post player, and the other baseline man, X4, played behind. X1 had the biggest job because he had the largest area to cover.

Diagram 10

(Diagram 11)   If the ball goes into the corner, X5 comes out a little. X1 would sag to the middle post.

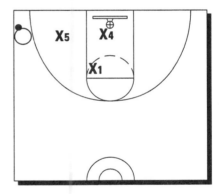

Diagram 11

(Diagram 12)   When the ball came to the wing, X1 would point the triangle.

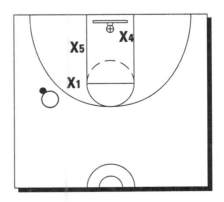

Diagram 12

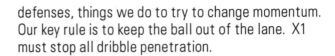
(Diagram 13)   If they skipped it over his head, X4 would come up to keep him from driving until X1 could get back.

Diagram 13

(Diagram 14)   We had to work with our people to overcome their natural tendencies. If the man was open at the elbow, we wanted him to shoot and see if he was going to make it. If he started making them, we got out of this defense.

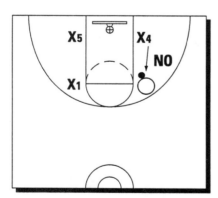

Diagram 14

(Diagram 15)   1-3 and a Chaser. We played it a little higher, but essentially it looks like a diamond. X2 will play man-to-man. The rules are the same as they are for a 2-3 zone. We make sure they realize man-to-man is our primary defense and that these things are changes of pace, special-situation

defenses, things we do to try to change momentum. Our key rule is to keep the ball out of the lane. X1 must stop all dribble penetration.

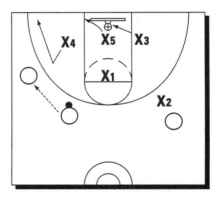

Diagram 15

(Diagram 16)   If the ball is passed to the wing, X4 comes up and stays with the ball all the way to the corner. X1, X5, and X3 move as shown. You must determine when and where to use them, how often to use them and how willing you are to stay in them. Playing hard, no matter what defense we are in, is the number one priority. We spend a significant amount of time working on our man-to-man defense. At least 60% of every practice is defensive-oriented early in the year. First, we must understand the man-to-man, then we put in the 2-3 zone. Then the 2-3 blitz. It was about a week before the first game when we got around to putting in the 1-3 and the chaser and the triangle-and-2. These defenses are particularly effective the second time around in our league. If you are going to change things defensively, you must have patience.

Question: What are the chaser's rules in the 1-3 and chaser?

Answer: All he does is face-guard. He absolutely disregards the ball. He stays with his man. Don't let him touch the ball if possible. We can also do that out of our man-to-man.

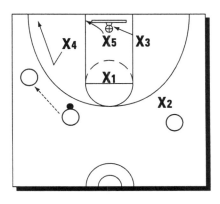

Diagram 16

(Diagram 17)   In our shell drill we can practice this. We will keep one man out on the shooter, and forget about the sagging and help rules.

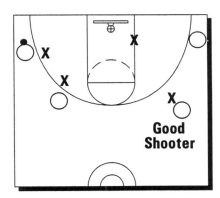

Diagram 17

Question: With your triangle-and-two, will you match up with the 5?

Answer: I have in the past. It would depend on the personnel of the other team. I found that when we played man on the two players who had the ability to feed the post, we negated them.

Special Situations

An argument could be made that you should work almost as much on special situations as on the rest of your defense, be it last-second plays, side out-of-bounds plays, or underneath out-of-bounds plays. For instance, rebounding foul shots. That is a special situation. There are offensive plays trying to get a shot off of missed foul shots. You must work on these.

(Diagram 1)   Several years ago, we were up three with three seconds to go. We did not put anyone on the ball. We planned to put pressure on whoever caught the ball, but our man goes for the ball, misses, and allows the man to catch the ball behind him. That was the key. You can't let the player catch the ball behind you. The player banks in a shot from mid-court. We lose in overtime.

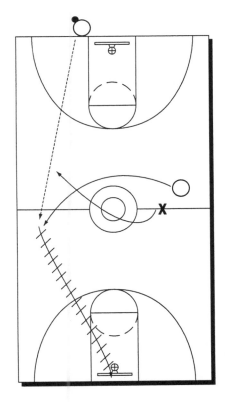

Diagram 1

(Diagram 2)   Several years later, we are up three, with six seconds to go. We had talked about it, but had never reached a consensus. This time we fouled the person who caught the inbound pass. We substitute with size. We have a four-man on the lane. But 4 has probably never blocked out from this spot on the lane. The shooter makes the first one, now we are up two. He misses the second, the ball bounds over everyone to this man going behind, and he shoots and ties the game. We lose in four overtimes. As I look back, our attention to detail probably wasn't what it should have been. Now, we pride ourselves on attention to detail. We go over them about five minutes near the end of practice.

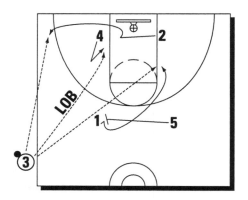

Diagram 3

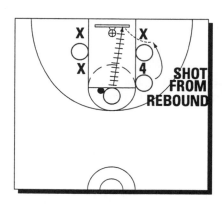

Diagram 2

(Diagram 3)   Side Out-of-Bounds. Box. 3 inbounds. First option is to 2, our shooter, in the corner. 5 back-screens for 1 who goes to the open area. That is the second option. If 4 is fronted, 4 moves the man higher, then seals him for the lob from 3.

(Diagram 4)   If the ball was passed over the top to 1, 1 takes it on the dribble while 5 back-screens for 3 cutting down the lane.

(Diagram 5)   Box Special. This is a counter. 2 starts to come off of 4, but comes back into the middle for the shot.

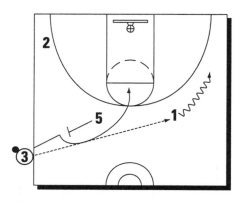

Diagram 4

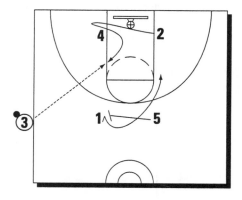

Diagram 5

(Diagram 6)   This is actually part of our man-to-man offense. 1 comes off the down-screen of 4. 5 down-screens for 2. 3 passes to 1 and 1 passes to 2.

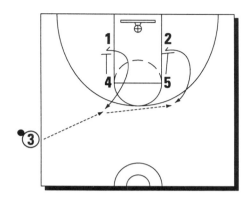

Diagram 6

of-bounds play to work, but the man must set up the screen. Go late on screens as opposed to going early. 2 cannot be in a rush to get to the corner. He must set up his man.

(Diagram 7)   2 has the ball, and 3 cuts low off of screens by 4 and 5. 4 then back-screens for 1 who goes to the wing. 2 can hit 3 or 1.

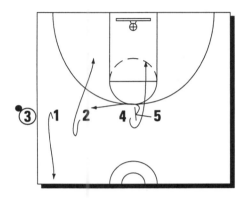

Diagram 8

Diagram 7

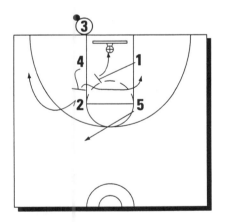

Diagram 9

(Diagram 8)   The Line. If 3 calls out an odd number, it means that 2 cuts to the basket and 1 goes to the back-court. 5 screens for 4 who curls to the basket, and then 5 comes to the ball.

(Diagram 9)   An Underneath Out-of-Bounds Play. These are tremendous scoring opportunities. Your players should know all positions of the out-of-bounds play and they should know the purpose of the play. We call this "up." 4 rolls and screens for 2 who breaks to the corner. 1 screens for 4 who breaks across the lane. 1 then rolls to the basket. 5 crosses for an outlet. You must screen to get an out-

(Diagram 10)   The counter to "up" is that 1 screens for 2 who goes to the basket. 1 then comes off the screen of 4 and goes to the corner. 5 crosses as an outlet. 3 looks for 1, then 2, then 5.

(Diagram 11)   "Slice." 1 inbounds to 3 who breaks to the corner. 1 comes off the screen set by 2 and the ball is reversed from 3 to 5 to 4 to 1.

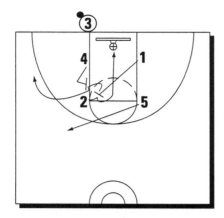

Diagram 10

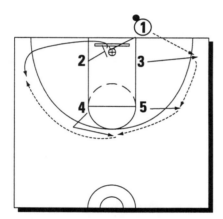

Diagram 11

(Diagram 12)   1 has the ball as 2 sets a diagonal screen for 5. 4 screens for 2. 1 can pass to 2 or to 5.

Diagram 12

(Diagram 13)   Slide Hole. 1 reverses the ball to 4, and if 1 is overplayed, he goes backdoor.

Diagram 13

(Diagram 14)   5 and 4 line up on the same side. 5 steps into the lane and then breaks to the corner to get the inbounds pass from 3. 4 screens diagonally for 1 who comes to the wing. 4 ducks into the lane.

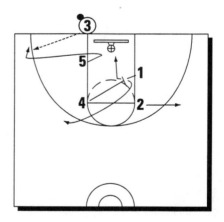

Diagram 14

(Diagram 15)   5 passes to 1 and screens down for 3 who is coming out to the corner. 1 can pass to 3, 4, or 2.

(Diagram 16)   The counter to this is that 3 would back-screen for 5, the ball is reversed to 2, and 4 comes high.

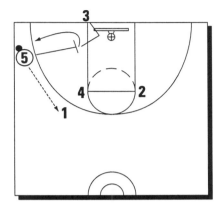

Diagram 15

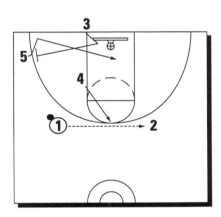

Diagram 16

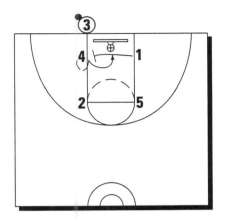

Diagram 17

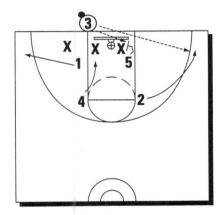

Diagram 18

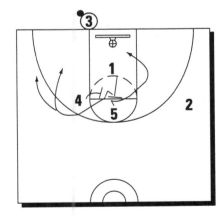

Diagram 19

(Diagram 17)   "Slice Again." Everybody is scientific in their scouting. This is a great idea. Say the word "again" to designate another play. If you yell to your team, "Slice again!" it does not mean to run the same play, but rather it designates another play. 4 would start out, but 1 will come across the lane and back-screen for 4 and 4 will reverse for the lob.

(Diagram 18)   Zone Out-of-Bounds. 2 breaks to the corner and can get a pass from 3 for the shot. 5 screens the bottom man in the zone. 1 breaks to the other corner, and 4 comes to the basket. On the counter, 5 will slip the screen for the pass from 3.

(Diagram 19)   Utah A. 1 has the option to screen 2, 5, or 4. If 1 screens for 5, 4 screens for 1.

(Diagram 20)   1 could screen for 4, and 5 could screen for 2.

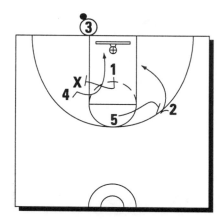

Diagram 20

(Diagram 21)   This is a counter for Utah A. We call it Utah B. 2, the shooter, comes off the staggered-screen of 5 and 4.

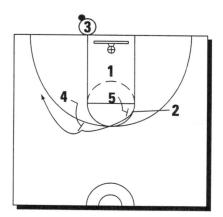

Diagram 21

I am going to show you three desperation plays. Which one you use will be determined by how much time is left. One play you throw the ball to half-court to get a time-out. If you have a little more time, you can throw the ball into the backcourt and attack. The last is to throw the ball the length of the floor.

(Diagram 22)   A Desperation Play. 1 and 2 break to the ball, then go deep. 5 screens down for 4. We want 4 to catch the ball. 4 meets the pass about the top of the circle. Depending on how much time you have, he could turn and shoot. Teams don't want to foul, and sometimes their momentum will carry them out of position. If there are more than two seconds, 4 catches the ball and dribbles, and hands the ball off to 1 who shoots the 3.

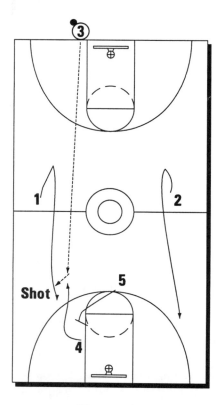

Diagram 22

(Diagram 23)   Throw the ball to half-court. We want 3 to catch the ball. 3 comes off of 4, our best screener. 1 goes deep. 2 is in the lane and comes down on the baseline to screen the defender of the inbounder. The ball is inbounded to 3. What happens depends on the amount of time remaining.

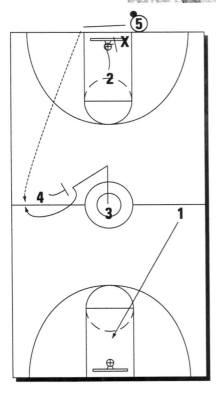

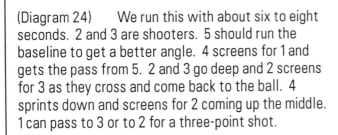

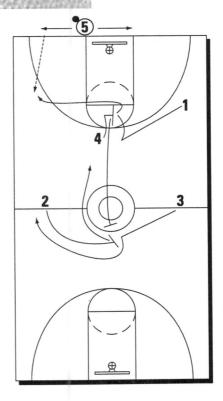

Diagram 23

Diagram 24

(Diagram 24)   We run this with about six to eight seconds. 2 and 3 are shooters. 5 should run the baseline to get a better angle. 4 screens for 1 and gets the pass from 5. 2 and 3 go deep and 2 screens for 3 as they cross and come back to the ball. 4 sprints down and screens for 2 coming up the middle. 1 can pass to 3 or to 2 for a three-point shot.

If you are going to have a good program, you must be disciplined in your approach and know what you are trying to get across to your kids, and you must cover these special situations so you can give them a chance to win.

INSTANT REVIEW BASKETBALL NOTEBOOKS

*Each volume features presentations made by several of America's most outstanding coaches. These instructional books are priced at **$22.95** each.*

Volume 1 • 1990
Featuring:
Jane Albright
Gene Bartow
Mike Krzyzewski
Ray Meyer
Billy Packer
Rick Pitino
Nolan Richardson
Norm Stewart
266pp • 8.5 x 11 paperback
ISBN 1-57167-266-4

Volume 3 • 1992
Featuring:
Geno Auriemma
Hubie Brown
Cheryl Burnett
John Calipari
John Kresse
Rick Majerus
Linda MacDonald
John Wooden
192pp • 8.5 x 11 paperback
ISBN 1-57167-268-0

Volume 4 • 1993
Featuring:
Jim Harrick
Marianne Hill-Stanley
Debbie Holley
Bob Huggins
Dave Odom
Kevin O'Neill
Ralph Sampson
Jerry Tarkanian
192pp • 8.5 x 11 paperback
ISBN 1-57167-269-9

Volume 7 • 1996
Featuring:
Steve Alford
Jim Baron
Lou Campanelli
Cliff Ellis
Angie Lee
Kelvin Sampson
Charlie Spoonhour
Dennis Wolff
224pp • 8.5 x 11 paperback
ISBN 1-57167-271-0

Volume 8 • 1997
Featuring:
Murry Bartow
Norm Ellenberger
Fran Fraschilla
Mike Jarvis
Andy Landers
Joye Lee-McNelis
Jerry Wainwright
Paul Westhead
292pp • 8.5 x 11 paperback
ISBN 1-57167-206-0

TO PLACE YOUR ORDER OR FOR A FREE CATALOG:
U.S. customers call
TOLL FREE: (800) 327-5557
or visit our website at
www.coacheschoice-pub.com
or FAX: (217) 359-5975
or write
COACHES CHOICE™
P.O. Box 647, Champaign, IL 61824-0647